W9-AUX-633

Jamaican Song and Story

Jamaican Song and Story

Annancy Stories, Digging Sings, Ring Tunes, and Dancing Tunes

Collected and Edited by

Walter Jekyll

With New Introductory Essays by
Philip Sherlock, Louise Bennett,
and Rex Nettleford

DOVER PUBLICATIONS, INC.
Mineola, New York

Copyright

Bibliographical Note

This Dover edition, first published in 1966 and republished in 2005, is an unabridged republication of the work first published for the Folk-Lore Society by David Nutt, London, in 1907. It contains new introductory essays by Philip Sherlock, Louise Bennett, and Rex Nettleford. This republication was made possible through the cooperation of the Western Reserve University Library, which kindly made available its copy of the original edition for reproduction.

Library of Congress Cataloging-in-Publication Data

Jekyll, Walter.

Jamaican song and story : Annancy stories, digging sings, ring tunes, and dancing tunes / collected and edited by Walter Jekyll ; with new introductory essays by Philip Sherlock, Louise Bennett, and Rex Nettleford.

p. cm.

"An unabridged republication of the work first published for the Folk-Lore Society by David Nutt, London, in 1907"—T.p. verso.

Includes bibliographical references.

ISBN 0-486-43720-5 (pbk.)

1. Folklore—Jamaica. 2. Folk songs, English—Jamaica. 3. Folk music—Jamaica. 4. Anansi (Legendary character) I. Title.

GR121.J2J4 2005
398'.097292—dc22

2005041348

Manufactured in the United States of America
Dover Publications, Inc., 31 East 2nd Street, Mineola, N.Y. 11501

THE LIVING ROOTS

by Philip Sherlock

KNOWING JAMAICA involves more than just being in Jamaica, more than just viewing the front garden, the sapphire radiance of the sea along the north coast, the gleaming beaches of white sand, the scarlet of the bougainvillea on the hotel lawns. Walter Jekyll knew Jamaica's inner rooms; he took one of the roads that lead from the flat lands along the coast up into the broken hill country and the mountainous interior. It was in these mountains that free Jamaica began, long before slavery was brought to an end.

This story begins with a definite event, the arrival of Columbus in 1494, when, on his second voyage to the new world, he discovered Jamaica, finding in the island an Amerindian people called the Arawaks whose original home was around the Orinoco River and whose forefathers had discovered Jamaica centuries earlier. There are no Arawaks left on the island, for they perished during the century and a half of Spanish occupation. Nor are there many traces left of the Spanish settlers; when the English conquered the island in 1655, most of the Spanish settlers withdrew to Cuba and Hispaniola. Jamaica was an empty island, save for a few bands of escaped African slaves called Maroons, who lived in the forests and mountains of the interior.

By 1700 Jamaica was a prosperous sugar island. At that period sugar meant slavery. The estates spread along the fertile strip of plain on the north coast from St. Ann's Bay to Falmouth and Montego Bay. This was the rich "northside" where the sugar plantations began at the sea's edge and ran back into the mountains—Cornwall, Cinnamon Hill, where lived ancestors of Elizabeth Barrett Browning, Little River, Rose Hall, where now the empty windows of the haunted great house look out on the sea. The estates spread along the south into Vere, and along the plains of Westmoreland and over the fertile inland valleys of Worthy Park, Appleton and Lluidas Vale. Since sugar is not a crop but the product of sugar cane, and since the juice must be extracted before it begins to ferment in the cut stalks, field and factory were joined. Each plantation was a little world linked to the outside world by rough dirt roads. Seaside estates had their own wharves along the coast for loading the hogsheads of molasses on to droghers that took them out to sloops waiting offshore. Many of the barques were from English ports, but a few were from Boston, Salem, Jamestown, and other American ports. The great houses were well built, their thick walls containing loopholes for muskets, since they were forts as well as homes. Beyond the fields were the villages where the slaves lived.

Sugar cane is not profitable when cultivated in small patches. It is a plantation crop requiring a large outlay of capital, and in the days before mechanization it required a huge labor force. The expansion of the West Indian sugar estates went hand in hand with the expansion of the West African slave trade. For two centuries and more the slave ships brought Africans of many tribes to the West Indies under the most wretched conditions. The people of the West Indies are of foreign ancestry, just as are those of Argentina and Chile, the United States and Canada; most North Americans, Argentineans and Chileans came from Europe, whereas most West Indians came from Africa. Sugar and the slave trade led to the Africanization of the Caribbean. In this region the dominant colors are black and brown.

The estates were on the flat land. Many estates had also some swamp land where one might find grass and even brackish water in times of drought, and some mountain land where one could cut wood for the fires in the boiling houses where the juice of the sugar cane had to be boiled until it crystallized. On the mountain land the slave grew his food, "ground provisions" like yams, sweet potatoes and cocos. He did not own this "piece of ground," but it was for his own use, even though he existed for the use of the estate, and generally he was free to sell or barter the produce of his "ground."

This patch of provision ground and the right of barter are the beginning of the internal marketing system of Jamaica, in which the women are the traders. The frenzy of a country market where women clamor before heaps of breadfruit, yams, sweet potatoes, where a man hawks lengths of tobacco twist or "jackass rope," his donkey tethered nearby, where the "higgler woman" sets off astride her donkey to sell her stock of provisions from cottage to cottage—the entire process originates in the provision ground and the Sunday market of the period of slavery.

But the plains meant servitude. Those who sought freedom escaped to the mountains. Because Jamaica is a large island with thickly wooded and almost inaccessible mountains, it has Maroons. "In a land where there was space for a Blue Mountain range there was space also for that freedom which mountain districts preserve for native races."[1] After slavery was brought to an end in 1834, many of the "new frees" moved away from the estates into the hill country to make homes and settlements of their own. So, as our poet Roger Mais says, mountains have a special meaning for Jamaicans:

All men come to the hills
Finally . . .

And it was in the hills and mountain valleys that Annancy lived. Jekyll heard the stories and songs in the mountains of Hanover. He knew that when the hoes stopped clacking someone had started telling an Annancy story. He knew that the stories are best told after sunset, when inanimate things come to life and the animals draw near—the Spider Man, his wife Crooky, Goat, Dog, Kisander the cat, Moos-Moos the mouse, Peafowl, Peacock, Crab, Jackass and Tiger. Here the riddles were told, like those still told in Iboland: "I was going to Ife, my face turn to Ife, I was coming from Ife, my face turn to Ife," which describes someone climbing a palm tree and descending from it, his face always turned upward. Here too men used proverbs sparkling with sunshine, in which the plants and animals of the field teach wisdom in vivid pictures: "When fish come out of de sea an' say alligator have fever,

[1] Lucas, Sir Charles, *Historical Geography of the British Colonies*, Oxford University Press, 1905.

believe him"; the reminder that familiarity breeds contempt, "Play wid puppy, puppy lick you mouth"; and "If snake bite you and you see lizard, you run," the Jamaican version of the West African "He whom a serpent has bitten dreads a slow-worm."

At a time when there were two Jamaicas, the semi-feudal Jamaica of the old plantation with its color lines and its emphasis on status and the Jamaica of the free black and brown peasant and the smallholder, Walter Jekyll saw the living roots of the future. He collected the stories and songs at a time when they were despised as "Negro talk" and "old-time sayings." In the Jamaica which now has found itself and is certain of its identity, which recognizes its heritage from both Africa and Europe and sets value on the Creole, and which is protected by the fact that in the hands of every adult rests the power of political decision through a free franchise; in this new Jamaica the work of Walter Jekyll has special significance. As Louise Bennett points out, it gives a new dimension to life because it is relevant, it belongs, it is peculiarly one's own. As Rex Nettleford emphasizes, it is a rich seedbed from which will spring new creations in the dance, pantomime and theater—creative works that will transform West Indian history from a footnote to European history into a story of achievement in its own right.

ME AND ANNANCY

by Louise Bennett

MY GRANDMOTHER used to tell me Annancy stories every night. All the stories had songs and she would sing a song over and over again, until I knew it and fell asleep singing it to myself. These were my favorite lullabies. At school my friends and I would swap Annancy stories during recess and lunch time, but before telling a story, each child had to mash (kill) an ant, or else something terrible might happen to her mother: the poor woman might turn into a bankra-basket! Annancy was a magic spider man, and a spider was always somewhere nearby. We could not always see him, but he was there, and we had to let him know that we knew he was there by killing an ant, or else——. At the end of each story, we had to say, "Jack Mandora, me no chose none," because Annancy sometimes did very wicked things in his stories, and we had to let Jack Mandora, the doorman at heaven's door, know that we were not in favor of Annancy's wicked ways. "Me no chose none" means "I don't choose to behave in any of these ways." It was sheer joy for us to recount how Annancy would "talk wid tie-toung" (lisp) and say "push" (put), "yicky" (little) and "sho" (so); how Annancy would "play fool fe ketch wise" (pretend to be stupid in order to outwit others) and "study up him brains fe work brains pon people." We reveled in telling how Annancy had certain powers at certain times and could call upon these powers when he needed them to help out a friend, to get food for his family or just to play a trick on someone he disliked. Everything that happened in the world was started by Annancy. *Is Annancy meck it?* We were fascinated by Annancy because we could never, never be like him. Of course we could study and make up a plan, but we couldn't work brains like Annancy could or carry out schemes like he did, because he was a spider man, a magic spider man!

Some years later, when I was collecting Jamaican folklore for use on the stage and trying desperately to remember some of the stories I knew as a child, a friend gave me a copy of Walter Jekyll's book of Jamaican stories and songs. I was overjoyed to find accurate retellings of many of the stories which I had forgotten. The book brought back memories too, for instance, of my first visit to a Dinky (a function held to cheer up the family of a dead person). For eight nights after the death, men, women and children sang, danced and laughed with unusual abandonment, because "nothing sad must happen at a Dinky." Much of the laughter was caused by the telling of Annancy stories, and my only regret was that I could not remember them all. Now here they all were in black and white. It was interesting and amusing to note that Annancy had somehow found his way into my versions of several of the stories Mr. Jekyll recorded without mention of him. For instance, in the story of the "Three Sisters" (p. 26), according to my Uncle Tom at the Dinky, it was Annancy who inveigled Snake to "try him luck and go a-courting." The words of the Ole Witch Sister's song were:

> My door is bar wit a screwtan bar oh,
> Fair an' grandilow still.

This means "My door is barred with a screwed on bar, in a fairly grand condition still." Then in the story of "Toad and Donkey" (p. 39), it was Annancy who, knowing that Toad had twenty pickney, set up Toad to trick Donkey in the race. In "Doba" (p. 46), Annancy was the fiddler and through greed, sang: "No meck de yicky one get 'way" and revealed Puss's plot to boy Ratta. I could go on citing examples of the implanting of Annancy into these stories, but suffice it to say that all Jamaican folk stories have now become Annancy stories. This shows the love of the Jamaican people for the little spider man.

In Jamaican theater, Annancy has developed into a lovable rascal, easily recognized in song, verse and drama:[1]

[1] The following verses are all by Louise Bennett.

The lover: You goes for me?
I goes for you,
Like how pick-pocket goes for money!

The coward pretending to be brave:

Let me go sah, meck me fight her,
For me tempa jusa bwile,
Lawd hamassy, hole me tight! Me
Nearly get way lickle w'hile!

The man who doesn't really want to work:

Dear Cousin Brown, me come to town,
Me dont start workin' yet,
But me hope to keep on strikin'
Till some big time job me get.

The city slicker:

Hi man, I glad to see you man! When I hear
that you come from, 'Merica man, I had to hire
a taxi come look you up man!
I know you would lend me a little smalls (money)
to drop pon (pay) the Taxi-man.

The samfy (con man) who has concocted a doubtful brew:

Fava wine? (look like wine),
Is wine! Real real wine,
Tas'e it!——Kiss me nek!
I hope is not poison.

Jamaican folklore is today an integral part of the Jamaican theater, and Walter Jekyll's book of Jamaican songs and stories is an important source of research in the development of our folk art. The present generation of Jamaicans and especially we in the theater are deeply indebted to Walter Jekyll for so faithfully and painstakingly recording the Jamaican folk stories and songs.

JAMAICAN SONG AND STORY AND THE THEATER

by Rex Nettleford

LOUISE BENNETT is right. *Jamaican Song and Story* remains a rich and valuable source book for Jamaican creative artists—particularly those of us in the performing arts. Brer Annancy—the nation's folkhero—supposedly expresses much of the Jamaican spirit in his ostentatious professions of love, in his wrong-and-strong, brave-but-cowardly postures of bluff, in his love for leisure and corresponding dislike for work, in his lovable rascality. This picaresque character misses no chance for chicanery in order to be on top, as though he lives in a world that offers him no other choice for survival. No doubt the character exists in folklore everywhere. In Jamaica this descendant of the West African semideity seems to take on special significance in a society which has its roots in a system of slavery—a system which pitted the weak against the strong in daily confrontations too well-known to be narrated. It is as though every slave strove to be Annancy and he who achieved the Spider-form became a kind of hero. People like Jekyll sensed this in the hero's descendants—the Negroes—for whom, he says, "language . . . is . . . the art of disguising thought" (p. 53). And, as if to be more positive, Jekyll notes also that "straightforwardness is a quality which the Negro absolutely lacks." Annancy's admirers will probably reply that in order to cope with an unstraight and crooked world one needs unstraight and crooked paths.

But Annancy is not this type of self-conscious moralist. And even he knows that he cannot be on top all the time, as is recorded in the story "Annancy and Candlefly" (p. 86). He remains the roguish imp in the theater characterizations which I have seen in Jamaica and in the end he is always the audience's hero. He has to be! The Annancy "pantomimes" staged by the Little Theater Movement in the middle 1950's gave to a popular Jamaican comedian an excellent vehicle for vaudeville, slapstick and even pathos. The character has definitely become a convention of Jamaican farce though he does not always carry the name Annancy. No dramatic work of recognized importance has yet been created around the Annancy character, and though the theater is the poorer for it, it may be that our playwrights and dramatists are sensitive to the uncertain role of Annancy in the changing scheme of things. Times have indeed changed, and the Jamaican prototype is probably finding it less necessary to resort to the old techniques for survival. The question can perhaps be asked: Is Annancy relevant to the twentieth century? An answer may be found in a careful study of this collection of stories which parabolically weave the virtues and failings of the human condition into a fabric of animal fantasies.

In terms of dance-theater Annancy is excellent material for creative mime and movement patterns. The character suggests a fleet-footed, high jumping, frisky, shifting plastic being. He is never still for long. He is elusive. This kinesthetic quality in turn helps to determine the designs which the dance-creator of Annancy must carve in space. The form of the Spider suggests a profusion of arms and legs and a beautifully curved back with a vigilant head that focuses in different directions almost all at the same time. The stories Jekyll relates abound in movement-ideas for the dance portrayal of this folk-character whose spindle-legged nimbleness has been a point of choreographic take-off for Jamaican dance creators.

The creative artist's debt to Jekyll goes beyond the Annancy stories. His recorded digging-sings and ring games do not exhaust the rich storehouse of Jamaica folk songs, but they represent a good cross section of the island's aids to labor and to self-amusement. Some of these still exist in the Jamaican countryside. The ravages of time and the process of urbanization have played havoc with many of these customs, but much has been transplanted to the stage by professional and amateur performers and through annual festivals which make a conscious attempt to continue a tradition which dates back many generations. "Jamaicans," said Edward Long in 1774, "have a good ear for music and mime is a necessary and integral part of the life of the country people." It is part of this tradition which Jekyll caught at the end of the last century for he insists that the Negro is a born actor, since gestures which give emphasis to words come naturally to him. Jekyll also invests the Jamaican peasant with a "keen sense of the ludicrous" for being able to give a funny turn to stories about his everyday experiences.

Such digging-sings as "Oh John Thomas!" (p. 177), "Me Know the Man" (p. 180), and "Rub Him Down Joe" (p. 183) are still heard in all forms of theater in Jamaica today and the first and the last of these have even forced their way into more sophisticated urban dance halls via recordings.

The quadrille, one of the few remaining traditional dances of Jamaica, can still draw on Jekyll for its tunes (p. 217). It remains today in certain parts of Jamaica and tends to surface at festival time, when competitive demonstrations are given largely by the generation that was young during the second decade of the present century. It depicts the leisurely and non-neurotic grace of the previous century. Jekyll reports in detail on the instruments used (p. 216), and some of them are still in use today. Some readers will no doubt be intrigued by the notations in 6/8 time of the well-known folk song "Linstead Market." The Jamaican's facility to adapt rhythms to his own purposes is as true today as it was in Jekyll's time.

In fact, the relevance of *Jamaican Song and Story* to present-day Jamaica more than justifies this new edition, for the book defines with clarity and charm an aspect of Jamaica which deserves general recognition now that the country seeks to find itself.

The Folk-Lore Society

FOR COLLECTING AND PRINTING

RELICS OF POPULAR ANTIQUITIES, &c.

ESTABLISHED IN

THE YEAR MDCCCLXXVIII.

Alter et Idem.

PUBLICATIONS

OF

THE FOLK-LORE SOCIETY

LV.

[1904]

JAMAICAN SONG AND STORY:

ANNANCY STORIES, DIGGING SINGS, RING TUNES, AND DANCING TUNES

COLLECTED AND EDITED BY

WALTER JEKYLL:

WITH AN INTRODUCTION BY

ALICE WERNER,

AND APPENDICES ON

TRACES OF AFRICAN MELODY IN JAMAICA

BY

C. S. MYERS,

AND ON

ENGLISH AIRS AND MOTIFS IN JAMAICA

BY

LUCY E. BROADWOOD.

"A few brief years have passed away
    Since Britain drove her million slaves
Beneath the tropic's fiery ray:
God willed their freedom; and to-day
    Life blooms above those island graves!"

Whittier

Published for the Folk-Lore Society by

DAVID NUTT, 57—59 LONG ACRE

LONDON

1907

CONTENTS.

PAGE

PART IV. : DANCING TUNES - - - - 216

DANCING TUNES—*Continued.*

INTRODUCTION.

MR. JEKYLL'S delightful collection of tales and songs from Jamaica suggests many interesting problems. It presents to us a network of interwoven strands of European and African origin, and when these have been to some extent disentangled we are confronted with the further question, to which of the peoples of the Dark Continent may the African element be attributed?

The exact relationship between the "Negro" and Bantu races,—which of them is the original and which the adulterated stock (in other words, whether the adulteration was an improvement or the reverse),—is a subject quite beyond my competence to discuss. It seems certain that the Negro languages (as yet only tentatively classified) are as distinct from the singularly homogeneous and well-defined Bantu family, as Aryan from Semitic. Ibo, at one end of the area, has possible Bantu affinities, which await fuller investigation; the same thing has been conjectured of Bullom and Temne at the other end (Sierra Leone); but these are so slight and as yet so doubtful that they scarcely affect the above estimate.

The difference in West Coast and Bantu folk-tales is not so marked as that between the languages; yet here, too, along with a great deal which the two have in common, we can pick out some features peculiar to each. And Mr. Jekyll's tales, so far as they can be supposed to come from Africa at all, are not Bantu. The name of "Annancy" alone is enough to tell us that.

Annancy, or *Anansi* is the Tshi (Ashanti)[1] word for "spider"; and the Spider figures largely in the folk-tales of the West Coast

[1] Fanti is a dialect of this language, which is variously called Twi, Chwi, Otyi, and Ochi.

(by which we mean, roughly, the coast between Cape Verde and Kamerun), while, with some curious exceptions to be noted later on, he seems to be absent from Bantu folk-lore. His place is there taken by the Hare (Brer Rabbit), and, in some of his aspects, by the Tortoise.

We find the "Brer Rabbit" stories (best known through *Uncle Remus*) in the Middle and Southern States of America, where a large proportion, at any rate, of the negro slaves were imported from Lower Guinea. Some personal names and other words preserved among them (*e.g.* "goober" = *nguba*, the ground-nut, or "pea-nut") can be traced to the Fiote, or Lower Congo language; and some songs of which I have seen the words,[1] *look* as if they might be Bantu, but corrupted apparently beyond recognition.

But the British West Indies would seem to have been chiefly supplied from Upper Guinea, or the "West Coast" proper (it really faces south, while Loango, Congo, etc., are the "South-West Coast"—a point which is sometimes puzzling to the uninitiated). Among the tribes to be found in Jamaica, Mr. Jekyll tells me are the Ibo (Lower Niger), Coromantin (Gold Coast), Hausa, Mandingo, Moko (inland from Calabar), Nago (Yoruba), and Sobo (Lower Niger).

Mr. Jekyll furnishes a bit of confirmatory evidence in the list of names (p. 156) given to children according to the day of the week on which they are born. These are immediately recognizable as Tshi. As given in Christaller's *Dictionary of the Asante and Fante Language called Tshi* (1881), the boys' names are identical or nearly so (allowing for the different systems of spelling) with those in Mr. Jekyll's list. They are: Kwasi,

[1] One is given by Mr. G. W. Cable in the *Century Magazine*, xxx. 820, as a Louisiana Voodoo song:

Héron mandé, tigui li papa, Héron mandé, dosé dan godo.

Another by Mr. W. E. Burghart Du Bois in *The Souls of Black Folk*, p. 254—apparently a lullaby:

Doba na coba gene me, gene me!
Ben d' nu li, nu li, nu li, nu li, bend'le.

I can make nothing of these. In the latter case, uncertainty as to the phonetic system adopted complicates the puzzle. One might be tempted to connect the last two words with Zulu *endhle* or *pandhle* = outside,—but I can find nothing else to support this resemblance, and such stray guesses are unprofitable work.

Kwadwo, Kwabena, Kwaku, Kwaw (or Yaw), Kofi, Kwame. (Mr. George Macdonald, in *The Gold Coast Past and Present*, gives Kwamina, instead of Kwame, probably owing to a difference of dialect. The girls' names are less easily recognizable, but a careful scrutiny reveals the interesting fact that in some cases an older form seems to have been preserved in Jamaica. Moreover, the sound written *w* by Christaller approaches that of *b*, which seems to be convertible with it under certain conditions, all the girls' names being formed by means of the suffix *ba* = a child. Conversely, *ekpo* in the mouth of a West Coast native sounds to a casual ear like *ekwo*.

Akosuwa [= Akwasiba] = Quashiba.
Adwowa = Jubba. (Cf. dw = dj in "Cudjo").
Abeua = Cubba.
Akuwa = Memba.
Ya [= Yawa] = Abba.
Afuwa = Fibba.
Amma [= Amenenewa] = Beniba.

The boys' names have "Kwa" (= *akoa*, a man, slave) prefixed to that of the day, or, more correctly speaking, of its presiding genius. These latter are: Ayisi, Adwo, Benã, Wuku, Yaw, Afi, Amin. The names of the days appear to be formed from them by the omission of the initial A (where it exists), and the addition of the suffix *da*, with some irregularities, which no doubt a fuller knowledge of the language would explain: Kwasida, Dwoda, Benada, Wukuda, Yawda, Fida, Memeneda (Meminda). The week of seven days does not seem to be known elsewhere in Africa, except as a result of Moslem or Christian influence. The Congo week of four days is puzzling, till one remembers that it, too, rests on a division of the lunar month: 7 × 4 instead of 4 × 7.[1]

The Tshi, Ewe and Yoruba languages are genderless, like the Bantu. (The word *ba* has come to mean "a daughter" when appropriated as a suffix to feminine names; but, properly, it seems to mean "a child" of either sex.) This fact explains the appearance of such personages as "Brother Cow" (see also Mr. Jekyll's note on p. 107), and the wild confusion of pronouns

[1] R. E. Dennett, *Folklore of the Fjort*, p. 8.

sometimes observed: "Annancy really want that gal fe marry, but he couldn' catch him."—"When the gal go, him go meet Brother Death,"—etc.

The few words given as "African" by Mr. Jekyll seem to be traceable to Tshi. "Massoo" (pp. 12, 13) is *mã so* = to lift. *Afu* ("hafoo," "afoo," p. 18) is not in Christaller's *Dictionary*, except as equivalent to "grass," or "herbs"; *fufu* is a food made from yams or plantains boiled and pounded; perhaps there is some slight confusion. *Nyam* is not "to eat," but *enãm* is Tshi for "meat," as *nyama* (in some form or other) is in every Bantu language. The nonsense-words in the songs may be corrupted from Tshi or some cognate language, but a fuller knowledge of these than I possess would be necessary in order to determine the point.

Transplanted African folk-lore has a peculiar interest of its own, and one is very glad to find Mr. Jekyll doing for Jamaica what Mr. Chandler Harris, *e.g.* has done for Georgia. But the African element in the stories before us is far less evident than in "Uncle Remus," and is in many cases overlaid and inextricably mixed up with matter of European origin. At least eleven out of the fifty-one stories before us can be set down as imported, directly or indirectly, from Europe. I say directly or indirectly, because an examination of Chatelain's *Folk-tales of Angola* and Junod's *Chants et Contes des Baronga* shows that some tales, at any rate, have passed from Portugal to Africa. Such are *La fille du Roi* (Ronga), which is identical with Grimm's *The Shoes that were danced to pieces*, and with the Slovak-gypsy story of *The Three Girls* (Groome, *Gypsy Folk-tales*, p. 141). But in the absence of more detailed and direct evidence than we yet possess, it would be rash to assume that they have passed to America by way of Africa, rather than that they have been independently transmitted.

The eleven stories above referred to are: II. Yung-kyum-pyung, III. King Daniel, VI. Blackbird and Woss-woss, X. Mr. Bluebeard, XVII. Man-crow, XVIII. Saylan, XXI. Tacoma and the Old-witch Girl, XXVI. The Three Pigs, XXXI. Pretty Poll (another version of III.), XXXIX. Open Sesame (variant of VI.), VII. The Three Sisters. But some of these, as I hope to show presently, also have genuine African prototypes, and it is a question how far these fading traditions have been amalgamated with fairy-tales told to the slaves by the children of their European masters. The last named is one of a small group of tales (VII., XXIV., XXXIV., L.) which I cannot help referring to a common African original.

By far the greater number of the stories in this book, whether, strictly speaking, "Annancy stories" or not, come under the heading of animal-stories, and are of the same type as "Uncle Remus," Junod's "Roman du Lièvre," and numerous examples from various parts of Africa. It will be remembered that, in most of these, the difference between animals and human beings is not very clearly kept in view by the narrators. As M. Junod says, "Toutes les bêtes qui passent et repassent dans ces curieux récits représentent des êtres humains, cela va sans dire. Ils sont personnalisés par un procédé linguistique qui consiste à mettre devant le nom de l'animal un préfixe de la classe des hommes." (This is a point we must come back to later on.) "Ainsi *mpfoundla*, le lièvre ordinaire, devient dans le contes Noua-mpfoundla .... La Rainette, c'est Noua-chinana, l'Eléphant, Noua-ndlopfou .... Leurs caractères physiques particuliers sont présents devant l'imagination du conteur pour autant qu'ils donnent du pittoresque au récit. Mais on les oublie tout aussi aisément dès qu'ils ne sont plus essentiels à la narration." This feature constantly meets one in Bantu folk-lore: the hare and the elephant hire themselves out to hoe a man's garden; the swallow invites the cock to dinner and his wife prepares the food, in the usual native hut with the fireplace in the middle and the *nsanja* staging over it; the hare's wife goes to the river to draw water, and is caught by a crocodile; the tortoise carries his complaint to the village elders assembled in the smithy, and so on. M. Junod seems to me to overrate the conscious artistic purpose in the narrators of these tales: the native mind is quite ready to assume that animals think and act in much the same way as human beings, and this attitude makes it easy to forget the outward distinctions when they appear as actors in a story. No doubt this haziness of view is increased by the popular conception of metamorphosis as a possible occurrence in everyday life. When, as has more than once been the case, we find men firmly believing, not only that they can, under certain circumstances, turn into animals, but that they actually have done so, we may expect them to think it quite easy for animals to turn into men.

The prefix given by the Baronga to animals, when they are, so to speak, personified in tales, may seem a slight point, but it is not without interest. The Yaos in like manner give them the prefix *Che* (*Che Sungula*, the Rabbit, *Che Likoswe*, the Rat, etc.), which, though usually translated "Mr.," is of common gender and used quite as often in addressing women as men. In Chatelain's Angola stories the animals sometimes (not always) have the honorific prefix *Na* or *Ngana*, "Mr."; the latter is sometimes translated "Lord." In Luganda folk-lore the elephant (*enjovu*) is called Wa Njovu. In Zulu, Ucakijana (to whom we shall come back presently) is the diminutive form of *icakide*, the Weasel, put into the personal class. I do not recall anything similar in Nyanja tales, but cannot help connecting with the above the fact that animals, whatever class their names may belong to, are usually treated as persons in the tales. Not to be unduly technical, I would briefly explain that *njobvu* (elephant) and *ng'ona* (crocodile) would naturally take the pronoun *i*, but in the stories (and, I think, sometimes in other cases) they take *a*, which belongs to the first, or personal class. Now, the reader will notice how often the animals in the stories before us are distinguished as "Mr." or "Bro'er" (cf. pp. 20, 23, 31, 86, etc.), though the Jamaica people seem to be less uniformly polite in this respect than Uncle Remus. "Brer Rabbit" is so familiar as to be taken for granted, as a rule, without further question; but, years before he had become a household word in this country, we find a writer in *Lippincott's Magazine*[1] remarking, "The dramatis personæ are honoured with the title *Buh*, which is generally supposed to be an abbreviation of the word 'brother,' but it probably is a title of respect equal to our 'Mr.'" The "but" seems hardly called for, since both assertions are seemingly true. We might also compare the Zulu *u Cakijana* (1st class), who is human or quasi-human, while *i-cakide* (2nd class) is the name for the Weasel.

[1] December, 1877, p. 751. The article is one on "Negro Folk-lore," by W. Owens, and contains several stories, some of these independent versions of "Uncle Remus" tales, while others are not to be found in that collection.

Annancy, then, is the Spider, and as such he is conceived throughout the folk-lore of West Africa. If he seems, as he continually does, to take on a human character, going to Freetown to buy a gun and powder (*Cunnie Rabbit*, p. 282), or applying to a "Mory man" for amulets (*ib.* p. 139), he only behaves like all other animals, as explained above. A Temne authority (*ib.* p. 93) maintains that "Spider was a person" in old times, and did not look the same as he does in these days, "he done turn odder kind of thing now." But this looks like an attempt at rationalising the situation, possibly in response to European inquiries. The change of shape alluded to at the end of the Temne Tar-baby episode is comparatively a minor matter: he was formerly "round lek pusson," but became flattened out through the beating he received while attached to the Wax Girl. In the Gold Coast stories, too, Anansi is quite as much a spider as Brer Rabbit is a rabbit; but in Jamaica, though he still retains traces of his origin, they are somewhat obscured—so much so that Mr. Jekyll speaks (pp. 4-5) of the "metamorphic shape, that of the Spider," which he assumes, as though the human were his real form, the other only an occasional disguise. In "Annancy and Brother Tiger" we find that he has to "run up a house-top" to escape the revenge of the monkeys, which accounts for some of his habits to this day. In "Yung-kyum-pyung" (a version of *Rumpelstilzchen*, or *Tom Tit Tot*), the only hint of his spider character is contained in a mere allusion (quite external to the story) to his "running 'pon him rope." In "Brother Death," Annancy and all his family cling to the rafters, hoping to escape from Death; but it scarcely seems in character that they should be incapable of holding on long. They drop, one after another, Annancy last (p. 33). He is always in danger from Cows (p. 107): "Anywhere Cow see him, he reach him down with his mouth"; and he lives in a banana branch (p. 119) for fear of Calcutta Monkey and his whip. His moral character is consistently bad all through; he is a "clever thief"—greedy, treacherous, and cruel, but intellectually he does not uniformly shine. He has to call in the help of a wizard in his love affairs; "Monkey was too clever for him" on more than one occasion; he has to be extricated from the slaughter-house (p. 23) by Blackbird and his army of Wasps, and in "Man-crow" he is signally discomfited. In other cases his roguery is successful, and he is described as the greatest musician and "the biggest rascal in the world" (p. 62). Much the same is the character given to Mr. Spider in "Cunnie Rabbit." Not one amiable trait is recorded of him.

A Gold Coast story,[1] however, shows him arbitrating between a Rat and a Panther in very much the same way as the Yao Che Sungula settles the difficulty between the Man and the Crocodile,[2] making the latter go back into the trap whence he had too confidingly been released, in order to show how it was done. Once having got the ungrateful Panther back into the trap, the Spider advises the Rat to leave him there.

As there is a Gold Coast tradition which affirms the human race to be descended from the Spider,[3] it might be expected that he should sometimes appear in a more favourable light, and also that those peoples who had lost this myth, or never possessed it, should concentrate their attention on the darker side of his character. At the same time, even in what may be called his own home, he does not appear as infallible. A very curious story, given by Zimmermann in his *Grammatical Sketch of the Akra or Gâ Language*, shows us the Spider and his son in the character of the two sisters who usually figure in tales of the "Holle" type,[4] and, strangely enough, it is the father who, by his wilfulness and indiscretion, forfeits the advantages which the son has gained. During a time of famine the young spider crawls into a rat-hole in search of a nut which has rolled into it,

[1] J. C. Christaller, in Büttner's *Zeitschr. für Afr. Sprachen.* M. Réné Basset says of a similar story included in Col. Monteil's *Contes Soudanais:* "L'Enfant et le caïman est le sujet bien connu de l'ingratitude punie que l'on retrouve dans tous les pays de l'ancien monde, et dont M. Kenneth Mackenzie vient d'étudier les diverses variantes." The idea is one so likely to occur independently that we must not in all cases resort to the hypothesis of borrowing.

[2] Duff Macdonald, *Africana*, ii. 346.

[3] Ellis, *Tshi-speaking Peoples of the Gold Coast.*

[4] No. 16 in the *Handbook of Folklore* (p. 122). It might also be referred to the "Golden Goose" type (51). Stories of this kind are the Ronga "Route du Ciel," and "The Three Women" in Duff Macdonald's *Africana.* But perhaps the tale referred to in the text comes nearer to "The Two Hunchbacks."

and there meets with three unkempt and unwashed spirits, who desire him to peel some yams and cook the peelings. He does so, and they are changed into large yams. They give him a large basket of yams to carry home, and teach him a spell which is not to be imparted to any one else. He repeatedly obtains supplies from the same source, but at last is followed by his father, who insists on going in his stead. He derides and disobeys the spirits, loses his yams, and is flogged into the bargain.

We have mentioned the comparative absence of the Spider from Bantu folk-lore. I have been able to discover only two references to him in East Africa, both to be found in Duff Macdonald's *Africana*. The first is in a creation-myth of the Yaos (i. 297), which informs us that when *Mulungu* was driven from earth by the conduct of mankind, who had set the bush on fire, he went, being unable to climb a tree as the Chameleon had done, to call the Spider. "The spider went on high and returned again, and said, 'I have gone on high nicely,' and he said, 'You now, Mulungu, go on high.' Mulungu then went with the spider on high. And he said, 'When they die, let them come on high here.'" The other is in the story of "The Dead Chief and his Younger Brother" (ii. 322)—also Yao. The dead chief gives his brother four bags to enable him to overcome the obstacles which his enemies put in his way; he opens the first on coming to a large tree in his path—a wood-moth comes out and gnaws a way through. From the second bag comes out a manis (scaly ant-eater), which digs a way under a rock, and from the third (which he opens when he comes to the bank of a river) a spider, which "went to the other side," and, presumably (though this is not expressly stated), made a bridge with its web for him to cross.[1]

Mr. R. E. Dennett (*Folk-lore of the Fjort*, p. 74) gives a Lower Congo story, telling how the Spider brought fire down from Nzambi Mpungu in heaven, and won the daughter of Nzambi (Mother Earth) by so doing. In an Angola story (Heli

[1] In Mr. Dudley Kidd's *Savage Childhood* (published since the above was written), I find that Zulu (or Pondo?) boys draw certain omens from spiders, in connection with dreams (p. 105), and that in Gazaland the rainbow is called "the spider's bow" (p. 153).

Chatelain, p. 131) the Spider is mentioned as affording a means of communication between heaven and earth, by which the Sun's maidservants go down to draw water, and his daughter is ultimately let down to be married to the son of Kimanaueze. But the Spider only comes in incidentally; it is the Frog whose resourcefulness makes the marriage possible. The notion of the spider's web as a ladder to heaven is one that might occur independently in any part of the world, and there is no need to suppose these tales to be derivatives of the Hausa one given by Schön.[1]

So far, the appearances of the Spider in Bantu folk-tales are so infrequent as to be almost a negligible quantity. We find him, however, playing a tolerably conspicuous part in the folklore of the Duala. These, living in the German territory of the Kamerun, may be considered the north-western outpost of the Bantu race, and their language, unmistakable in its general character, has departed, perhaps more widely than any other, from the normal Bantu standard. Herr Wilhelm Lederbogen, formerly of the Government School, Kamerun, has collected a large number of stories, some of which are published in the *Transactions* of the Berlin Oriental Seminary (see *Afrikanische Studien* for 1901-1903). These comprise 67 "*Tierfabeln*" and 18 tales of the ordinary *märchen* type. The latter (some of them recognizable as variants of tales current in Bantu Africa) introduce animals along with human beings, and the incident of the Spider being consulted as a soothsayer repeatedly occurs. "*Die Spinne tritt immer als Wahrsagerin auf*" says the collector in a note. But the malignant aspect of Anansi seems to be absent.

The late W. H. J. Bleek, who supposed the animal-stories which he had collected from Hottentots and Bushmen to be characteristic of and peculiar to these races, had built up a somewhat elaborate theory, scarcely borne out by the facts as known to us to-day, in connection with this point. Briefly, it amounted to this: that a fundamental limitation in the Bantu race, which had prevented, and always would prevent, their advancing beyond a certain point, was denoted by the absence of grammatical gender in their languages, their supposed incapacity for personifying nature, and their worship of ancestors, as opposed

[1] *Magana Hausa*, 63.

to the alleged moon-worship of the Hottentots.[1] The Zulus, he says, believe that the spirits of the dead appear to them in dreams, and also show themselves to the waking eye in the shape of animals, usually serpents. "No personification of the animal takes place, however, such as we find, for instance, in the mythical world of our earliest [Teutonic] literature. The imagination of the ancestor-worshipper does not even, as a rule, show us the animal as possessing the gift of human speech; it is only supposed to perform acts well within its capacity as an animal, though such acts are considered, in the case of individual animals supposed to be possessed by the spirits of deceased persons, as emanating from the spirits." Thus, a serpent, known by various tokens to be an *idhlozi*, may enter a hut and consume the meat left for it, or it may engage in combat with other snakes which must be supposed to represent the enemies of the deceased. Animals thus revered by ancestor-worshippers always have the distinguishing characteristic that they have once been human beings; and spirits, unless they appear as animals, are always invisible. "A personification of the animal world (such as we find in our own fables), or even of other things (as in the mythologies of Europe), is utterly absent from this primitive, prosaic way of looking at things." The poetic impulse implied in such personification can only arise, in Bleek's view, among the speakers of a sex-denoting language. The linguistic argument I cannot here reproduce in detail; its tendency is sufficiently shown by the following quotation, which bears directly on our subject:

"The form of a sex-denoting language, by exciting sympathy even for creatures not connected with us by human fellowship, leads in the first instance to the humanization of animals, and thus especially gives rise to the creation of fables. Even on the lowest stage of national development, we find the Hottentot language accompanied by a literature of fables, for which we may vainly seek a parallel in the literatures of the prefix-pronominal languages."

The validity of Bleek's theory was seriously doubted by the late Dr. C. G. Büttner, in 1886, and the masses of fresh material which have come to light during the last forty years, have com-

[1] See *Ursprung der Sprache* (Weimar, 1868), pp. xix, xxiii (Introduction).

pletely altered the aspect of the question. The Hottentot myth of the Hare and the Moon, to take but one example, which appears among the Zulus as the tale of Unkulunkulu and the Chameleon, is told by the Anyanja (of the Shire Highlands and Lake Nyasa) of the Chameleon. The Duala have the same Chameleon story; and there is a Gold Coast version, in which the two messengers are the Sheep, who linger on the way to graze, and the Goat, who arrives first with the tidings that man shall not return after death. The Krūmen of the Ivory Coast say that *Nemla* (a small antelope probably representing, if not identical with, the "Cunnie Rabbit" of Sierra Leone), maliciously, not accidentally, rendered inoperative the remedy against death provided by the fetich Blenyiba. Who is responsible for the original version it is perhaps impossible to settle. But there can be no question of *recent* borrowing; and supposing that the Bantu did derive the myth from their predecessors (now represented by the remnant of the Bushmen, and perhaps the Pygmies), this would surely prove them at least capable of assimilating fresh ideas and thus advancing beyond the line so inexorably traced for them from the beginning. It may be remarked in passing that there seems some probability of the Bantu Anyanja in the Shire district having largely absorbed, instead of exterminating as was elsewhere the case, a smaller-sized race who previously occupied the country. In the same way, the Abatembu of the Cape Colony are the descendants of a Bantu clan amalgamated with the Bushman tribe of the 'Tambuka, and traces of similar fusion could no doubt be discovered elsewhere. But we doubt its being *necessary* to the introduction of animal-stories into folk-lore,—or, in general, of ideas connected with the personification of nature.

The Zulu tales which Bleek had before him present a character very different from that of the Hottentot beast-fables. But a comparative study of Bantu folk-lore suggests at least the possibility that they may have been developed out of animal-stories. Hlakanyana is conceived of as certainly human, and reminds us of Tom Thumb; but some of his adventures are identical with those of the Hare, the Jackal, or Brer Rabbit. Cakijana shows still clearer traces of animal origin. The episode of Hlakanyana's demanding a digging-stick in exchange for the birds he accuses his companion of having eaten, and the sequence of exchanges which culminates in his acquiring a cow,[1] is in substance the same as the story told by the Anyanja about the Hare (*kalulu*) which was given in *Folk-Lore* for Sept. 29th, 1904. This again reminds us of "The Man who Lived by Overreaching Others" (Dr. Elmslie in *Folk-Lore*, vol. iii.), and of a Sukuma story given by Herrmann,[2] in which a boy gives his grandmother some honey to keep for him, and, coming back after a time, and finding she has eaten it, makes her give him some corn in exchange. The corn is then exchanged for an egg, the egg for sticks, the sticks for a knife, and the knife for a cow's tail, for which, by the same trick as in Dr. Elmslie's story, he obtains a cow. There is no suggestion of trickery in the Nyanja story, whereas it is brought out very strongly both in Hlakanyana and the Sukuma example.

We shall have occasion to refer, later on, to more than one instance where a story is found in two forms, one having animals, the other human beings, as its characters.

The animals figuring in folk-tales must necessarily vary with the locality of the tale, and in cases where a story has travelled (or possibly where the same idea has arisen independently in different places) it is interesting to note the changes in its *dramatis personæ*. Thus, the incident of the race between the swift creature and the slow seems to be found in the folk-lore of every country. In Africa the winner is always, so far as I know, the Tortoise, as Brer Terrapin is in "Uncle Remus." The Jamaica version in the volume before us substitutes the Toad, while the defeated party is the Donkey. In a Konde (North Nyasa) variant, the protagonists are the Elephant and the Tortoise, in a Duala one, the *Ngoloñ* (a large kind of Antelope) and the Tortoise. Another version of the Duala story, contained in *Märchen aus Kamerun*, by the late Frau Elli Meinhof, has the Hare and the Tortoise, but with the explanation that by "hare" is meant "eine kleine Antilopenart, *eseru* genannt." The curious thing is that Njo Dibone, the native authority for the tales, himself suggested the name of "hare," but added "Hase ist nicht wie hier,[3] sondern hat kleine

[1] McCall Theal, *Kaffir Folk-Tales*, pp. 96-98.

[2] "Afrikanische Studien," 1898 (*Transactions* of the Berlin Oriental Seminary, vol. i.) p. 194.

[3] He had been brought to Europe by a German naval officer in 1885, and remained for some time an inmate of Professor Meinhof's family.

Hörner." It is not stated whether he had himself seen the European hare, but apparently he thought the two animals so far similar that *Hase* would be the nearest available rendering for *eseru*. This may throw some light on the question why the *Dorcatherium* gazelle, or possibly the Royal Antelope, *Neotragus*, is called "Cunnie Rabbit" in Sierra Leone English.

The Tortoise plays a conspicuous part in the folk-lore both of Bantu and West African Negroes. In Yoruba tradition he takes the place of the Spider with the Fantis, all mankind being descended from him. Perhaps this is not strange, when we consider how much there is about him which would appeal to the primitive mind as uncanny and mysterious. A recent writer in the *West African Mail*[1] says on this subject: "The original conception of the tortoise culminated in a belief concerning its attributes that, in the eyes of these [Niger] Delta natives, elevated it to the sovereignty of the beasts of the forest. . . . Absolutely harmless and inoffensive in himself, the tortoise does not prey on even the smallest of insects, but subsists entirely on the fallen fruits of the forest"—or, in some cases, on fungi. "In the gloomy forests of the Delta there are only two enemies capable of doing him any serious harm. The one is man, who is able to lift him up and carry him bodily away, which, however, he does not do, except in those instances in which the animal is regarded as sacred, and required in connection with certain religious ceremonies. His other and most dangerous enemy is the python, who having first of all crushed him by means of the enormous power of constriction which it can apply, swallows him alive, shell and all. But pythons large enough to do this, unless the tortoise happens to be very young and small, are very scarce, so that he has not much to apprehend in that quarter. To the elephant—herbivorous, like himself—he is too insignificant, for unlike the mosquito or the sand-fly, he has no sting; and although they meet in fable, in real life the hippopotamus and himself are not much thrown together. From the leopard or the bush-cat, he has nothing to fear, for their teeth cannot penetrate his shell, nor can [their] claws do him any damage. Thus it is that . . . the tortoise has been practically immune from attack and therefore destruction—a fact that in a great measure explains his longevity."

[1] May 25, 1906, p. 202.

If we add to this his power of living for a long time without food, his silence, the extreme slowness and caution of his movements, his instinct of keeping out of sight, and the peculiar air of dogged determination with which he sets about overcoming or circumventing obstacles, it is "easy to understand how in process of time the word which stood for tortoise became a synonym for cunning and craft, and a man of exceptional intelligence was in this way known among the Ibo as 'Mbai,' and among the Ibani as 'Ekake,' meaning a tortoise. For although he of the shell-back was slow, he was sure, as the old Greek Aesop tells us. . . . This sureness, in the native mind, implied doggedness and a fixed determination, while silence and secrecy implied mystery and a veiled purpose behind which it is impossible to get."

The tortoise of African folk-lore is sometimes, in fact usually, the land-tortoise (as implied in the above extracts), of which there are several species, living either in forest-country or in deserts like the Kalahari. In Angola, the story of "Man and Turtle" (Chatelain, p. 153—identical with "Mr. Fox tackles Old Man Tarrypin" in "Uncle Remus") refers to a kind which, if not aquatic, is evidently amphibious. We find tortoise stories all over Negro and Bantu Africa; we have Temne, Bullom, and Yoruba examples, besides Duala, Konde (Nyasa), Yao, Nyanja, Herero, Bemba, Congo (Upoto), Angola and Sesuto ones. This does not exhaust the list I have made out, and further research would no doubt bring to light many more. One of these is the well-known "tug-of-war" story, which in "Uncle Remus" has the title "Mr. Terrapin shows his strength." We have two versions of this (agreeing in their main points) from the Kamerun, one told by the Duala, the other by the Yabakalaki-Bakoko tribe. Here it is the Elephant and the Hippopotamus whom the Tortoise induces to pull against each other. The American Negro substitutes the Bear for one of these competitors, and then, apparently at a loss for a wild animal strong enough to take the place of the other, makes "Brer Tarrypin" tie "Miss Meadows's bed-cord" to a root in the bed of the stream. But it is interesting to find two native African versions in which other animals are substituted for the Tortoise. The Temne (*Cunnie Rabbit*, p. 117) gives his part to the Spider, while the Bemba people (North-eastern Rhodesia) make the Hare the hero of the adventure. Col. Monteil gives a

Mandingo variant, introducing a different motive for the contest: the Hare has borrowed a slave apiece from the Elephant and the Hippopotamus, and when pressed for payment hands each of his competitors in turn the end of a rope, with the words, "Tu n'as qu'à tirer sur cette corde, le captif est au bout."[1]

Another Temne story collected by Miss Cronise, "Mr. Turtle makes a riding-horse of Mr. Leopard," is paralleled by an Angola one (Chatelain, p. 203) in which it is Mr. Frog who plays the trick on Mr. Elephant. In the New World, it will be remembered that Brer Rabbit has usurped the part.

In M. René Basset's *Anthology of African Folk-tales*[2] is included a tale about a monkey and a tortoise from Baissac's *Folklore de l'Ile Maurice* which recalls a Nyanja one obtained by me at Blantyre and printed in the *Contemporary Review* for September, 1896. In the latter it is the iguana, not the monkey who robs the Tortoise; but in both, the Tortoise exacts retribution with a cold-blooded relentlessness suggestive of Shylock. A Brazilian negro story is also given, which looks like a variant of one told in Calabar to account for the fact that the Tortoise's shell is composed of separate plates, as though it had been broken to pieces and put together again.

But we look in vain for the tortoise in these stories of Mr. Jekyll's. Even in the race-story, as we have seen, the part which in Africa is so peculiarly his own, is taken by the Toad. Probably this is because the land-tortoise is not found in Jamaica, and the great turtle of the seas is not a creature whose ways would come under the daily observation of the peasantry. In the same way familiar animals have been substituted for unfamiliar ones in a great many cases, though not in all. Mr. Jekyll thinks "Tiger" is a substitute for "Lion," but it seems equally possible that "Leopard" is meant. All over South Africa, leopards are called "tigers" by Dutch, English, and Germans, just as hyenas are called "wolves," and bustards "peacocks" (*paauw*). "Tiger" is used in the same sense in German Kamerun, and probably elsewhere in West Africa.

[1] *Contes Soudanais*, p. 49.

[2] P. 425. Another Mauritius negro tale from the same source is identical with the Yao one of the Elephant and the Hare (Duff Macdonald, ii. 353)—also found elsewhere in East Africa.

Lion and elephant are known—perhaps by genuine tradition—to Uncle Remus; but they seem to have faded from the recollection of the Jamaica negroes; indeed, the lion is not found in their original homes, being absent from the whole West Coast as far as Sierra Leone.

"Brer Rabbit," so characteristic a figure of Bantu folk-lore that his adventures are related from one side of Africa to the other (though in the west he is less frequently met with north of Angola), only appears in two of Mr. Jekyll's stories, in none of which we can recognize anything of his traditional character. In "Annancy and his Fish-pot," he is unscrupulously victimised by Annancy, and subsequently dies of fright and worry; in "Snake the Postman," he escapes from Annancy's machinations, but there is no indication that he could ever be considered a match for "that cravin' fellah." In "John Crow and Fowl-hawk" he is merely alluded to (p. 142, "This company was Rabbit"). In "Dry Bone," he is induced by Guinea-pig to carry the unwelcome load, but succeeds in passing it on, for the time being, to Annancy. Finally, in "Gaulin," he cuts a poor figure as the unsuccessful suitor. A Bantu story by no means complimentary to the Hare's intelligence is given by M. Junod,[1] and seems to have reached Louisiana[2] as "Compair Lapin et Michié Dinde," where the Rabbit gets his head cut off under the belief that the Turkey has removed his when he puts it under his wing to sleep. M. Junod thinks this must refer to a second species of Hare, a by-word for stupidity, as the other is for cuteness; but it is at least worth noting that the same story is told by the Basumbwa (south of Lake Victoria) of the Hen and the Tiger-cat.

Besides Annancy himself, and the "Tiger" already mentioned, we have, in these stories, either domestic or quasi-domestic animals: Cow, Hog, Dog, Puss, "Ratta," etc., or creatures indigenous to Jamaica, such as John-Crow, Chicken-Hawk, Sea-Gaulin, Candle-Fly, Crab and Tarpon. Some stories, for which I fail to recall any exact parallel, either in Africa or Europe, may be of purely local origin; this is most likely to be true of those which profess to explain some elementary fact in

[1] *Chants et Contes*, p. 135, see also the preceding story, and some remarks on p. 86, footnote 2.

[2] Alcée Fortier, *Louisiana Folklore*, p. 24.

natural history, such as the inability of two bulls to agree in one pasture ("Timmolimmo"), or the hostility between dogs and cats. Even were this not so, the amount of local colour introduced (as always where tales are transmitted orally) could change them almost beyond recognition. This often has a very quaint effect, as in "Parson Puss and Parson Dog," who are evidently conceived as ministers of some rival Methodist denominations, and in the references to weddings, funerals, and dances possibly ending up with a free fight, as in "Gaulin," "How Monkey manage Annancy," "Doba," etc. Annancy's inviting the animals to his father's funeral and slaughtering them (with the exception of Monkey, who is too clever for him) reminds us of the Temne "Mr. Leopard fools the other animals,"[1] but in this, Leopard himself pretends to die. Cunnie Rabbit's test, "Die pusson nebber blow," is less ingenious than that applied by Brer Rabbit in "Uncle Remus":[2] "When a man go to see dead folks, dead folks allers raises up der behime leg en hollers *wahoo*!" (In Mr. Owen's version, they "grin and whistle.") In the Sesuto story[3] the Monkey suspects a trick and escapes, when the Hare persuades the Lion to entrap the other animals by shamming death. Perhaps the baptism of the crabs ("Annancy in Crab Country") may be connected with "Mr. Spider initiates the fowls,"[4] where the Temne Spider, assuming for the nonce a quasi-religious character, gathers his victims together to celebrate the Bundo mysteries, and massacres them wholesale.

"Annancy and Hog" (XXXII.) is a fragmentary story, not very easy to understand as we have it, but something has evidently dropped out. The sentence "An' when Hog think him done up Annancy him done up him own mother" may point to some original similar to the Fiote story given by Mr. Dennett, in which the Leopard's wife is induced to eat her husband's head.[5] But in that case it is difficult to understand the connection with the opening incidents.

In "John-Crow and Fowl-hawk" (XLVI.) we *may* have a reminiscence of the class of stories represented by the Yao "Kalikalanje," in which an unborn child is promised by the

[1] *Cunnie Rabbit*, p. 219.

[2] "Mr. Wolf makes a failure."

[3] Jacottet, p. 19.

[4] *Cunnie Rabbit*, p. 133.

[5] *Folklore of the Fjort*, pp. 82-84.

mother in return for a service rendered her by some person or animal. The resemblance, however, is not very marked, and the incident is quite lost sight of in the later part of the story.

"Annancy and Death" is curious, and, as it stands, not very intelligible. Death, as a person, is introduced into several African stories,[1] and even (in one from the Ivory Coast) together with the Spider, but none of these have anything parallel with the one before us. The last part, however, where Annancy and his children are clinging to the rafters, and Death waiting for them below, recalls the story to be found on pp. 224-226 of *Cunnie Rabbit.* The Spider and his family take refuge in the roof when pursued by the Leopard, and he sits on the ground and catches them as they drop one by one. Last of all, the wife, Nahker, "he say he done tire, en Spider say: 'Yo' wey (=who) big so? Fa' down now, yo' go get de trouble.' Nahker fa' down, Lepped yeat um. Spider he one lef' hang." He escapes, however.

In "Dummy," Annancy wins a bet and the hand of the King's daughter by inducing "Peafowl" to make the dumb man talk. This "Peafowl" does by the sweetness of his song; but in a Duala story given by Lederbogen as "Der Tausendfuss und das stumme Kind," the means adopted more nearly resemble the time-honoured recipes for detecting changelings in this country. The Mouse advised the dumb child's parents to consult the Spider, who told them to hang up a centipede over the fireplace, set on a pot of water just underneath it, and leave the child sitting beside the fire. They did so, and went out. As soon as the steam rose from the water, the centipede, feeling the heat, began to struggle, and the dumb child watching it cried out in his excitement, "Father! there is a centipede going to fall into the pot."

"William Tell" is puzzling. There is no single point of contact between the owner of the witch-tree and the mythical archer of Europe. It is most probable that the name (a likely one to remain in the memory) had been picked up by some negro story-teller who did not know the tale belonging to it and simply attached

[1] *Kalunga* in Angola, *Ko* by the Né Kru-men. Some curious episodes connected with the latter are given by M. Georges Thomann in his *Essai de Manuel de la langue néonlá* (Paris: E. Leroux).

it to the first character that came handy. The "sings" by means of which Annancy fells the tree occur frequently in native African stories; we need only mention the incident (found not only in the Xosa "Bird that made Milk," but in a Duala tale, and elsewhere) of the song which made the hoed garden return to grass and weeds, and that of Simbubukwana's sister[1] who sang "Have legs, have arms," and the boy who was without those members immediately grew them. The notion of spells to be sung, however, does not seem to be confined to any country or race.

I do not remember any exact parallel to "Dry River" (XXXIII.), but the incident of the river rising is found in Africa with several different sequels. In a Nyanja story which I have in MS., some children go out into the bush to gather wild fruit, and are cut off on their return by the rising of the river. They are helped across by "a big bird, with one wing, one eye and one leg" (one of the "half-beings"[2] whose place in Bantu folk-lore has not yet been fully worked out), and charged not to tell who took them over. One boy tells his mother, and is drowned on the next expedition, his companions getting across in safety. In "The Village Maiden and the Cannibal" (Mrs. Martin's *Basutoland, its Legends and Customs*), the girls cannot cross the swollen stream till they have thrown a large root into the water, and complied with the directions. The last girl, who is reluctant to obey, but finally gives in, is not drowned, but she and her sister have an adventure with cannibals of a not uncommon kind, which may be referred to Mr. Jacobs's "Flight from Witchcraft" type. Two other stories, a Kinga (North-east Nyasa) and a Machame (Kilimanjaro) one, have the same opening incident (in the one case, however, it is a rock and not a river which enlarges itself and blocks the way), but continue in quite a different way—the girls are helped by an animal (in one case a jackal, in another a hyena) who subsequently insists on marrying one of them. The Machame tale, to which we shall have to return presently, as it belongs to the group to which we refer "Yellow Snake" and some

[1] McCall Theal, p. 68.

[2] See Junod, *Chants et Contes des Baronga*, p. 197; also a note in Chatelain, *Folk-tales of Angola*, p. 254, and Callaway, *Zulu Tales*, p. 199.

others, goes on to relate how the girl escaped from the hyena's village; the Kinga one takes an entirely different course.

"Leah and Tiger" is one of the stories which can be most unhesitatingly identified as African; and, as it happens, the examples at present known to me are nearly all Bantu. Perhaps the closest parallel is the Suto "Tselane" (Jacottet, p. 69),[1] where, however, the girl, instead of being secluded by her father to avoid the trouble which her refusal to marry threatens to bring upon him, herself insists on staying in the house her parents are leaving. As in the Jamaica version, they bring her food every day, and sing to let her know of their approach. The cannibal on the prowl (represented in Jamaica by the "tiger") imitates the mother's voice, but fails; after swallowing a red-hot hoe, he succeeds at the first trial. He does not eat Tselane, however, and so end the story with a warning against obstinacy; he puts her into a bag to carry her home, and rests on his way at a hut, which proves to be her uncle's. While he is resting inside the hut, leaving his bag outside, the family discover the girl and let her out, substituting a dog and some biting ants. In other versions it is bees and wasps, or snakes and toads; but the result is always the same—the death of the cannibal. The incident of swallowing red-hot iron to soften the voice is found also in "Demane and Demazana" (Theal) and elsewhere. In a curious Masai story, "The Old Man and his Knee" (Hollis, *The Masai: Language and Folklore*, p. 153), the "enemies" (not said to be cannibals) carry off the old man's two children by means of the same stratagem. After failing in the first attempt they consult a medicine-man to find out how they can "make their voices resemble an old man's." He tells them merely to go back, and eat nothing on the road. They eat a lizard and an ant, and their voices do not produce the desired effect. On trying again, and this time complying exactly with the doctor's directions, they deceive the children and get the door opened. This incident is preserved in "Leah," and, like the Masai "enemies," Tiger thinks that such a trifle as the guava and "duckanoo" cannot possibly do any harm. The Masai story concludes with the killing of the old man by making him swallow a hot stone—a incident which crops

[1] This story is also given by Arbousset.

up in various connections in the Hare stories, but seems out of its place in this one. On the whole (though I do not like to hazard a conjecture) it seems more probable that the Masai had picked up this tale from some of their Bantu neighbours than that the Bantu should have adopted it from them.

As regards the imported stories, it seems reasonably clear that "Yung-Kyum-Pyung" is a "Rumpelstiltzchen" story which has accidentally become associated with Annancy. Though the superstition on which these stories are based exists in Africa as well as in other parts of the world, and is one of the factors in the custom of *hlonipa*, I do not remember any tale embodying it in this form, though there are numerous examples of those which turn a *tabu* of some sort.

"King Daniel" is the story of the jealous sister, best known, perhaps, in the ballad of "Binnorie." But it has African prototypes as well, though the resemblance to these is not so close, in which the crime is discovered by the song of a bird—sometimes the metamorphosed heart of the victim. In "Masilo and Masilonyane" and the Kinga "Die Reiherfeder,"[1] one brother (or companion) kills the other; in "Unyengebule" (Callaway) the husband kills the wife, and here it is her feather head-dress which turns into a bird. "Pretty Poll" (XXXI.) is a variant of this story.

Another pair of variants, apparently, are "Blackbird and Woss-woss" and "Open Sesame." But the former of these, it seems to me, corresponds much more closely with a Nago story of the Lizard and the Tortoise, given by M. Basset (*Contes populaires d'Afrique*, p. 217); and it should be remembered that the Nagos of Yoruba are one of the tribes represented among the Jamaica negroes. The lizard finds a rock containing a store of yams, and overhearing the words used by the owner "*Stone, open!*" obtains food for himself in time of famine. He imparts the secret to the tortoise, and they go together, but the tortoise lingers behind to load himself with all he can carry, and not knowing the word fails to get out, and is killed when the owner returns. He revives, however, and gets the cockroach to stick his shell together, thus presenting a

[1] R. Wolff, "Grammatik der Kingasprachen" (*Archiv für das Studium deutschen Kolonialsprachen*, iii.), p. 135.

point of contact with other aetiological myths about the Tortoise. The rescue by the army of wasps I have been unable to match.

"Man-crow" is the story, which exists in so many variants, where the hero is robbed of the fruit of his achievement by an impostor stepping in at the last minute. The nearest parallel which occurs to me is "Rombao" (probably obtained from a Portuguese source by the Quilimane natives who related it to Mr. Duff Macdonald), where the hero kills the whale and cuts out its tongue; the captain who finds it dead claims his reward, but is discomfited by Rombao's appearance with the tongue.

"The Three Pigs" will be readily recognized as the familiar English story, and corresponds pretty closely to the version in Mr. Jacobs's *English Fairy Tales.* A version current among the negroes of the Southern States is given by Mr. Owens in the paper in *Lippincott's Magazine* already referred to. This version, entitled "Tiny Pig," omits the two incidents of the apple-tree and the butter-churn; but curiously enough these appear as "Buh Rabbit" episodes in another part of the same paper, the apple-tree having become a pear-tree, and the churn a tin mug which Buh Rabbit puts over his head, while he hangs various articles of tinware about his person.

"Sea-Mahmy" introduces several different elements. The mermaid herself is probably of European extraction,[1] and the device by which Blackbird brings Annancy to the feeding-tree *might* be a far-off echo of the Daedalus and Icarus myth. But Annancy's trick for conveying Trapong to his house and eating him recalls one of the stock incidents of Bantu folk-lore—the one where Hlakanyana, or the Hare, or some other creature, induces his dupe to get burnt or boiled by pretending to undergo the process himself and to escape with impunity. The Suto Hare[2] commends this as a device for attaining immortality—in which there is a faint suggestion of Medea's caldron. I was at first disposed to refer this episode to the "Big Klaas and Little Klaas" (or the "Getting-to-Heaven-in-a-Sack") group; but the inducement to enter the sack, which is so great a point in these, is here wanting. It is found in a

[1] One kind of duppy is a mermaid—but I can find no indication that she came from Africa.

[2] Jacottet, p. 15.

Zanzibar story ("Abu Nuwasi na waziri na Sultani") in Dr. Velten's collection,[1] where Abu Nuwas is sewn up into a sack to be thrown into the sea, and induces another man to take his place by saying that he is to be drowned for refusing to marry the Sultan's daughter. This is evidently an Arab tale, though I do not remember it in the *Arabian Nights.*

The exotic tales to be found in Bantu Africa come mainly from two sources—Arab and Portuguese. The former is exemplified at Zanzibar and all down the Mozambique coast; the latter in Angola and Mozambique. We have already referred to an example obtained at Delagoa Bay by M. Junod; but "Bonaouaci" (*Chants et Contes*, p. 292), though the names are Portuguese, and the local colouring goes so far as to introduce the Governor of Mozambique in person, is in substance identical with one of the "Abu Nuwas" stories given by Dr. Velten, the incident of the egg-production being nearly the same in both, as well as the two other impossible tasks set the hero—sewing a stone and building a house in the air. I fancy the same is the case with "Djiwao," though the incidents have been a good deal remodelled, and the concluding episode—the boiling of the chief Gwanazi in the pot he had intended for Djiwao, is the purely Bantu one alluded to in the last paragraph—in a somewhat unusual setting. "Les trois vaisseaux,"[2] again, is an *Arabian Nights* story, of which a curious version has been obtained at Domasi, probably brought from the coast by some member of a Yao trading caravan. Mr. Dennett's No. III., "How the wives restored their husband to life," looks like a much altered and localized form of this. If so it might have reached the Congo through the Portuguese. We also find it on the Ivory Coast[3] where it might have come from an Arab source through Mandingoes or Hausas.

The stories of "Fenda Maria" and "Fenda Maria and her elder brother Nga Nzuá"[4] ("The Three Citrons" and "Cinderella"), are good examples of transplanted stories invested with local colour by successive generations of narrators, till, as

[1] *Suaheli Märchen*, p. 154 (p. 241 in the German translation).

[2] *Ib.* p. 304.

[3] See Thomann, *op. cit.*, "Trois maris pour une femme."

[4] Chatelain, No. I. and No. II.

Mr. Chatelain says, "the fundamental idea of exotic origin has been so perfectly covered with Angola foliage and blossoms, that science alone can detect the imported elements, and no native would believe that [these tales] are not entirely Angolan."

A curious stage in the migration of stories is exemplified by the "Taal" (or Cape Dutch) versions of Oriental stories imported into South Africa by the Malays, and existing in a purely traditional form among the coloured people. One of these was printed by Mr. H. N. Müller in *De Gids* for Jan., 1900, but I think hardly any attempt has been made to collect them. And here I may mention that Herr Seidel's *Lieder und Geschichten der Afrikaner*[1] contains a Nama version of the Lear story, taken down and translated by Herr Olpp, of the Rhenish Mission, who seems quite unaware of its real origin, in spite of the very obvious parallel in Grimm's *Hausmärchen*. He says in a note: "Diese Begebenheit kann sich nur in der Kap-Kolonie ereignet haben zu einer Zeit in welcher Kolonisten sich schon angesiedelt hatten und unter den Eingeborenen wohnten. Der Name der Tochter spricht dafür und enstammt dem Holländischen." Now the youngest daughter's name is "Katje Leiro" —surely, all things considered, not such a very far cry from Cordelia.

It is interesting to trace the African elements in these imported tales as distinct from those which are merely derived from West Indian surroundings. Thus Mr. Bluebeard's three-legged horse (compare also the three-legged horse in "Devil and the Princess") is, as explained in the footnote, a "duppy"; and the duppy, whatever the derivation of his name, seems to be West African in origin. Duppies are the souls of the dead, "capable of assuming various forms of men and other animals."[2] Some of these forms are monstrous, as the "three-foot horse" already alluded to, the "long-bubby Susan," and the "rolling calf." The informant who is responsible for these statements also says that "the duppy in human form generally moves along by spinning or walking backwards." Perhaps this may explain the mysterious "Wheeler" (LI.) who has his habitation in a hollow tree, and seizes the hand of any unwary person who puts it into the hole. What he would

[1] P. 135, "Liebe bis zum Salz."

[2] See *Folk-Lore*, March, 1904, p. 90.

have done if not requested to "Wheel me mile an' distant," remains obscure; but apparently the persons making the request are whirled through the air and then dropped at the place where Annancy (who has previously passed through the experience unscathed) has prepared a trap for them. The story suggests—though the resemblance is not very close—the episode of "The Stone that wore a Beard" in *Cunnie Rabbit* (p. 167), where the Spider, having had a narrow escape from the magic powers of the bearded stone (a transformed "devil") utilises them for the destruction of his acquaintances. Those who remark on the peculiarity of the stone are struck down unconscious, and Spider exercises all his ingenuity in inducing his victims to say, "Dah stone get plenty bear'-bear'!" Cunnie Rabbit will not say the words till Spider has himself done so, and has suffered the consequences; both are afterwards rescued by Trorkey (Tortoise). Somewhat similar to "Wheeler" is the magic jar in XLV.—which might, however, be due to a distorted reminiscence of "Bluebeard." Spirits are often believed on the Gold Coast to take up their abode in trees, as well as to assume the form of animals. The usual Tshi name for them appears to be *bonsum* or *bossum*: the word "duppy" I have been unable to trace.

The method of divination in "Mr. Bluebeard" is one I do not remember to have met with, though it may be akin to the "magic mirror of ink." The magic drum by which Calcutta Monkey (XXXVIII.) finds out Annancy's whereabouts is African. I do not recall any parallel story, but drums are much used by witch-doctors and in ceremonial dances, and in some cases auguries are drawn from their sound. But Monkey first discovers Annancy to be the thief by cutting the cards, which of course is European.

Two stories, "Annancy and the Old Lady's Field" (XVI.) and "Devil's Honeydram," introduce the incident of a woman compelled to dance against her will—in one case to dance herself to death. In both cases the music seems to be the compelling power; but it is not clear whether, in "Devil's Honeydram," the knowledge (and use in the song) of the woman's name has anything to do with the spell. If so, the idea is so universal that one can scarcely refer to it as specially African. It is interesting, though perhaps scarcely pertinent to the matter in hand, to note that the Akikuyu believe their images (of which Mr. Scoresby

Routledge has brought home specimens) to have the power, if held up before people, of compelling them to dance.

The folk-lore of Jamaica, as given in the interesting papers published in *Folk-Lore*, 1904-5, is decidedly of a composite character. The negroes have, as there pointed out (1904, p. 87), "adopted many of the most trivial of English superstitions," while at the same time preserving some reminiscences of their African beliefs. These are especially seen in the notions respecting "duppies," which again are perceptibly influenced by Christian ideas, cf. the efficacy of the name of Christ (p. 90) and the statement that the "rolling calf" is the spirit of a person not good enough for heaven or bad enough for hell, or the recipe of "sitting on a Bible" to get rid of a duppy. The directions for "killing a thief" (p. 92) belong to the system (universal throughout Negro and Bantu Africa) of guarding crops by means of "medicine," or "fetish," or whatever one likes to call it: the technical name in Chinyanja is *chiwindo*. I do not remember any of the particular forms of *chiwindo* here enumerated; and the silver threepence to be planted with the "guinea yam" is a civilized addition, but the principle is the same. The methods of "finding out the thief," on the other hand, which follow on p. 93, are certainly English—the Bible and key, and the gold ring, hair and tumbler of water. There is a third alternative:—"A curious kind of smoke, which, when it rises, goes to the house of the thief, etc."—but it is too vaguely stated to enable us to pronounce upon it.

Among funeral customs we find the following (p. 88): "If a person dies where there are little children, after the body is put into the coffin, they will lift up each little child, and calling him by name, pass him over the dead body." According to a Sierra Leone paper this custom is observed there; but it is not stated by which of the tribes who make up the extremely mixed population. It may even be found on investigation that some of the freed slaves brought the notion back from the New World. The same authority states that it is considered unlucky to whistle, and adds the rationalizing explanation that whistling attracts snakes, lizards, and other undesirable creatures into the house. In Jamaica, you must not "whistle in the nights, for duppies will catch your voice."

The proportion of native and acquired, or African and European ideas in these superstitions can only be determined by a much more detailed examination than I can make here, and one based on fuller materials than are yet accessible.

In conclusion, I would briefly glance at five stories which I have grouped together as derived from a common African original, and which present several features of interest, though I am unable to examine them as much in detail as I should like to do. These are "The Three Sisters" (VII.), "Gaulin" (XXIV.), "Yellow Snake" (XXXIV.), "John Crow" (XLIII.), and "Devil and the Princess" (LI.). The type to which these may be referred resembles the one registered by Mr. Jacobs as the "Robber-Bridegroom"; but the African prototypes are certainly indigenous, and it might seem as if the stories Mr. Jacobs had in view were late and comparatively civilized versions of the corresponding European and Asiatic ones, the Robber being the equivalent of an earlier wizard or devil, who, in the primitive form of the story, was simply an animal assuming human shape. The main incidents of the type-story are as follows:

(1) A girl obstinately refuses all suitors.

(2) She is wooed by an animal in human form, and at once accepts him.

(3) She is warned (usually by a brother) and disregards the warning.

(4) She is about to be killed and eaten, but is saved by the brother whose advice was disregarded.

A Nyanja variant of this story, where the bridegroom is a hyena, corresponds very closely with the Temne "Marry the devil, there's the devil to pay" (*Cunnie Rabbit*, p. 178)—even to the little brother who follows the newly-wedded couple, against the wishes of the bride, and who is afflicted—in the one case with "craw-craw," in the other with sore eyes. A translation of the Nyanja story may be found in the *Contemporary Review* for September, 1896. In Mrs. Dewar's *Chinamwanga Stories* (p. 41) there is a variant,—"Ngoza,"—where the husband is a lion. In the Machame story, previously alluded to, the hyena, having befriended a girl, marries her, and she escapes with some difficulty from being eaten by his relations. Yet another variant is "Ngomba's Balloon" in Mr. Dennett's *Folklore of the Fjort.*" Here the husband is a *Mpunia* (translated "murderer")—apparently a mere human bad character, and Ngomba escapes by her own ingenuity.

In the Jamaican stories it strikes one that the idea of transformation is somewhat obscured. We are told how "Gaulin" (Egret) and "John Crow" provide themselves with clothes and equipages—the latter a carriage and pair, the former the humbler local buggy;—and this seems to constitute the extent of their disguise. Yellow Snake is said to "change and fix up himself"—but the expression is vague. Gaulin, however, can only be deprived of his clothes (and so made to appear in his true shape) by means of a magic song. The "old-witch" brother, who has overheard the song, plays its tune at the wedding and thus exposes the bridegroom, who flies out at the door. "John-Crow" is detected by a Cinderella-like device of keeping him till daylight, and his hurried flight through the window (in which he scraped the feathers off his head on the broken glass) explains a characteristic feature of these useful but unattractive birds.

In neither of these is the bride in any danger: but in "Yellow Snake" her brothers save her when already more than half swallowed; in "Devil and the Princess," she escapes by the aid of the Devil's cook, who feeds the watchful cock on corn soaked in rum. In this story, too, it is not the girl's brother, but the "old-witch" servant-boy, who warns her; and, as he is cast into prison for his pains, he has no hand in the release. In two cases ("Gaulin" and "John Crow") Annancy is one of the unsuccessful suitors, and, in the former, "Rabbit" is another. (He, apparently, takes no steps to change his shape, being rejected on the ground that he is "only but a meat," *i.e.*, an animal.) In the Nyanja story, Leopard and Hare are mentioned as meeting with refusals, before the Hyena arrives on the scene. "The Three Sisters," while keeping one or two points of the original story, is much altered, and seems to have introduced some rather unintelligible fragments of an English ballad (as to which see Appendix, p. 286). The Snake is never accepted; and the youngest of the sisters, who answers him on behalf of all, would seem to represent the "old-witch" brother who detects his true character. His "turning into a devil" is another alien element—perhaps due to Biblical recollections, and the concluding assertion that he "have chain round his waist until now" seems to refer to something which has dropped out, as there is no previous allusion to a chain in the story as it stands. Of all the five, "Yellow Snake" is, on the whole, the closest to what we may suppose to have been the original; "Devil and the Princess" is in some respects complete, but has acquired several foreign features, and "John Crow" has quite lost the characteristic conclusion. It is to be hoped that we may one day succeed in discovering, if not all the African variants of this story, yet enough to render those we possess more intelligible, and to afford materials for an interesting comparative study.

A. WERNER.

AUTHOR'S PREFACE.

THE stories and tunes of this book are taken down from the mouths of men and boys in my employ. The method of procedure has in every case been to sit them down to their recital and make them dictate slowly; so the stories are in their *ipsissima verba*. Here and there, but very rarely indeed, I have made a slight change, and this only because I thought the volume might find its way into the nursery. The following list exhausts the emendations: (1) It was not his fat that Tiger took out when he went bathing, but his viscera; (2) The "Tumpa-toe" of one of the stories is "Stinking-toe"; (3) Dog always swears, his favourite expression being, "There will be hell here to-night," and the first line of one of the dance tunes runs really: "Hell of a dog up'tairs"; (4) "belly" is replaced by a prettier equivalent.

The district in which I live is that of the Port Royal Mountains behind Kingston. Other districts have other "Sings," for these depend upon local topics. The Annancy Stories are, so far as I know, more or less alike throughout the island. This title seems to include stories in which Annancy himself does not figure at all, but this is of course an illegitimate use of it. The collection in this book is a mere sample both of stories and tunes.

The book as a whole is a tribute to my love for Jamaica and its dusky inhabitants, with their winning ways and their many good qualities, among which is to be reckoned that supreme virtue, *Cheerfulness*.

W. J.

JAMAICA, *January*, 1906.

JAMAICAN SONG AND STORY.

PART I. ANNANCY STORIES.

WHEN the hoes stop clicking and you hear peals of laughter from the field, you may know that somebody is telling an Annancy story. If you go out, you will find a group of Negroes round the narrator, punctuating all the good points with delighted chuckles. Their sunny faces are beaming, and at the recital of any special piece of knavery on Annancy's part ordinary means of expression fail, and they fling themselves on the ground and wriggle in convulsions of merriment.

Annancy is a legendary being whose chief characteristic is trickery. A strong and good workman, he is invariably lazy, and is only to be tempted to honest labour by the offer of a large reward. He prefers to fill the bag which he always carries, by fraud or theft. His appetite is voracious, and nothing comes amiss to him, cooked or raw. No sooner is one gluttonous feast over than he is ready for another, and endless are his shifts and devices to supply himself with food. Sometimes he will thrust himself upon an unwilling neighbour, and eat up all his breakfast. At another time he carries out his bag and brings it home full of flesh or fish obtained by thieving. He is perfectly selfish, and knows no remorse for his many deeds of violence, treachery and cruelty. His only redeeming point is a sort of hail-fellow-well-met-ness, which appeals so much to his associates that they are ready almost, if not quite, to condone his offences.

Annancy has a defect of speech owing to a cleft palate, and pronounces his words badly. He speaks somewhat like Punch, through his nose very rapidly, and uses the most countrified form of dialect. He cannot say "brother," and has to leave out the *th* owing to the failure of the tongue to meet the palate, so he says "bro'er." He even pretends he cannot say "puss," and turns it into "push." Strings of little words he delights in, such as, in the Brother Death story, the often-repeated "no mo so me no yerry," an expressive phrase difficult to render into good English. It means "I must have failed to hear." The words are "no more so me no hear," equivalent to "it must be so (that) I (do) not hear," the "no more" having something of the force of the same words in the colloquial phrases, "no more I do," "no more I will." When, for instance, to the remark, "I thought you didn't like the smell of paint," we make the rejoinder "no more I do," Priscian strives in vain to disentangle the words and reduce them to rule of syntax, but they mean "Well! I do not." Thus "no more me hear" would be "Well! I do not hear." The "so" introduces the hypothetical element and the "no" before "yerry" is a reduplicated negative.

Thus far for the sense. Now for the pronunciation. The accent indicates where the stress of the voice falls, and unless the accent is caught, the phrase will not run off the tongue. This is how it goes:

nŏ mŏ | sō mĕ nŏ | yerry.

As an illustration of the necessity of right placing of the accent, take the name of that town in Madagascar, which we so often saw in our papers a few years ago, Antananarivo. Most of us just nodded our heads at it, but never tried, or at least only feebly, to articulate it. With all this "an an" it was the same sort of hopeless business as the deciphering of the hieroglyphics of those writers whose words seem to be composed of nothing but *m*'s. And yet how simple, and easy to say, the word is when we catch the accent. First "an"; then stop a little; "tánana," same values as traveller; and finally "rivo." French sounds for the vowels of course, An-tananarivo. This grouping of accents is that which in music is known as rhythm. Rightly grouped they make musical sense, wrongly grouped—and alas! how often we hear it—musical nonsense. See the stuttering hopelessness and helplessness of án-tán-án-á—there might be any number more of "an-an"s to follow, and compare with this the neat satisfying form Antánanarivo. So let no bungler read in the story of Brother Death "no mó so mé no yerry" with halting and panting, but let him reel off as quickly as he can "no mo so me no yerry" with just the accent that he would use in this phrase;—"It is here that I want you." Remember, too, that the *o*'s have the open sound of Italian, and not the close sound of English. So is exactly like *sol* (the musical note) with the *l* left out, and not as we pronounce it. And above all, speed.

When the stranger lands in Jamaica and hears the rapid rush of words, and the soft, open vowels, he often says: "Why, I thought they talked English here, but it sounds like Spanish or Italian!" The difficulty in understanding a new language lies in the inability to distinguish the point where one word ends and the next begins. The old puzzle sentence, *Caille a haut nid, taupe a bas nid*, shows this very well. The ear catches the sound but fails to differentiate the words, and, their real identity being disguised, the listener has a sort of impression of modern Greek or Italian, writing these fragments in his brain *oni, bani.*

Just as hopeless is negro English to the new-comer, and the first thing to do is to set about learning it. And well it repays investigation. It is the boast of the English language that it has got rid of so much superfluous grammatical matter in the way of genders, inflections and such-like perplexities. True, it has abolished much that was evil, and enables us to speak and write shortly and to the point. But negro English goes a step further, and its form is still more concise. Compare these expressions:

NEGRO.	ENGLISH.
Corn the horse.	Give the horse some corn.
Care the child.	Take care of the child.
Him wife turn fire.	His wife became a shrew.
You middle hand.	The middle of your hand.
My bottom foot.	The bottom of my foot.
Out the lamp.	Put out the lamp.
The boy too trick.	The boy is very tricky.
I did him nothing.	I did not provoke him.
See the 'tar up a 'ky.	Look at the star up in the sky.
No make him get 'way.	Do not let him get away.
Me go buy.	I am going to buy.
A door.	Out of doors.
Short-mout'ed.	Quick at repartee.
Bull a broke pen.	The bull has broken out of the pen.
Bell a ring a yard.	The bell is ringing in the yard.
Same place him patch.	In the place where it was patched.
To warm fire.	To warm oneself by the fire.
You no give.	If you do not give.
Bring come.	Bring it here.
A bush.	In the bush.[1]

These are a few typical sentences out of a host which might be cited to show the neat, short turn they take in the mouth of the Jamaica Negro.

The rapidity of utterance natural to all the Blacks is exaggerated by Annancy. He generally affects, too, a falsetto tone as in "Play up the music, play up the music," in Yung-kyum-pyung. He has a metamorphic shape,

[1] These idioms are very similar to those of Cape Dutch, especially as spoken by the coloured people, and may help to illustrate its development. Cf. *Jy is te skellum,—ek gaan* (or better, *Corp*) korp, etc. "To warm fire" reminds one of the Bantu *Ku ot a moto*, of which it is almost a literal translation. (A. W.)

that of the Spider. At one moment he is a man "tiefing (thieving) cow," the next he is running upon his rope (web).

As he is the chief personage in most of the stories in this book, it is well to have a perfectly clear idea of the pronunciation of his name. Unnahncy does not represent it badly, but the first letter has actually the sound of short French *a* as in *la*. The accent falls strongly on the middle syllable. In "Tacoma" all the syllables are very short. The first has the sound of French *ta*, and takes the accent; *co* is something between English *cook* and Italian *con*, and it is impossible to determine whether to write the vowel *o* or *u*; *ma* again as in French. The exact relation in which Tacoma stands to Annancy is obscure. In one case he is described as Annancy's son, but, according to most of the stories, he appears to be an independent neighbour.

The stories are obviously derived from various sources, the most primitive being no doubt those which are concerned only, or chiefly, with animals. These may be of African origin, but we should have expected to find the Elephant and not the Tiger. I have a suspicion that Tiger was originally Lion, and that he is the Ogre of Jack the Giant-killer, and other fairy stories brought to Jamaica from England. Ogre would easily be corrupted to Tiger, and with the information, which might have been acquired at the same time, that Tiger was a fierce animal which ate men, his name would find its way into stories repeated from mouth to mouth. This is, however, pure conjecture. How much the stories vary may be seen from the two versions of Ali Baba, in one of which the point is so entirely lost that the door is not kept shut upon the intruder.

The tunes are in the same case as the stories. What I take to be certainly primitive about them is the little short refrains, like "Carry him go 'long" (Dry Bone) and "Commando" (Annancy and Hog). These suggest tapping on a drum. Again, the same influence that has produced the American Plantation Songs is occasionally visible, as in "Some a we da go to Mount Siney" (Annancy in Crab Country). This kind of patter is just what the Negro likes. Some of the tunes are evidently popular songs of the day, as, for instance, the vulgar "Somebody waiting for Salizon" (Snake the Postman). But others are a puzzle, showing as they do a high order of melodic instinct. Such are the melodies in "The Three Sisters" and "Leah," and the digging-tunes, "Oh, Samuel, Oh!" and "Three Acres of Coffee." These digging-tunes are very pleasant to hear, and the singers are quick at improvising parts. They are an appropriate accompaniment to the joyous labour of this sunny, happy land.

One more word with regard to the tunes. They gain a peculiar and almost indescribable lilt from a peculiarity in the time-organisation of the Negro. If you ask him to beat the time with his foot, he does it perfectly regularly, but just where the white man does not do it. We beat *with* the time; he beats *against* it. To make my meaning quite plain, take common measure. His first beat in the bar will be exactly midway between our first and second beats. The effect of this peculiarity in their singing is, that there is commonly a feeling of syncopation about it. The Americans call it "rag-time."

The men's voices are of extraordinary beauty. To hear a group chatting is a pure pleasure to the ear, quite irrespective of the funny things they say; and their remarks are accompanied with the prettiest little twirks and turns of intonation, sometimes on the words, sometimes mere vocal ejaculations between them. The women's voices have the same fine quality when they speak low, but this they seldom do, and their usual vivacious chatter is anything but melodious.

I. ANNANCY AND BROTHER TIGER.

ONE day Annancy an' Bro'er Tiger go a river fe wash'kin. Annancy said to Bro'er Tiger:—"Bro'er Tiger, as you are such a big man, if you go in a de blue hole with your fat you a go drownded, so you fe take out your fat so lef' it here."

Tiger said to Bro'er Annancy:—"You must take out fe you too."

Annancy say:—"You take out first, an' me me take out after."

Tiger first take out.

Annancy say:—"Go in a hole, Bro'er Tiger, an' make me see how you swim light."

Bro'er Annancy never go in.

As Tiger was paying attention to the swimming, Annancy take up his fat an' eat it.

Then Annancy was so frightened for Tiger, he leaves the river side an' go to Big Monkey town.

Him say:—"Bro'er Monkey, I hear them shing a shing a river side say:—

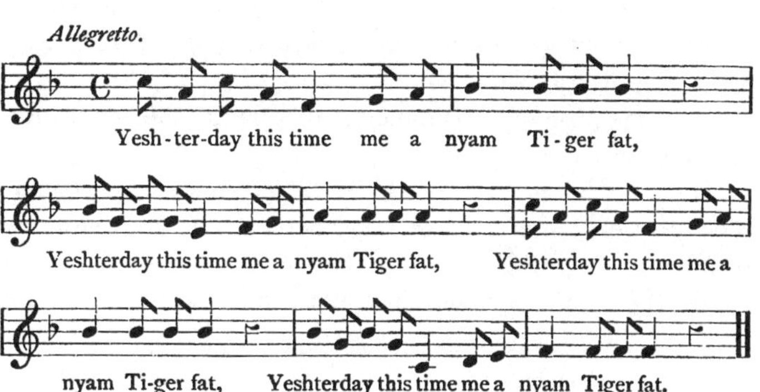
Allegretto.
Yesh-ter-day this time me a nyam Ti-ger fat,
Yeshterday this time me a nyam Tiger fat, Yeshterday this time me a
nyam Ti-ger fat, Yeshterday this time me a nyam Tiger fat.

The Big Monkey drive him away, say they don't want to hear no song.

So him leave and go to Little Monkey town, an' when him go him said :—

"Bro'er Monkey, I hear one shweet song a river side say :—

"Yeshterday this time me a nyam Tiger fat.
Yeshterday this time me a nyam Tiger fat."

Then Monkey say :—"You must sing the song, make we hear."

Then Annancy commence to sing.

Monkey love the song so much that they made a ball a night an' have the same song playing.

So when Annancy hear the song was playing, he was glad to go back to Bro'er Tiger.

When him go to the river, he saw Tiger was looking for his fat.

Tiger said :—"Bro'er Annancy, I can't find me fat at all."

Annancy say :—"Ha ha! Biddybye I hear them shing a Little Monkey town say :—

Yeshterday this time me a nyam Tiger fat.
Yeshterday this time me a nyam Tiger fat.

Bro'er Tiger, if you think I lie, come make we go a Little Monkey town."

So he and Tiger wented.

When them get to the place, Annancy tell Tiger they must hide in a bush.

Then the Monkey was dancing an' playing the same tune.

Tiger hear.

Then Annancy say :—"Bro'er Tiger wha' me tell you? You no yerry me tell you say them a call you name up ya?"

An' the Monkey never cease with the tune ;—

Yeshterday this time me a nyam Tiger fat.
Yeshterday this time me a nyam Tiger fat.

Then Tiger go in the ball an' ask Monkey them for his fat.

The Monkey say they don't know nothing name so, 'tis Mr. Annancy l'arn them the song.

So Tiger could manage the Little Monkey them, an' he want fe fight them.

So the Little Monkey send away a bearer to Big Monkey town, an' bring down a lots of soldiers, an' flog Bro'er Tiger an' Annancy.

So Bro'er Tiger have fe take bush an' Annancy run up a house-top.

From that, Tiger live in the wood until now, an' Annancy in the house-top.

Jack Mantora me no choose any.

NOTES.

Go a river fe wash 'kin, go to the river to wash their skins. Pronounce **fe** like **fit** without the **t.**

in a de, into the.

A go drownded, will be drowned.

fe take, short for **must have fe take,** must take.

so lef', and leave.

fe you, for you, yours.

me me, I will. Annancy is fond of these reduplications.

in a hole, in the hole.

make me see, let me see. **Make** and **let** are always confused.

frighten, frightened. Past participles are seldom used.

take, eat, leave, go, takes, eats, leaves, goes. This shortening is always adopted. If a final **s** is used, it is generally in the wrong place.

shing a shing, sing a song. Annancy's lisp will not always be printed, but in reading, it should be put in even when not indicated.

a river side, at the river's side. The **v** is pronounced more like a **b,** and the **i** in **river** has the sound of French **u.**

me a nyam, I was eating, I ate. **Nyam** is one of the few African words which survive in Jamaica.

make we hear, and let us hear it.

have the same song playing; the past participle again avoided, and its place supplied by the present participle. Song and tune are interchangeable terms, and, even when there is no singing, the fiddle speaks words to those who are privileged to hear; see "Doba" and other stories.

Biddybye, by the bye.

a Little Monkey town, in Little Monkey town. So already in this story we have had *a* standing for **to, in, the, at, will,** besides being interjected, as **in me a nyam** and elsewhere.

make we go, let us go.

in a bush, in the bush, in the jungle.

dancing an' playing. No mention of singing, observe.

a wha' me tell you, etc. What did I tell you? Did you not hear me tell you they were talking about you up here? A good phrase to illustrate the use of the interjected **say. Call you name,** mention your name.

Monkey them; another common addition.

nothing name so, nothing called so.

a bearer. Bearers are important people in the Jamaica hills where post-offices are few. They often bear nothing but a letter, though some carry loads too.

Jack Mantora, etc. All Annancy stories end with these or similar words. The Jack is a member of the company to whom the story is told, perhaps its principal member; and the narrator addresses him, and says: "I do not pick you out, Jack, or any of your companions, to be flogged as Tiger and Annancy were by the monkeys." Among the African tribes stories we know are often told with an object. The Negro is quick to seize a parable, and the point of a cunningly constructed story directed at an individual obnoxious to the reciter would not miss. So when the stories were merely told for diversion, it may have been thought good manners to say: "This story of mine is not aimed at any one."

II. YUNG-KYUM-PYUNG.

A KING had t'ree daughter, but nobody in the world know their name. All the learned man from all part of the eart' come to guess them name, an' no one could'n guess them.

Brother Annancy hear of it an' say :—" Me me I mus' have fe fin' them ya-ya gal name. Not a man can do it abbly no me."

So one day the King t'ree gal gone out to bathe, an' Brother Annancy make a pretty basket, an' put it in a the house where he knew they was going to come fe eat them vittle.

He leave it there, an' go under the house fe hear the name.

When them come, them see the basket, an' it was the prettiest something they ever see in their life.

Then the biggest one cry out :—

> Yung-kyum-pyung ! What a pretty basket !
> Marg'ret-Powell-Alone ! What a pretty basket !

And the next one say :—

> Marg'ret-Powell-Alone ! What a pretty basket !
> Eggie-Law ! What a pretty basket !

And the youngest bahl :—

> Eggie-Law ! What a pretty basket, eh ?
> Yung-kyum-pyung ! What a pretty basket, eh ?

Brother Annancy hear it all good, an' he glad so till him fly out a the house an' gone.

Him go an' make up a band of music with fiddle an' drum, an' give the musicians them a tune to sing the names to.

An' after a week him come back.

When him get where the King could yerry, him give out :—" Play up the music, play up the music."

So they play an' sing :—

Allegro.
Yung-kyum-pyung Eg-gie-Law Marg'ret-Powell-A - lone.

After six times sing the Queen yerry.

She say :—" Who is that calling my daughter name ? "

Annancy tell them fe play all the better.

Then the Queen massoo himself from up'tairs, an' t'row down broke him neck.

Dat time de King no yerry, so Annancy harder to play de music still.

At last the King yerry, an' him say :—" Who is dat, calling me daughter name ? "

Annancy let them sing the tune over and over :—

Yung-kyum-pyung Eg-gie-Law Marg'ret-Powell-A - lone.

An' the King t'row himself off a him t'rone an' lie there 'tiff dead.

Then Annancy go up an' take the t'rone, an' marry the youngest daughter an' a reign.

Annancy is the wickedest King ever reign. Sometime him dere, sometime him gone run 'pon him rope an tief cow fe him wife.

Jack Mantora me no choose none.

NOTES.

Me, me I mus' have, etc., I will find out those girls' names. Anybody else would have said :—" Me mus' have fe find them ya (those here) gal name," but Annancy likes to add a few more syllables. His speech is **Bungo talk.**

The Jamaican looks down on the Bungo (rhymes with Mungo) who "no 'peak good English."

abbly no me, except me.

go under the house. It is no absurdity to the narrator's mind to picture the King's house on the pattern of his own. This is a two-roomed hut, consisting of the hall or dining-room and a bedroom. It is floored with inch-thick cedar boards roughly cut and planed, so that they never lie very close. An air space is left underneath, and anybody who creeps under the hut can hear all that goes on above.

bahl, bawl.

hear it all good, hears everything perfectly.

Play up the music. He almost sings, like this :—

Play up the mu-sic.

all the better, all the harder.

massoo himself, lifts herself up. "Massoo" is an African word. The hall seems to have a sort of gallery.

t'row down, etc., throws herself down and breaks her neck. They always say **to broke.**

Dat time de King. The turning of **th** into a **d** or nearly a **d** is characteristic of negro speech. To avoid the tiresomeness of dialect-printing, and for another reason to be mentioned by and by, this is not always indicated. The change is introduced occasionally to remind readers of the right pronunciation.

let them sing, makes them sing.

Sometime him dare, sometimes he is there (at home), sometimes he goes and runs upon his web and steals cows for his wife. Other stories will show Annancy's partiality for beef, or indeed anything eatable.

tief, thieve.

Spiders' webs of any kind are called **Annancy ropes.**

III. KING DANIEL.

THERE was two young lady name Miss Wenchy an' Miss Lumpy. The King Daniel was courtening to Miss Wenchy, an' the day when they was to get marry Miss Lumpy carry Miss Wenchy an' show him a flowers in the pond. Miss Wenchy go to pick it, an' Miss Lumpy shub him in the pond.

An' she said :—"T'ank God! nobody see me."

Now a Parrot sat up on a tree, an' jes' as Miss Lumpy say "T'ank God! nobody see me" the Parrot say :—"I see you dough!"

Then Miss Lumpy said to the Parrot :—"Do, my pretty Polly, don't you tell, an' I'll give you a silver door an' a golden cage."

And the Parrot sing :—

Moderato.
No, No, I don't want it, for the
same you serve an - o - ther one you will serve me the same.

"Oh do, my pretty Polly, don't you tell, an' I'll give you a silver door an' a golden cage."

But the Parrot wouldn' stay, and he fly from houses to houses singing this tune :—

Allegro.
I brought, I brought a news to the young King Daniel; Miss

Lumpy kill Miss Wenchy loss, on becount of young King Daniel.

At last the Parrot got to the table where the young King Daniel was.

An' Miss Lumpy was into a room crying. Many pocket-handkerchief she got wet with tears. An' the Parrot sing the same song:—"I brought, I brought a news to the young King Daniel; Miss Lumpy kill Miss Wenchy loss on becount of young King Daniel."

Then Miss Lumpy call out:—"Oh drive away that nasty bird, for Miss Wenchy head hurting her."

But King Daniel wouldn' have it so, but said:—"I heard my name call. I would like to know what is it."

An' the Parrot fly near upon the King's shoulder an' tell him what become of Miss Wenchy. An' they go an' look in the room an' find her not.

An' pretty Polly take them to the pond an' show them where Miss Wenchy is, an' she was drown.

Then the King call Miss Lumpy an' head him up into a barrel an' fasten it up with tenpenny nails, an' carry him up to a high hill an' let him go down the gully, an' he drop in the gully pom-galong.

An' the Parrot laugh Ha! Ha! Ha! Ha!

Jack Mantora me no choose none.

NOTES.

I see you dough. The first three words are pitched high and the voice falls as low as possible on the **dough** and dwells upon it.

Do, my pretty Polly, etc. I have heard this story many times, and these words never vary. Obviously it was once a silver cage with a golden door.[1]

I brought; brought for bring, as we had **broke** for break.

---

[1] The well-known and lately-current ballad of *May Colvin*, in which this incident occurs (though it is the false lover, not the sister, who is murdered), has a cage of gold with an ivory door. (C. S. B.)

loss. It is doubtful what this word represents. It may be loss or lost. Observe **becount.**

I would like to know what is it, I should like to know what it is, what the matter is. The perverse misplacing of these words strikes a newcomer to the island. In questions they misplace them again and say "What it is?"

find her not. The **not** has a heavy accent.

gully, precipice.

pom-galong imitates the sound of the barrel as it goes bumping down. The o's have the Italian sound.

IV. TOMBY.

ONE day there was a gal, an' Annancy really want that gal fe marry, but he couldn' catch him. An' Annancy ask a old-witch man—the name of him was Tomby—an' the old-witch man had a 'mash-up side, an' him was the only man could gotten the gal for Annancy. An' Annancy give the old-witch man a t'reepence to give the gal when him goin' to the market to buy a t'reepence of youricky-yourk. An' the gal take the t'reepence. An' as she walk along the pass to market she meet up one of her friend call Miss Princess Johnson an' she said:—"Good mornin' me love," an' the answer:—"How you do, me dear? Where you a come from now?"

An Miss Justina say:—"Me a come from Tomby yard, an' see de t'reepence he give me fe go buy youricky-yourk."

"Never you bodder with somet'ing 'tan' so. Gi' ahm back him fuppence because him goin' to turn trouble fe you."

"How I manage fe gi' him the fuppence?"

"When you go to the market come back tell him you no see no youricky-yourk."

"An' what you go go buy, Miss Princess?"

"Me go buy me little salt fish an' me little hafoo yam, t'reepence a red peas fe make me soup, quatty 'kellion, gill a garlic to put with me little nick-snack, quatty ripe banana, bit fe Gungo peas, an' me see if me can get quatty beef bone."

"Ah! me missis, Cocoanut cheap a market ya."

"Yes, me love, make me buy sixpence."

An' as they talking they get to market. They buy what they want an' turn back, an' when they reach up Princess yard they tell goodbye an' Justina call in to Tomby.

An' Justina bring back the t'reepence an' sing:—

Andante.
Me go to market, me look, Tomby; look oh! me
look, Tomby, look oh! me look, Tomby, see no youricky-yourk; Me
went to Lingo Starban, 'cornful day, me went to Lingo Starban, 'cornful
day, me went to Lingo Star - ban, 'cornful day.

An' Tomby very vex as, being a old witch, he knew all what the gal do already. An' he answer:—

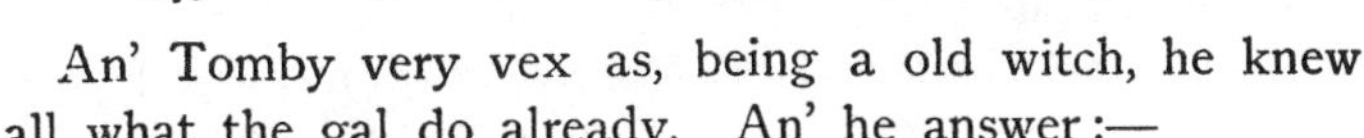
Allegretto.

Hm hm! hm hm! me have me mash-up side gee oh! a
him make you say Ta-ta - lin-go ya you bit oh! 'cornful day.

An' he won't take the t'reepence. Now the rule is that anybody take something from old-witch an' can't give it back, it give him power to catch him. An' so comes it that Tomby catch Justina an' send for Mr. Annancy an' make him a present to be a wife. His name was Miss Sinclair, but she becomes now Mrs. Annancy Sinclair.

Jack Mantora me no choose none.

NOTES.

Old-witch, a person of either sex possessed of supernatural powers, not necessarily old in years, as will be seen in other stories. The name "white witch" applied to men is familiar to dwellers in the West of England.

'mash-up, smashed up, wounded, lacerated.

youricky-yourk, a nonsense word for some kind of plaster.

pass, path.

Miss Princess. Prince and Princess are common names for boys and girls.

good mornin'. This broad **o** is always pronounced ah.

yard, a house with its immediate surroundings.

Never you bodder, don't you bother with something which stands so, with that sort of commission.

ahm, frequently used for him.

fuppence, with Italian **u** having a turn towards **o**, fivepence in the old Jamaica coinage, equal to threepence English. Princess advises the return of the fuppence because it is going to get Justina (English **u** and Italian **i**) into trouble, coming as it does from an old-witch. It would not be guessed that the Jamaica coinage is identical with that of England. Such is, nevertheless, the case in spite of these curious names:

3 farthings 1 gill.
2 gills 1 quatty (quarter of sixpence, pronounced quotty).
2 quatties 1 treppence or fuppence (old coinage).
3 quatties 1 bit.
4 quatties 1 sixpence or tenpence (old coinage).
5 quatties, bit-o-fuppence.
7 quatties, bit-o-tenpence.
8 quatties 1 shilling or maccaroni.
10 quatties, mac-o-fuppence.

go go buy. It is not only Annancy who uses reduplications. The close English **o** is replaced in the Negro's mouth by an Italian open **o**.

hafoo (pronounced hahfoo, really **afoo**, an African word), a kind of yam.

'kellion, skellion or scallion, a kind of onion which does not bulb.

Gungo, Congo. This pea is not only excellent for soup, but the growing plant improves the soil by introducing nitrogen into it.

ya, do you hear? a common ending to any remark.

tell goodbye. They **tell** howdy (how do you do?) and goodbye.

Lingo Starban. This should probably be Lingo's tavern, Lingo's tahvern; **v** and **b** being indistinguishable as in Spanish and Russian.

'cornful day, a day of scorning or flouting. Justina wishes Tomby to believe that she tried everywhere to get some youricky-yourk, but met only with flouts and jeers.

Hm, hm, grumbling.

a him, it is him, it is that which makes you say:—"Tatalingo, here's your bit," your three quatties. She only had a treppence but the Negro is above accuracy as the Emperor Sigismund was above grammar.

Tatalingo. Lingo's name is now transferred to Tomby. Italian vowels in Tata. In "Finger Quashy" we find Tatafelo as one of the cats' names.

make him a present, make her (Justina) a present to Annancy.

Mrs. Annancy Sinclair. They are not particular in the matter of surnames. A remarried widow is constantly called by the surname of her first husband.

V. HOW MONKEY MANAGE ANNANCY.

ONE day Mr. Annancy an' his wife sat under a tree an' don't know that Mr. Monkey was on the tree. Mr. Annancy say to his wife :—" You know I really want little fresh." The wife say to Annancy:—"What kind a fresh?"

" How you mean, me wife, fe ax me dat question? Any meat at all. Me wife, you know wha' we fe do. Make we get a banana barrel an' lay it on de bed, make him favour one man, so get white sheet an' yap him up from head to foot, an' sen' go call Bro'er Cow, Bro'er Monkey, Bro'er Sheep, Bro'er Goat an' Bro'er Hog. An' when them come we mus' put all the strange friend them inside de house an' den you fe stay inside de room wi' dem."

Now Bro'er Annancy send fe all his friend, Sheep, Goat, Hog, Monkey. Cow was the minister.

When they come to Annancy yard they met him was crying.

Parson Cow say :—" Don't cry so much, my good friend, because it is the all a we road."

Annancy say :—" Ah, ah! Bro'er Cow, you no know the feeling me have fe me one puppa. Bro'er Cow, as you is the parson, take you frien' in, you will see de ole man 'pon bed."

During this time Mrs. Annancy was inside the room. The Reverend Cow went in to raise up the sheet.

Mrs. Annancy say :—" No; me husban' say nobody fe look on the ole man face till in the morning."

So Cow don't rist.

Mr. Monkey who hear all what Annancy was saying, he an' his wife wouldn' go in the house.

Mr. Annancy say :—" Bro'er Monkey, go inside. Go see the last of the ole man."

Monkey say:—"No, Bro'er Annancy, me sorry fe you too much. If a go in dere a we cry whole a night."

"No, Bro'er Monkey, go in, go keep them other one company for you are me nearest frien'."

Monkey never go.

He has to left Monkey, for Monkey was too clever for him.

An' by that time Mr. Annancy hid his cutlass back of his door well sharpen an' go in the house an' shut the door. It was the only door in the whole house, so he sat back of the door after lock it.

An' after, Bro'er Annancy ask Bro'er Cow to say a word of prayer.

During the praying Annancy was crying.

Hog with an old voice say:—"Keep up Mr. Annancy, keep up Mr. Annancy."

He cry much the better.

The prayer was finish. Mr. Annancy ask Cow to raise a hymn.

The Cow commence with hundred a de hymn, hundred a de page.

Lagrimoso.
Me gullen ho St. John, me gullen ho St.
John, me see the last to-day ya, me see the last, puppa gone.

Bro'er Annancy want fe kill Parson Cow, begin with a big confusion, say that him don't like that hymn.

During this time his door was well lock, an' same time Bro'er Annancy draw his cutlass an' raise a fight, say that him don't like that hymn.

An' the poor friend them didn' have anything to fight. He kill the whole of them.

In the morning Monkey laugh, say:—"Bro'er Annancy, If me min come in a you house you would a do me the same."

Annancy say "No."

Him give Monkey a piece of the meat.

Jack Mantora me no choose none.

NOTES.

fresh, fresh meat. In the country districts the only meat to be had as a rule is ancient salt beef out of a tub.

favour, look like. In some parts of England the word is still used in this sense.

met him was crying, found him crying.

all a we. All of us have to tread the road of death.

one, own.

who hear, who had heard previously when he was on the tree.

cutlass. Every Negro carries one. It is used for every sort of purpose, but seldom murderously as here.

old voice, voice of simulated grief.

much the better, all the more.

hundred a de, hundredth.

me gullen ho, nonsense words.

confusion, quarrel.

min, been. If I had come in you would have done the same to me.

VI. BLACKBIRD AND WOSS-WOSS.

ONE day there was a place where they usual to kill plenty of meat. An' Mr. Blackbird has a certain tree, hiding himself. An' every cow them kill Mr. Blackbird see how them kill it. An' going into the house, the house don't lock with no key nor either open with no key. When they want to go in them use a word, say "one—two—t'ree—me no touch liver," an' the door open himself. An' when them want to come out of the house them use the same words "one—two—t'ree—me no touch liver." An' Mr. Blackbird tief them fe true, an' them never find it out.

An' one day Mr. Blackbird write his friend Mr. Annancy to take a walk with him, an' him will show him where he is getting all these meat. An' when he is going him tell Mr. Annancy all the rule, that when he go on the tree he must listen, an' him will hear what them say to open the door both going in an' coming out.

What Mr. Annancy did; when he see the butcher them passing with the meat, Annancy was trembling an' saying:—"Look a meat,—Look a meat."

"Bro'er Annancy hush you mout', you a go make dem shot me."

When the butcher them gone, Mr. Blackbird come down, he an' Mr. Annancy, an' go inside the house the very same as the butcher them do, say "one—two—t'ree—me no touch liver." As they go into the house Blackbird tell him that him mustn't take no liver. An' Mr. Annancy took liver an' put in his bag. An' when Blackbird started out with the same word Mr. Annancy left inside was tying his bag.

Now Mr. Annancy ready fe come out of the house, count "one—two—t'ree—me no touch liver," and by this time he has the liver in his bag.

The door won't open.

Blackbird call him "Come on."

He say :—"The door won't open."

Then he count more than what he was to by get so frighten. He say :—"One—two—t'ree—four—five—six—seven—eight—nine—ten—me no touch liver."

The door won't open.

Mr. Blackbird say :—"Look in your bag, you must be have liver."

The fellow so sweet-mout' say in a cross way "No."

Blackbird leave him.

When Blackbird go home he look an' can't see Mr. Annancy, so him fly a bush an' get up a whole regiment of soldier. Who these soldier was, was Woss-Woss. Mr. Blackbird was the General, march before. When them reach to the place they were just in time, for the butcher were taking Mr. Annancy to go an' tie him on a tree to cut him with hot iron. Word of command was given from Mr. Blackbird, an' by the time the butcher them come to the door with Mr. Annancy the whole world of Woss-Woss come down on them.

They have to let go Mr. Annancy. Not one of the butcher could see. Mr. Blackbird soldier gain the battle an' get 'way Mr. Annancy. They take all the butcher meat an' carry home. Then Mr. Blackbird take Mr. Annancy under his wing an' all his soldiers an' fly to his own country. From that day Woss-Woss is a great fighter until now, so bird never do without them to guard their nest.

Jack Mantora me no choose any.

NOTES.

Woss-Woss. The West Indian wasp hangs its paper nest to the twigs of bushes and trees as a rule, though it does not despise the shelter of the verandah. The wasps live in colonies, making many small nests instead of one big one. The nests are shaped like the rose of a watering-pot with the shank turned upwards.

This story clearly owes its origin to Ali Baba. The conversion of Sesame, which meant nothing to the negro, into one-two-three, which at least means something, is not unnatural.

fe true, literally **for true** is an expressive phrase conveying the idea of intensity. **It hot fe true,** it is intensely hot. **He tief fe true,** he steals terribly. **It rain fe true,** it is raining very hard. **He wort'less fe true,** he is a regular scamp. **He sinnicky fe true,** he is a horrid sneak. **His ears hard fe true,** his ears are outrageously hard, said of a boy who will not do as he is told. **He nyam fe true,** he eats immensely. **Lazy fe true,** abominably lazy. **Ugly fe true,** exceedingly ugly. **The water cold fe true,** the water is very cold. **White yam burn fe true,** the white yam is sadly burnt. **Orange bear fe true,** the oranges bear heavily. **Puss catch ratta fe true,** the cat catches any amount of rats. **Him favour tiger fe true,** he looks for all the world like a tiger, said of a man who has a sullen expression. **Me head hurt me fe true.** I have a very bad headache. **Boot burn me fe true,** my boots gall me dreadfully.

by get so frighten, through fright; literally, owing to his getting so much frightened.

must be have, must have.

sweet-mout', sweet-mouthed, greedy.

VII. THE THREE SISTERS.

THERE was t'ree sister living into a house, an' everybody want them fe marry, an' them refuse.

An' one day a Snake go an' borrow from his neighbour long coat an' burn-pan hat an' the whole set out of clothing. Then he dress himself, an' him tell his friends that him mus' talk to those young lady. An' what you think the fellow does? He get up a heap a men to carry him to the young lady yard. An' when him got there the door was lock with an iron bar. An' when he come he say:—"Please to open the door, there is a stranger coming in." An' he sing like this:—

Andante.
My el-des' sis-ter, will you o-pen the door? My el-des'
sis-ter, will you open the door oh? Fair an' gande-low steel.

An' the eldest one was going to open the door. An' the last one, who was a old-witch, say to her sister:—"Don't open the door," an' she sing:—

Andante.
My door is bar— with a scotran bar, My door is
bar— with a scotran bar oh, Fair an' gandelow steel.

Then the Snake ask again to the same tune:—

My second sister will you open the door?
My second sister will you open the door oh?
Fair an' gandelow steel.

An' the youngest, which was old-witch, sing again:—

My door is bar with an iron bar,
My door is bar with an iron bar oh,
Fair an' gandelow steel.

An' the Snake turn to a Devil, an' the t'ree sister come an' push on the door to keep it from open.

An' the Devil ask a third time:—

My youngest sister will you open the door?
My youngest sister will you open the door oh?
Fair an' gandelow steel.

But the last sister won't have it so, an' she said with a very wrath:—

The Devil ro - guer than a woman-kind, The Devil ro-
guer than a woman-kind oh, Fair an' gandelow steel.

An' the Devil get into a great temper an' say:—

What is ro - guer than a woman-kind? What is ro-
guer than a woman-kind oh? Fair an' gandelow steel.

Then the Devil fly from the step straight into hell an have chain round his waist until now.

Jack Mantora me no choose none.

NOTES.

Snake is pronounced with an indefinite short vowel between the **s** and **n**, senake.

burn-pan hat, the tall hat of civilized towns. The **pan** is the usual cylindrical tin vessel used for cooking. When blackened by fire it is a **burn-pan** or burnt pan. It is pronounced like French *bonne.*

Gandelow, scotran. The meaning of these words is lost.

roguer. This word is doubtful. Sometimes it sounds like rowgard, at others like rowgod. It may mean "more roguish." The boy who gave me this story often quotes this line from a hymn:

"To break the bonds of cantling sin."

One day I asked him to point it out in his hymnbook. It was **conquering.** He can say it perfectly well, but he still goes on with **cantling.** It is not surprising, therefore, that we cannot recover words passed from mouth to mouth for generations.

womankind. Again it is doubtful whether this is a single word or two words. The article would fix it as the latter in pure English, but in negro speech it goes for nothing.

old-witch, though she was a young girl: see notes to No. IV. (Tomby).

VIII. WILLIAM TELL.

ONCE there was a man who name William Tell, an' him have a lots of cow. An' in the yard there was a tree, an' the tree no man can fall it. Any animal at all go under that tree it kill them, an' the name of the tree is Huyg.

An' William Tell wanted the tree to cut down.

An' him offer a cow to any man that kill the Huyg. They shall get the cow.

An' first of all Tacoma went to cut down the tree, an' him couldn' bear the itch, I mean 'cratch of the tree.

An' William Tell made a law that any man come to cut the tree they must not 'cratch their 'kin or else they would lose the cow.

An' Mr. Tacoma were very sorry, an' he was to leave the cow just to save his life.

An' that great man Mr. Annancy heard about the cow an' him got a very sharp axe. An' when Mr. Annancy come, William Tell show him the cow—Annancy glad when he see the cow—an' after he show Mr. Annancy the tree.

Then Mr. Annancy say :—" Ho, me good massa, don't you fret of the tree. If one sing don't send 'way the tree another one must send him 'way."

An' the first sing was :—

Allegro.
Big chip, fly! little chip, fly!

He repeat the word over an' over, but the tree don't fall yet.

So him take up another sing again:—

Allegro.
Me go to Ricky-lan - jo, eye come shine, come
show me your mo - tion, eye come shine.

An' Mr. Annancy never cease till him cut down the tree an' receive his reward.

NOTES.

Huyg for Hag, as they say **buyg** for bag. The spelling is awkward but it seems the only convenient one to adopt. The sound will be best understood from the second example. Say **buy** and put a hard **g** after it. The **Huyg** seems to combine the qualities of the Upas and Cow-itch (*Mucuns pruriens*). The last, a common Jamaica weed, looks like a scarlet runner. It bears pods covered with a pretty velvet of hairs which "scratch" or irritate the skin.

sing. Further on there is a collection of these **sings.**

show me your motion, let me see you begin to topple.

IX. BROTHER ANNANCY AND BROTHER DEATH.

ONE day Brother Annancy sen' gal Annancy fe go a Brother Deat' yard fe go beg fire.

When the gal go, him go meet Brother Deat' dis a eat fe him breakfas' enough eggs. Brother Deat' give gal Annancy one. Gal Annancy take the egg an', after eat done, put the shell 'pon him finger.

Brother Annancy wait an' wait but can't get the fire, till at last he see the gal a come.

When him see the gal with the egg shell 'pon him finger, him run an' bit off the gal finger slap to the hand. Him take 'way the fire, out it, an' go back to Deat' say:— " Bro'er Deat', de fire out."

Brother Deat' give him fire an' one egg, tell him fe go home.

" Say, Bro'er Deat', I goin' to give you me daughter fe marry to."

So Annancy do marry off Deat' an' him daughter the same day. So him lef' them gone for a week, then come back again fe come see him son-in-law.

When him come him say:—" Bro'er Deat', me son, me hungry."

Brother Deat' no 'peak.

So Annancy begin fe talk to himself: " Bro'er Deat' say me fe go make up fire, but no mo so me no yerry."

After five minutes him call out:—" Bro'er Deat', me make up de fire."

Deat' no 'peak.

" Bro'er Deat' say me fe wash de pot, but no mo so me no yerry.

When the pot wash done, him call out :—" Pot wash."

Deat' no 'peak.

"Bro'er Deat' say me fe to put him on, but no mo so me no yerry."

Soon him say :—" Bro'er Deat', where de vittle ?"

Deat' no 'peak.

"Him say me fe look somewhé dé me see enough yam, me fe peel dem put dem a fire, but no mo so me no yerry."

Annancy cook all Deat' food.

When it boil, him take it off. Him say :—" Bro'er Deat', him boil."

Deat' no 'peak.

"Bro'er Deat' say me fe share, but no mo so me no yerry."

Annancy eat fe him share, then turn back say :—" Bro'er Deat', you no come come eat ?"

Deat' no 'peak.

"Bro'er Deat' say him no want none, but no mo so me no yerry."

So Annancy eat off all the food him one.

Then Deat' get vex in a him heart, and him run into the kitchen.

"Bro'er Annancy a whé you mean fe do me, say a come you come fe kill me ?"

So Deat' catch Annancy an' say :—" Me no a go let you go again, no use, no use."

Then, after, Deat' carry Annancy in a him house an' leave him, gone to get his lance to kill him.

So, after Annancy sit a time an' about to go away, him say :—" Bro'er Deat' say me fe go take piece a meat, but no mo so me no yerry."

When Annancy go to the meat cask, him see the cask full with meat. Him take out two big piece of meat. Then he see fe him daughter hand with the missing finger. Him jump out of the house an' bawl out :—" Bro'er Deat', you b'ute, you b'ute, you kill me daughter."

Deat' catch him again an' was going to kill him, but the feller get 'way, run home a fe him yard.

Brother Deat' follow him when him go home.

Annancy take all him children an' go up a house-top, go hang up on the rafter. Brother Deat' come in a de house, see them up a de house-top.

Annancy say to his family—there was two boy an' the mumma—"Bear up! If you drop de man a dirty dé a go nyam you."

Here come one of the boy say:—"Puppa, me han' tired."

Annancy say:—"Bear up!"

The boy cry out fe de better.

Annancy say:—"Drop, you b'ute! No see you dada a dirty dé?"

Him drop.

Deat' take him and put him aside.

Five minutes the other one say:—"Puppa, me han' tired."

Annancy say again:—"Drop, you b'ute! No see you dada a dirty dé?"

Him drop.

Deat' take him an' put him aside.

Soon the wife get tired, say:—"Me husban', me han' tired."

Annancy say:—"Bear up, me good wife!"

When she cry she couldn' bear no more, Annancy bawl again:—"Drop you b'ute! No see you husban' a dirty dé?"

She drop.

Deat' take her.

At last Annancy get tired. Das de man, Bro'er Deat' been want. Annancy was so smart, no want fe Deat' catch him, so he say:—"Bro'er Deat', I goin' to drop, an' bein' me so fat, if you no want me fat fe waste, go and fetch somet'ing fe catch me."

"What me can take fe catch you?"

"Go in a room you will see a barrel of flour an' you fe take it so fe me drop in dé."

Deat' never know that this flour was temper lime.

Deat' bring the barrel an', just as he fixing it up under where Annancy hanging, Annancy drop on Deat' head PUM, an jam him head in a the temper lime an' blind him. So he an' all him family get 'way.

Jack Mantora me no choose any.

NOTES.

dis a eat, just as he had eaten.

no mo so me no yerry, I must have failed to hear. See page 3.

Deat' no 'peak, Death won't speak. The comedy is well sustained. Annancy goes through the various stages of preparation for breakfast, pretending that he is carrying out orders from Death which he fails to hear.

put him on, put the pot on the fire.

somewhé dé, somewhere there. The **e**'s are like French **é**, and **dé** is said with a strong accent and made very short.

enough yam, plenty of yams.

say a come you come, say do you come.

me no a go etc., I am not going to let you go again.

no use, no mistake about it this time.

bawl. Remember to pronounce it **bahl.**

b'ute, brute, pronounced byute like the island Bute.

a fe him yard, to his yard.

a dirty dé, etc., on the ground there will eat you.

fe de better, all the more.

Das, that's.

temper lime, tempered lime originally no doubt, but now meaning quick lime. Temper, I am told, means cross. And in further explanation my informant adds: "You can't fingle (finger) temper lime as you have a mind; it cut up your hand."

pum with the shortest possible vowel represents the thud of Annancy's fall upon Death's head.

The Kitchen is outside the house, often at a considerable distance from it.

X. MR. BLUEBEARD.

THERE was a man named Mr. Bluebeard. He got his wife in his house an' he general catch people an' lock up into a room, an' he never let him wife see that room.

One day he went out to a dinner an' forgot his key on the door. An' his wife open the door an' find many dead people in the room. Those that were not dead said :—"Thanky, Missis; Thanky, Missis."

An' as soon as the live ones get away, an' she was to lock the door, the key drop in blood. She take it up an' wash it an' put it in the lock. It drop back into the blood.

An' Mr. Bluebeard was a old-witch an' know what was going on at home. An' as he sat at dinner, he called out to get his horse ready at once. An' they said to him :—"Do, Mr. Bluebeard, have something to eat before you go."

"No! get my horse ready."

So they bring it to him. Now, he doesn't ride a four-footed beast, he ride a t'ree-foot horse.

An' he get on his horse an' start off itty-itty-hap, itty-itty-hap, until he get home.

Now, Mrs. Bluebeard two brother was a hunter-man in the wood. One of them was old-witch, an' he said :—"Brother, brother, something home wrong with me sister."

"Get 'way you little foolish fellah," said the biggest one.

But the other say again :—"Brother, brother, something wrong at home. Just get me a white cup and a white saucer, and fill it with water, and put it in the sun, an' you will soon see what do the water."

Directly the water turn blood.

An' the eldest said:—"Brother, it is truth, make we go."

An' Mrs. Bluebeard was afraid, because he knew Mr. Bluebeard was coming fe kill him. An' he was calling continually to the cook, Miss Anne:—

Moderato.
Sister Anne, Sister Anne, Ah! you see an-y one is coming?
Sis-ter Anne, Sis-ter Anne, Ah! you see an-y one is coming?

An' Sister Anne answer:—

Moderato.
Oh no, I see no one is coming,
But the dust that makes the grass so green.

An' as she sing done they hear Mr. Bluebeard coming, itty-itty-hap, itty-itty-hap.

Him jump straight off a him t'ree-foot beast an' go in a the house, and catch Mrs. Bluebeard by one of him plait-hair an' hold him by it, an' said:—"This is the last day of you."

An' Mrs. Bluebeard said:—"Do, Mr. Bluebeard, allow me to say my last prayer."

But Mr. Bluebeard still hold him by the hair while he sing:—

Sister Anne, Sister Anne, Ah! you see any one is coming?
Sister Anne, Sister Anne, Ah! you see any one is coming?

An' Sister Anne answer this time :—

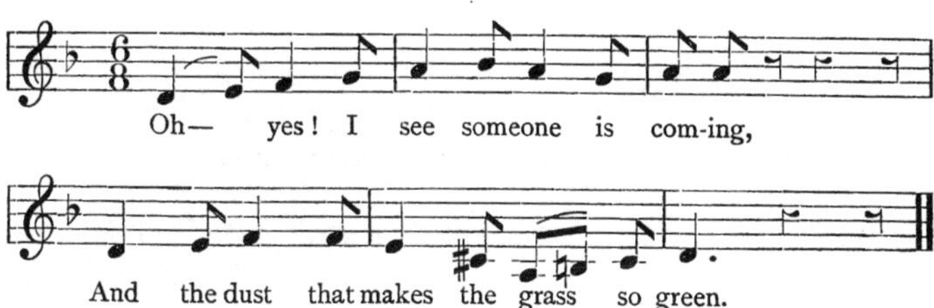
Oh— yes! I see someone is com-ing,
And the dust that makes the grass so green.

Then Mr. Bluebeard took his sword was to cut off him neck, an' his two brother appear, an' the eldest one going to shot after Mr. Bluebeard, an' he was afraid an' begin to run away. But the young one wasn't going to let him go so, an' him shot PUM and kill him 'tiff dead.

Jack Mantora me no choose none.

NOTES.

three-foot, three-legged.[1] **Hand** is used for arm in the same way.

itty-itty-hap, imitating the halting gait of the three-legged horse. The voice rises on **hap** which is said with a sharp quick accent.[1]

fe kill him, to kill her. The use of masculine for feminine pronouns is bewildering at first.

[1] "The 'three-foot horse' is believed to be a kind of duppy with three legs, hence its name; and is able to gallop faster than any other horse. It goes about in moonlight nights, and if it meet any person it blows upon him and kills him. It will never attack you in the dark. It cannot hurt you on a tree." *Folklore of the Negroes of Jamaica*, in *Folklore*, Vol. XV., p. 91. (C.S.B.).

XI. ANNANCY, PUSS, AND RATTA.

ONE day Annancy an' Puss make a dance, an' invite Ratta to the ball. Annancy was the fiddler. The first figure what him play, the tune say :—

Presto.

Ying de ying de ying, Ying de ying de ying, take care you go talk oh,

min' you tattler tongue ying de ying, min' you tattler tongue ying de ying,

min' you tat-tler tongue ying de ying.

The second tune he say :—

Allegro Vivace.

Ban-dy-wichy wich, Ban-dy-wichy wich, Ban-dy-wichy wich,

Timber hang an' fall la la, fall la la, fall la.

Then, as the Ratta dance, the high figure whé him make, him slide in the floor an' him trousies pop. Then the shame he shame, he run into a hole, an' him make Ratta live into a hole up to to-day day.

Jack Mantora me no choose none.

NOTES.

This story should be rattled off as quick as possible.

Ratta, rat or rats.

Ying de ying imitates the "rubbing" of the fiddle, as they call it.

take care you go talk, mind you don't talk, mind your tattling tongue.

figure whé him make, caper that he cuts.

trousies pop, trousers burst.

XII. TOAD AND DONKEY.

ONE day a King made a race and have Toad and Donkey to be the racer. An' Toad tell Donkey that him must win the race, an' Donkey mad when him yerry so. And the race was twenty mile.

An' Donkey say :—"How can you run me? I have long tail an' long ear an' a very tall foot too, an' you a little bit a Toad. Let me measure foot an' see which one longer."

An' Toad say to Donkey :—"You no mind that man, but I must get the race."

An' Donkey get very vex about it.

An' Donkey say to the King :—"I ready now to start the race."

An' the King made a law that Donkey is to bawl at every miles that he might know where he got.

Now that little smart fellah Toad says to the King that he doesn't fix up his business yet, an' will he grant him a little time.

An' the King grant him a day, an' say to the two of them :—"Come again to-morrow."

An' Donkey wasn't agree, for he know that Toad is a very trickified thing.

But the King wouldn' hear, an' say :—" No, to-morrow."

Now Toad have twenty picny. An' while Donkey is sleeping, Toad take the twenty picny them along with him on the race-ground, an' to every milepost Toad leave one of his picny an' tell them that they must listen for Mr. Donkey when he is coming. " An' when you yerry that fellah Mr. Donkey bawl, you must bawl too." An' Toad hide one of his picny behind every milepost until him end the twenty mile.

So the race begin.

Donkey was so glad in a him heart that he was going to beat Toad that he say to himself :—" Tche! That little bit a fellah Toad can't manage me, so I must have plenty of time to eat some grass."

So him stand by the way, eat grass and poke him head through the fence where he see some potato-slip, an' try a taste of Gungo peas. An' he take more than an hour fe catch up the first mile-post, an' as him get him bawl :—

Moderato.
Ha ! Ha ! Ha ! me more than Toad.

An' there comes the first picny call out :—

Jin - ko - ro - ro, Jin-kok-kok-kok.

An' Donkey quite surprise, an' say :—" Tche! How him manage to be before me ? "

An' he think :—" Me delay too long with that grass, I must quicker next mile."

An' him set off with a better speed an' only stop a minute for a drink of water. An' as him get to the next post him bawl :—

Ha! Ha! Ha! me more than Toad.

An' there come the second picny call out:—

Jin - ko - ro - ro, Jin-kok-kok-kok.

An' Donkey say:—"Lah! Toad travel fe true. Never mind, we will chance it again."

So him 'tart, an' when him reach the third mile-post him bawl:—

Ha! Ha! Ha! me more than Toad.

An' the third picny behind the post say:—

Jin - ko - ro - ro, Jin-kok-kok-kok.

Jackass get vex when he hear Toad answer him, an' he go fe 'mash Toad, an' Toad being a little man hide himself in a grass.

Then Donkey say:—"Hi! fellah gone ahead; make I see if I can catch up the next mile-post before him." An' he take him tail an' touch it like a horsewhip an' begin fe gallop.

An' him get to the fourth mile-post an' bawl:—

Ha! Ha! Ha! me more than Toad.

An' there comes the fourth picny answer him :—

Jin - ko - ro - ro, Jin-kok-kok-kok.

When him yerry, him 'tand up same place an' trimble, say :—"My goodness King! a whé me a go do? Make me gallop so I knock off all me hoof self upon the hard hard dirty because I must beat the race."

An' he gallop so fast than he ever do before, until when he get to the fifth mile-post he was really tired an' out of breath.

But he just have enough to bawl :—

Ha ! Ha ! Ha ! me more than Toad.

When he hear :—

Jin - ko - ro - ro, Jin-kok-kok-kok.

This time he really mad, an' race on harder than ever. But always the same story. Each mile-post he catch him bawl :—"Ha! Ha! Ha! me more than Toad." An' always come answer :—"Jinkororo, Jinkokkokkok."

An' Donkey begin to get sad in his mind for he see that he lost the race. So through Toad smartness Donkey can never be racer again.

Jack Mantora me no choose any.

NOTES.

tall foot, long leg. A tall bridge is a long one, not one that stands high above the river.

wasn't agree, didn't agree. Auxiliaries are a snare.

picny. This is the almost universal form of picaninny in Jamaica, varied occasionally by picany.

Tche! the Pshaw! of books and the Tush! of the Psalms. There is a world of contempt in this ejaculation, which is accompanied by an upward jerk of the chin. The vowel is that of French **le.**

potato-slip. The sweet potato (*Ipomœa Batatas*) is cultivated by slips or cuttings. Our kind of potato is called "Irish potato."

Jinkororo, etc. This is a capital imitation of the Toad's croaking chuckle. The second bar should be made as out of tune as possible and the **kok** is on the lowest note of the voice. It is the repeated k's that make the croak so life-like.

take him tail. They are fond of this expression. Other examples are:— "The horse take him mout' fe 'cratch him foot," the horse scratches his leg with his mouth. "Me take me owny yeye an' see it," I saw it with my own eyes.

a whé me a go do? What am I going to do, what shall I do?

dirty, ground.

XIII. SNAKE THE POSTMAN.

ONE day Annancy ask Snake to be his postman.

Snake ask him how much he is going to pay him.

An' Annancy tell Snake that he know he is a man love blood, an' when him come in the night he will give him a bite off his head.

An' Snake did agree.

An' the first night he give Annancy a bite in his head, an' Annancy feel it very much.

An' the second night when Snake is to come back Annancy invite his friend Mr. Rabbit. An' Annancy usual to sleep out in the hall. An' that night, when his friend Mr. Rabbit did come, he move an' go in the room an' make a very high bed. An' his friend Mr. Rabbit didn' know what Annancy mean to do.

So Annancy put him out in the hall, an' tell him

that one of his cousin is sleeping in here too, so he will come in later on; an' when him hear him call he must just get up an' open the door an' see who it is.

An' when Annancy out lamp Rabbit think it very hard, an' say to himself:—"Bro'er Annancy up to some trick."

An' Rabbit wake up an' begun to dig a hole, an' him dig a hole until him get outside the door an' find himself back to his yard.

When Snake come in the night to get the other bite from Annancy him call Annancy.

Annancy wouldn' give answer as him being put Rabbit outside in the hall, an' Snake continually calling until Annancy give answer.

An' when him give answer he begin to wake Rabbit an' thought Rabbit was inside the house. He didn' want was to receive his bite, an' he begun to call Rabbit "Cousin Yabbit," that Rabbit may glad an' give him answer. When him couldn' hear, him say "Godfather Yabbit." An' him call again "Bro'er Yabbit," an' him couldn' hear him. An' he call again "Puppa, Puppa!" an' he couldn' hear.

An' him light the lamp an' come out the hall an' begin to s'arch for Rabbit. An' when him look, him see Rabbit dig a heap of dirt an' come out.

An' Annancy beguns to cry inside the house an' wouldn' open the door. An' he begin to complain to Snake that the first bite him gi' him he 'mash up the whole a him head.

An' Annancy 'tudy a 'cheme, catch up a black pot an' turn it down over him head.

An' as he put out him head Snake bite the pot, t'ought it's Annancy him catch. An the whole of Snake mouth was in sore. An' when he get home he send back to Annancy that he sick an' won't manage to come back another night.

An' Annancy was very glad an' send go tell him that himself is in bed.

An' when the bearer start for home him sing this song:—

Andante.
Somebody waiting for Sa - li - zon, Somebody waiting for Sa-li-zon,

Somebody waiting for Sa - li-zon, Take up your letter an' go.

An' from that day Snake broke friend with Annancy. *Jack Mantora me no choose none.*

NOTES.

The house would have two rooms, first the hall and then the inner room or bedroom. From Rabbit's burrowing operations it appears to have no floor. This was a common condition in the old times, but now it gets rarer and rarer. Only Coolie (East Indian) houses are unfloored.

him being put, he had put.

'tudy a 'cheme, studies a scheme. It is more usual **'tudy a plan.** This common, vulgar song is evidently of late origin and probably does not really belong to the story.

XIV. DOBA.

ONE day Puss make a ball an' invite the whole world of Ratta.

All the Ratta dress in long coat an' silk dress. There was t'ousand of them women, an' men. When them come they bring a little boy an' the mother with a young baby.

When all the Ratta settle, the door was shut, an' the Puss them have them junka 'tick secretly in a them trousies' foot. They made a bargain between themselves that, when the Ratta deep in dancing, Doba must out the lamp, then the licking-match commence.

When the music begin, it sweet Ratta so that they dance till their white shirt-bosom was wet.

The fiddler was Dandy Jimmy Flint.

An' this is what the fiddle say:—

Allegro.
Dobo, Doba, Do - ba no make de little one get 'way
Ball - an - to - ny Bap! twee twee, Ball - an - to - ny Bap! twee twee.

The boy Ratta take notice of what the fiddle say.

Him go to him dada an' whisper:—"Puppa, you no yerry what the fiddle say?"

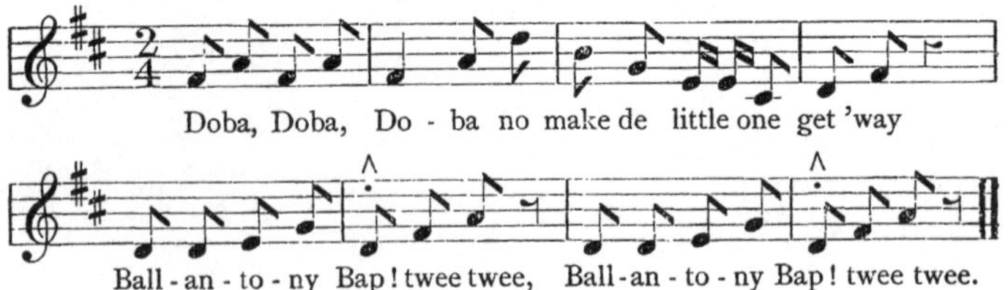
Doba, Doba, Do - ba no make de little one get 'way
Ball - an - to - ny Bap! twee twee, Ball - an - to - ny Bap! twee twee.

The father say:—"Get 'way, Sir, you little fellah you! It the worst fe carry any little boy out fe met. Go, off, Sir, you lying fellah!"

During this time the boy hear what the music say in truth, went an' dug a hole fe him an' him mumma.

When Ratta in hot dancing the gate-man Puss, Mr. Doba, out the lamp. Then the junka 'tick fly round an' all the Ratta was kill. Blood was cover the floor an' all the Puss take their share.

Only boy Ratta an' his mumma an' the young baby, get way.

If the puppa did take what the boy say him wouldn' dead.

Puss ball was flourish with meat.

If boy Ratta an' his mumma didn' get 'way we wouldn' have no Ratta in dis ya-ya-world again.

Jack Mantora me no choose any.

NOTES.

Ratta, rats.

Puss them. These words are closely joined together.

junka 'tick, short sticks.

trousies' foot, the legs of their trousers. The Negroes are expert in the art of hiding things about their person.

Fighting with sticks is called a **licking-match.**

sweet (a verb), pleased, delighted.

In these stories the fiddle is often made to sing words which some have the gift of hearing.

Bap! is the knock of the stick, or "lick of the stick" as they say.

twee twee, the squeak of the rat.

no make, don't let.

it the worst fe carry, etc. It is very troublesome to take a little boy out to a meeting. Met, dance, spree, picnic are convertible terms.

Carry is seldom used as in English. They say:—Carry the mule a pastor (to the pasture). When a man carries you over a river on his back he "crosses you over."

Doba, long **o** as in Dover.

Blood was cover, etc., the floor was covered with blood.

Dis ya-ya, the vulgar English "this here." **Ya-ya** is said very quickly. It does not come into common speech but is reserved for Annancy stories and is generally found only in Annancy's mouth.

XV. DRY-BONE.

ONE day Rabbit invite Guinea-pig to his yard.

An' when Guinea-pig go, Rabbit ask Guinea-pig to go an hunting.

An' Rabbit meet up Dry-bone.

An' when him meet up Dry-bone, him t'row down his gun an' him call to Guinea-pig an' tell him :—"I meet with a luck."

An' Guinea-pig tell Rabbit :—" I won't carry none of the Dry-bone, but you must make me carry the birds what we kill."

Rabbit wasn't agree to let him carry the birds, but Guinea-pig coax him until Rabbit consent an' they fix up the bargain : Rabbit was to carry Dry-bone, an' Guinea-pig was to carry the birds.

So they put Dry-bone into the bag, an' Rabbit ask Guinea-pig to help him up.

An' Guinea-pig help him up an' pick up the gun an' carry it.

An' they start home to their yard.

An' when Rabbit got half part the road he found the load getting heavier an' heavier, an' him ask Guinea-pig to take it for a while.

Guinea-pig tell him that he made no promise was to help him with Dry-bone.

Rabbit walk on till the load get so heavy him begin to cry, say that him going to t'row down Dry-bone.

An' Dry-bone fasten on his head an' begin to talk.

He say to Rabbit:—"You take me up you take up trouble."

An' that time Guinea-pig was laughing after Rabbit.

Just then that cravin' fellah Mr. Annancy was passing an' see Rabbit with his load. He thought that it was something good, an' he ask Rabbit that he will help him carry it.

An' Rabbit was very glad to get relief of his trouble.

So Annancy take Dry-bone from Rabbit an' put him on his own head.

An' when Annancy 'tart, he t'ought that Rabbit was coming.

An' Rabbit turn back an' hide a bush an' leave the trouble to Annancy.

When Annancy get home to his yard him find that it was Dry-bone, an' it vex him in a him heart.

An' Annancy want to leave Dry-bone an' go away.

An' Dry-bone find out what Annancy mean to do.

Annancy have a cock in the yard.

Dry-bone tell him that him must watch Annancy, keep him a yard, an' he will pay him.

An' the Cock ask Dry-bone:—"What is your name?"

An Dry-bone say:—"'Tis Mr. Winkler."

So Dry-bone live in Annancy yard.

An' one day Annancy ask him if him don't want to warm sun.

Dry-bone say:—"Yes."

An' Annancy tell him that to-morrow he will put him out a door.

Annancy went away an' make a bargain with Fowl-hawk, that him have a man name of Mr. Dry-bone, him must come to-morrow an' take him up an' carry him an' drop him in the deepest part of the wood.

An' so Fowl-hawk did do.

When the Cock see Fowl-hawk take up Mr. Winkler him sing out:—

Andantino.

Mister Wink - ler, Winkler come give me me pay.

An' Annancy look up a 'ky an' sing:—

Andantino.

Carry him go 'long, An - nan-cy say so, Carry him go 'long,
Me'll pay fe cock, Carry him go 'long, An - nan-cy say so,
Carry him go 'long, Me'll pay fe cock, Carry him go 'long.

Jack Mantora me no choose any.

NOTES.

help him up, to get the load on to his head. In this story and some others the load once taken up cannot be put down. It sticks to the head of the bearer and, until it reaches its destination, can only be transferred to another head.

cravin', craving, greedy, often sounds like craven. A man who is **cravin'** is generally **cubbich**, covetous. This has lost its original meaning of desiring possession of other people's things and is used only in the sense of close-fisted. A **cravin'** man wants to get hold of what others have got, a **cubbich** (ends with the sound of rich) one will not part with what he has.

laughing after, laughing at.

him must watch. The Cock must watch Annancy and not let him leave the yard, Dry-bone is helpless, and requires attention.

to warm sun, to warm himself in the sun. So they have:—"Puss warm fire," the cat warms herself by the fire.

a 'ky, in the sky.

Me'll pay fe cock, I will pay the Cock's wages which Dry-bone agreed to give. *We* pay a person for a thing, but the Negro pays for the person as well.

Walk, talk, warm, hawk, all have the vowel ah. This story refers to the time of slavery. It is almost indisputable that in certain cases, when a slave was in a weak state owing to incurable illness or old age, he was carried out and left to die. To his pitiful remonstrance, "Massa me no dead yet," the overseer made no reply, but went on with his directions to the bearers, "Carry him go along." This kind of barbarity was not practised by owners living in Jamaica. By them the slaves were well treated and such a thing would have been impossible. But when the masters went away they left the control in the hands of overseers, men of low caste who had neither scruples nor conscience.

XVI. ANNANCY AND THE OLD LADY'S FIELD.

ONE day there was a old lady work a very nice field on a rock, an' an old-witch boy is the watchman.

An' one day Annancy heard about the old-witch boy, an' Annancy send an' invite him to his yard. An when the old-witch boy come, Annancy ask him what his name. An' he says to Annancy that his name is John-John Fe-We-Hall.

An' the boy ask Annancy why him ask him like that.

An' Annancy say:—"Don't be afraid my frien', I very love you; that's why I ask whé you name."

An' by this time the old lady didn't know that the old-witch boy gone to Annancy yard.

An' Annancy have a son is a very clever tief, call Tacoma.

An' Annancy made a bargain that, when him see John-John Fe-We-Hall come, he must walk to the back door an' come out, an' go to the old lady ground an' destroy the provision.

An' when Tacoma come home, Annancy leave John-John out the hall, an' tell him that he is going to get some breakfast for him.

Now the old lady make a law that, if the watchman eat any of his provision, it going to make him sick in a way that he will find out if it is the same watchman tiefing him.[1]

An' being the boy is old-witch, he know that the food Annancy is getting ready is from the old lady field. So when Annancy bring the breakfast he won't eat it.

Annancy tell him that he must eat the food, he mustn't be afraid.

An' the boy say :—" No."

An' Annancy send an' tell the old lady that the man is here clever more than him.

An' when the old lady receive the message from Annancy, he sent to the ground to tell the old-witch boy that he must look out for Mr. Annancy, for him receive a chanice from Annancy.

An' this time the old lady didn't know that the watchman is at Annancy yard.

An' the old-witch boy is a fluter, an' when the old lady want to dance it's the same boy playing for the old lady. An' the old lady have a tune which he is dancing with. An' Annancy ask the boy to play the tune when he is going home, an' Annancy know if the tune play the old lady will dance till she kill herself.

When the boy going home, him took up his sing with the flute :—

Giocoso.
Old lady you too love dance, turn dem, Old lady you too love dance, turn
dem, Turn dem make dem lay, turn dem, Turn dem make dem lay, turn dem.

[1] This is evidently a reminiscence of the "medicine" (Nyanja, *chiwindo*) used in Africa to protect gardens. Sometimes it kills the thief, sometimes makes him ill. (A. W.)

An' when the old lady hear the sing she beguns to dance an' wheel until she tumble off the rock an' dead.

An' Annancy becomes the master of the field until now.

Jack Mantora me no choose none.

NOTES.

A rock would be a bad place for a field. Her house was on a rock probably, and her field or provision-ground elsewhere. For Provision-grounds and their contents see Digging-Sings.

old-witch. Join these words as closely as possible wherever they occur.

Fe-We-Hall. Very humble houses are called So-and-so Castle and So-and-so Hall. **Fe we**, for us, our. He was John of our Hall.

destroy, take away, so that they are lost to the owner and destroyed as far as she is concerned.

out the hall, out in the hall.

breakfast, the principal repast of the day at twelve o'clock.

the man is here. They delight in this enigmatic language. Annancy speaks of himself. He sends word that the man here (himself) is more clever than her (the old lady). Straightforwardness is a quality which the Negro absolutely lacks. If you try to get at the truth of any story he brings, and cross-question him upon it, he will shuffle and change it little by little, and you cannot fix him to any point. Language with him is truly, as the cynic said, the art of disguising thought.

chanice, more usually **chalice**, challenge.

Boys constantly carry their musical instruments about with them. The Flute, a cheap kind of fife, and the Concertina are the favourites. They play as they walk along the road.

The tune, which is quick, is sung over and over and gets uproariously and deliriously merry; gasps on an inward breath, which there is no time to take properly, doing duty for some of the notes.

The words are fragments of a song referring to fowls and eggs. It runs:—

Mother Bonner me hen a lay, turn dem,
Them a lay t'ree time a day, turn dem,
Turn dem make dem lay, turn dem.

XVII. MAN-CROW.[1]

ONCE there was a bird in the wood name Man-crow, an' the world was in darkness because of that bird.

So the King offer thousands of pounds to kill him to make the world in light again.

An' the King have t'ree daughter, an' he promise that, if anyone kill Man-crow, he will make them a very rich man an' give one of his daughter to marry.

So t'ousands of soldiers go in the wood to kill Man-crow. An' they found him on one of the tallest trees in the woods. An' no one could kill him, an' they come home back.

So there was a little yawzy fellah call Soliday.

An' he say to his grandmother :—" Gran'mother I am very poor. I am going in the wood to see if I can kill Man-crow.

An' the grandmother answer :—" Tche, boy, you better go sleep a fireside than you go to the wood fe go dead."

" Gran'mother, I goin' to town fe buy six bow an' arrow."

So he went to Kingston an' bought them.

An' when him return home he ask his grandmother to get six Johnny-cake roast, an' he put it in his namsack, an' he travel in the wood.

He s'arch until he find the spot a place where Man-crow is, an' he see Man-crow to the highest part of the tree.

[1] Cf. the story of "Rombas" in Duff Macdonald's *Africana* II., which would seem to have reached Africa through the Portuguese. Rombas kills the whale which has swallowed the girl, and removes the tongue. (A. W.)

An' he call to him with this song:—

Andante.

Good marnin' to you, Man-crow, Good marnin' to you, Man-

crow, Good marnin' to you, Man-crow, How are you this marnin'?

An' the bird answer:—

Good marnin' to you, So - li - day, Good marnin' to you, So - li -

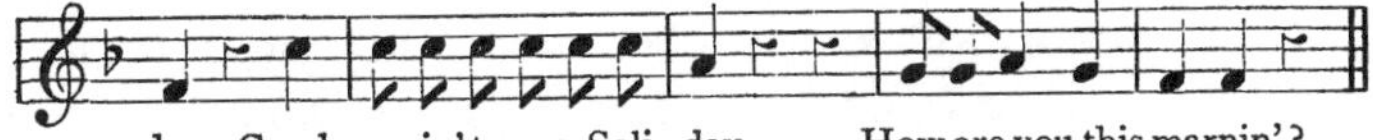
day, Good marnin' to you, Soli - day, How are you this marnin'?

An' Soliday shot with his arrow at Man-crow an' two of his feather come out.

An' Man-crow come down to the second bough.

An' Soliday sing again:—

Good marnin' to you, Man-crow, Good marnin' to you, Man -

crow, Good marnin' to you, Man-crow, How are you this marnin'?

An' Man-crow answer as before:—

Good marnin' to you, So - li - day, Good marnin' to you, So - li -

day, Good marnin' to you, Soli - day, How are you this marnin'?

An' he fire after Man-crow an' two more feather fly out.

An' so the singing an' shotting go on.

At every song Man-crow come down one branch, an' Soliday fire an arrow an' knock out two feather, till five arrows gone.

So Brother Annancy was on a tree watching Soliday what he is doing.

An' the song sing for the sixth time, an' Man-crow jump down one more branch.

An' Soliday put his last arrow in the bow an' took good aim an' shot after Man-crow.

So he killed him an' he drop off the tree.

An' Soliday go an' pick up the bird an' take out the golden tongue an' the golden teeth, an' shove it in a him pocket, an' Soliday come straight home to his grandmother.

An' Annancy come off the tree an' take up the bird, put ahm a him shoulder, cut through bush until he get to the King gate, an' he rakkle at the gate.

They ask :—"Who come?"

He say :—"Me, Mr. Annancy."

An' they say :—"Come in."

An' the King said :—"What you want?"

"I am the man that kill Man-crow."

An' they take him in an' marry him to one of the King daughter an' make a very big table for him an' his family.

They put him in the middle of the table, but he refuse from sit there. He sit to the doorway to look when Soliday coming. (The King then do know that that fellah up to trick.) An' directly Annancy see Soliday was coming, he stop eating, ask excuse, "I will soon be back." An' at that same time he gone outside into the kitchen.

An' Soliday knock at the gate.

An' someone answer him an' ask:—"What you want?"

"I am the boy that kill Man-crow."

An' they said:—"No, impossible! Mr. Annancy kill Man-crow."

An' he take out the golden tongue an' teeth an' show it to the King, an' ask the question:—"How can a bird live without teeth an' tongue?"

So they look in the bird mouth an' found it was true.

An' they call Annancy.

An' Annancy give answer:—"I will soon be there."

An' they call him again.

An' he shut the kitchen door an' said:—"Me no feel well."

All this time Brother Annancy shame, take him own time fe make hole in the shingle get 'way.

They call him again, they no yerry him, an' they shove the kitchen door.

Annancy lost in the shingle up to to-day.

An' the King marry Soliday to his daughter an' make him to be one of the richest man in the world.

Jack Mantora me no choose none.

NOTES.

Yawzy. Yaws is a disease very prevalent among the Negroes. It causes ulcers to form on the soles of the feet. In old slave days every estate had its yaws-house for the accommodation of the sufferers. This complaint does not attack the Whites.

six bow an' arrow, a bow and six arrows, we suppose.

Johnny-cake, journey cake made of flour and water fried in lard.

spot a place, spot of place, exact place.

ask excuse, asks to be excused. Pronounce the **s** like **z.**

shame, etc., was ashamed and was quietly making a hole in the shingle roof so as to get away.

XVIII. SAYLAN.

THERE was a man have two daughter. One of the daughter belongs to the wife an' one belongs to the man. An' the wife no love for the man daughter, so they drive her away.

An' she get a sitivation at ten shillings a week, an' the work is to look after two horses an' to cut dry grass for them.

An' every night she put two bundles of dry grass in the 'table.

An' the mother was very grudgeful of the sitivation that she got.

An' one night she carry her own daughter to the pastur' an' they cut two bundles of green grass. An' they go secretly to the horse manger an' take out the dry grass an' put the green grass in its place.

So the horse eat it, an' in the morning they dead.

An' the master of that horse is a sailor.

The sailor took the gal who caring the horse to hang her.

An' when he get to the 'pot a place to hang her he take this song:—

Andante.
Mourn, Say-lan, mourn oh! Mourn, Say-lan, mourn; I
come to town to see you hang, hang, you mus' be hang.

An' the gal cry to her sister an' brother an' lover, an' they give her answer:—

Allegretto.
Sister, you bring me some silver? No, my child, I bring you none.
Brother, you bring me some gold? No, my child, I bring you none.
Lover, you bring me some sil-ver? Yes, my dear, I bring you some.
Lover, you bring me some gold? Yes, my dear, I bring you some. I
come to town to see you save, save you mus' be saved.

An' the lover bring a buggy an' carry her off an' save her life at last.

An' the mumma say :—"You never better, tuffa."

Jack Mantora me no choose any.

NOTES.

This is quite an unusual form of story, but appears to be of some antiquity in my district, where it ranks as an Annancy story.[1]

caring, taking care of. This is so convenient a word that it is used by everybody.

You never better, you will never be good for anything.

tuffa, with Italian **u** imitates spitting, a sign of contempt.

[1] Cf. *The Maid Freed from the Gallows*, F. J. Child, *Ballads*, vol. ii., p. 346. (C. S. B.)

XIX. ANNANCY AND SCREECH-OWL.

ONE day Annancy made a dance, an' ask 'creech-owl to be the musician. An' Annancy send an' invite all his friend.

An' when they come Ratta was in long coat an' Guineapig too, for Ratta tell Guineapig they must wear long coat an' they will get all the gal to dance with.

An' 'creech-owl is a great player, but the only danger he cannot sing in the day.

An' 'creech-owl has a Cock in his yard, an' he sent an' ask Annancy if he can bring a friend along with him.

An' Annancy send an' tell him that 'tis no objectin to bring the friend, an' Annancy tell 'creech-owl that he will get a lots of drink.

At that time Annancy didn't know the friend as yet.

So, as he being hate 'creech-owl, he didn't wish to see no friend of his.

So when the friend come the friend was a Cock.

An' Annancy was very sorry for he knew that the Cock going to crow when day clean, an' 'creech-owl going to know when day is cleaning an' go away.

An' Annancy got some corn, an' get a pint of 'trong rum, an' t'row the rum in the corn, an' let the corn soak in the rum.

An' when the Cock call out to 'creech-owl that he is hungry, he says to Mr. Annancy that he must treat his friend Mr. Cock, an' Annancy took some of the corn an' give to the Cock.

An' it so being that he love corn, Annancy continually feed him with the corn until he get drunk an' fast asleep.

An' Annancy feel very glad in his heart that he is going to kill Brother 'creech-owl for his breakfast.

An' when 'creech-owl playing, his mind was on his dear friend Mr. Cock, an' he continually listen to hear him crow, an' he couldn' hear him.

An' he ask for him.

Mr. Annancy tell him that he is having a rest.

An' 'creech-owl play an' play till day catch him.

An' Annancy got a kettle of boiled water an' dish it out an' ask his friend them to have some tea.

An' 'creech-owl get very sad to see day catch him.

An' Annancy didn' know whé make 'creech-owl wouldn' drink the tea.

So Annancy begin to raise a confusion over it, say, as he won't drink the tea he must made up him mind to sarve him breakfast.

An' 'creech-owl began to cry.

An' the same time Annancy (that wicked fellah!) take up 'creech-owl music, an' ask young ladies an' young gentlemen to assist him in a noble song which he is going to kill Mr. 'creech-owl with.

An' this the song:—

There's a blind boy in a ring, tra la la la la, There's a
blind boy in a ring, tra la la la la, There's a blind boy in a ring,
tra la la la la, He like su-gar an' I like plum.

An' when Annancy sing the sing done, he catch up 'creech-owl an' wring off him neck, an' get him cook for his breakfast an' becomes the master of 'creech-owl's band of music.

An' from that day Mr. Annancy becomes the greatest player an' the biggest raskil in the world.

Jack Mantora me no choose none.

NOTES.

the only danger, the only danger is. This omission is frequent.

At daylight, or soon after, it is the custom to drink tea. This is generally hot water and sugar with, or more often without, milk. Sometimes they make an infusion of the leaves of lime, orange, mint, fever-grass, cinnamon, pimento or search-me-heart. Coffee and chocolate are also occasionally used. These all grow in Jamaica, but, owing to its high price, actual tea is beyond the reach of the peasant. Lime is, of course, not the English tree of that name, but the tropical one which bears that small juicy fruit which is so much better than the coarser lemon. Fever-grass (*Andropogon citratus*) has the exact smell and taste of lemon-scented verbena. Search-me-heart (*Rhytidophyllum tormentosum*) is a pretty wild plant with leaves of green velvet, which on moist days give out a delicious aromatic smell much like *Humea.*

raise a confusion, get up a quarrel. Annancy resorted to the same artifice when he killed Cow and the other animals at the mock obsequies of his father.

sarve him breakfast, serve for his breakfast.

The song will be found again among the dance tunes.

sing the sing done, finished the song.

'creech-owl sounds like creechole.

XX. ANNANCY AND COW.

ONE day Annancy tell his family that he is going in the wood.

Before he start he get some cane-liquor an' pour it into a big gourdy, an' he tell him wife that " me gone."

An' he travel so till he meet three Cow.

An' he tell one of the Cow marnin', say :—" Marnin', Bro'er Cow."

Cow say :—" Marnin', Brother Annancy."

Annancy say :—" Beg you a little water, Bro'er Cow."

When Annancy get the water he said :—" The water no sweet not 't all." An' he say to Cow :—" Come taste fe me water." An' he no make Brother Cow know say a cane liquor him got.

When Cow taste it him lick him tongue.

Annancy say :—" No say fe me water sweeter more than fe you ?"

Cow said " Yes."

Annancy said :—" Bro'er Cow, you want to go home with me becausen me have it dé a run like a river ? Bro'er Cow, if you want to go with me you fe make me put one wiss-wiss over you harn. But, Bro'er Cow, me have some picny a me yard, dey so fooyish, when time we most yech, dey ma go say ' Puppa bring Cow.' When them say ' Puppa bring Cow ' you mus' say ' A so him do.' "

Annancy carry Cow into his yard an' tie him upon a tree, an' tell Cow him goin' to get a yitty breakfus' for him. (Annancy 'tudy trick fe nyam Cow ; he was very anxious for his beef.)

An' he get into his house and take his tumpa bill coming to Cow force ace fe chop off Cow's neck. He miss the neck an' chop the wiss-wiss, an' Cow take him tail put on him back an' gallop away.

Annancy a bawl, a call:—"Say, Bro'er Cow, a fun me a make, me a drive fly, come back."

Cow no a yerry but gallop till him get home an' tell him wife an' picny, said Annancy want fe kill him:—"Thank God me get 'way; the whole family must sing we own tune to-day ya":—

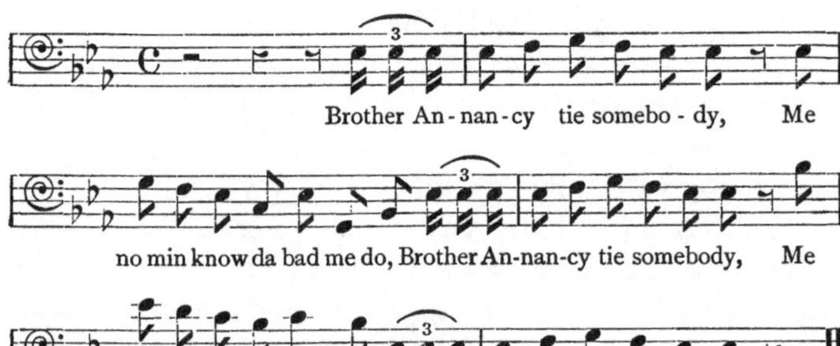
Brother An-nan-cy tie somebo-dy, Me
no min know da bad me do, Brother An-nan-cy tie somebody, Me
tie, me tie, me tie oh! Brother Annancy tie some-bo-dy.

Jack Mantora me no choose none.

NOTES.

cane liquor, juice of sugar-cane.

gourdy, the dried shell of the gourd-like fruit of the Calabash (*Crescentia Cujete*).

wiss-wiss, withe. There are many kinds of these natural ropes to be found in the bush.

fooyish, foolish.

most rech, almost reach, are just getting to the yard.

day ma go say, they may go and say.

A so him do, so he does. The reciter imitates lowing here, the voice falling to a deep prolonged note on the last word.

carry, lead.

yitty, little.

nyam, eat.

tumpa, stumpy, short.

force ace, post haste.

a fun me a make, it's fun I am making, I was only pretending.

min, been, wrong auxiliary for did. I did not know that I had done anything wrong.

Substitute the vowel **ah** in water, all, bawl, call.

XXI. TACOMA AND THE OLD-WITCH GIRL.

ONE day there was a old-witch gal, an' Tacoma want the gal to marry. An' Tacoma went to the gal yard an' ask the gal to courten to. An' the gal tell Tacoma that he don't want a husband as yet.

So Tacoma get very sad in his heart, an' he comes home back to his yard, an' when he come he 'tudy a plan. An' when he 'tudy the plan he fix a day to go back to the gal yard.

An' Tacoma get a buggy, an' get Ratta for his Coachman, an' get a pair of brown-coloured mongoose to be the horse.

An' when Tacoma was going he sent to notice the the gal that he is coming such a day.

An' Tacoma went to his friend Annancy an' borrow long boots an' dress himself nicely, an' borrow a gold watch an' chain, an' got a helmet to his head.

An' when Tacoma ready he order his coachman to harness up the horses. An' when he start he carry lots of present, an' hitch a grey horse behind the buggy, an' take along with him t'ree pieces of music.

An' this time Tacoma didn' know the gal was a old-witch, an' all what Tacoma talk from home the gal really know everything.

An' he reach up the yard an' sing:—

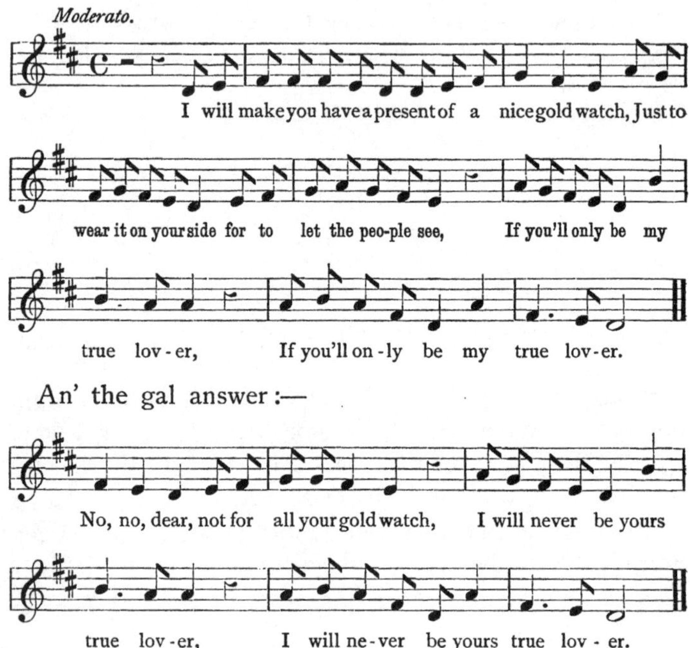
Moderato.
I will make you have a present of a nice gold watch, Just to
wear it on your side for to let the peo-ple see, If you'll only be my
true lov - er, If you'll on - ly be my true lov - er.
An' the gal answer :—
No, no, dear, not for all your gold watch, I will never be yours
true lov - er, I will ne - ver be yours true lov - er.

An' Tacoma have plenty more t'ing is to make a present to the gal. An' he promise to give her a nice silk dress, an' a nice silver bangle, an' a nice gold egg, an' a nice grey horse, an' tell the gal that everyt'ing, which is going to make him a present to, he must wear it along the street to let the people see, if you will only be my true lover.

An the gal say to Tacoma:—"No, for I want the best thing which you have."

An' Tacoma guess an' guess an' he couldn' find out.

An' the gal say if Tacoma find out she will marry Tacoma.

An' Tacoma guess an' guess until he made the gal a promise that he will give him the key of his heart.

An' then the gal was so glad an' said to Tacoma that I'll ever be yours true lover.

An' Tacoma sent for the gal's parents an' his parents an' marry off the gal, an from that day the gal becomes Tacoma wife.

NOTES.

mongoose, see the note to the dance tune "Mahngoose a come."

yours true lover, always **yours.** Generally it is "you" for "your." They say "this is yours" correctly and then add "and this is mines."

t'ing is, things.

which is going, etc., which he is going to make her a present of.

When, commenting on Tacoma's directions, I objected that the girl could not wear the grey horse, the boy who was telling the story saw it at once and said:—"No, he must **carry** it." When the story was done (it is reproduced exactly from his dictation) he sang all the missing verses with the girl's answer to each verse, and instead of his usual "carry" which did not fit he substituted "lead it in the street." The singer will see at once where to make the necessary alterations. The words "silver bangle" want four quavers instead of two crotchets, and it will be worn on the hand as they call the wrist or any part of the arm. "Just to keep it in your hand" follows "gold egg." "The silk dress is worn 'long the street," and after "the key of my heart" comes "just to keep it in your own." I was looking out in this last verse for a change in the words "for to let the people see," but none came. To the last verse the answer is:—"Yes, yes, dear, for the key of your heart I will ever be yours true lover." [Cf. Baring-Gould, *Songs of the West*, No. xxii.; Fuller-Maitland and Broadwood, *English County Songs*; and *Journal of the Folk-Song Society*, Vol. ii., pp. 85-87. (C. S. B.)]

XXII. DEVIL'S HONEY-DRAM.

ONE day Devil set his honey-dram near a river side.

An' Annancy has a little son name of John Wee-wee, an' when the boy find out Devil honey-dram he continually tiefing all the dram.

An' Devil couldn' find out who was doing it.

An' Devil put out a reward that if any one can prove who is tiefing his dram he will pay them a good sum.

An' one day Annancy miss his son, an' Annancy guess that the little boy must be gone to Devil honey-dram.

An' as Annancy being a tief himself he went an' s'arch for the boy. An' when he go he found him drunk an' fast asleep. An' Annancy lift him up an' bring him home.

An' when the boy got sober, about three days after, he got so use to the dram an' he went back.

An' Devil gone out to hunting. An' when he was going he ask his mother to give a heye upon his dram until he come in. An' the mother went down to the dram an' he found the boy drunk the very same again.

An' there was no one know the woman name except Mr. Annancy.

An' Annancy went an' look for his son.

An' when he go the woman catch the boy already an' carry him to Devil yard. An when the boy go the woman gi' him some corn to beat.

An' Annancy went an see his son was beating corn, an' he ask the woman what the boy is doing here. An' the woman tell him that this is the boy was tiefing all Devil honey-dram, an' now him catch him, an' him wouldn' let him go until the master come.

An' Annancy ask the woman if he don't have any more corn to beat.

The foolish woman say:—"Yes, Brother Annancy, but not all the corn you going to beat you won't get your son till the master come."

An' Annancy begin to fret for him know when Devil come he won't have no more son again, for Devil will kill him an' eat him.

An' the woman name is Matilda.

An' Annancy took the corn an' begun to beat an' he start to sing:—

Allegretto.
Wheel oh! Wheel oh Ma - til - da.
Turn the wa - ter-wheel oh Ma - til - da! Ma - til - da mah - my
los' him gold ring, Turn the wa - ter-wheel oh Ma - til - da.

An' the woman begun to dance an' wheel. An she dance an' dance till she get tired an' fall asleep. An' Annancy (the clever fellah) took his son out an' light Devil house with fire.

An' when Devil in the bush look an' see his house is burning he t'row down his gun an' 'tart a run to his yard.

Until he come the house burn flat to ground.

An' Devil couldn' find Matilda his faithful mother, an' Devil take to heart an' dead.

An' Annancy take Devil honey-dram for himself an' build up a house in Devil own place, an' from that day Mr. Annancy becomes the smartest man.

Jack Mantora me no choose any.

NOTES.

Honey dram. The ingredients are honey, water, chewstick, ginger and rum. When mixed the dram is put in the sun to ripen. Chewstick (*Gouania domingensis*) is bitter and takes the place of hops.

beating corn, i.e. maize, to separate the grain from the husks, called also **huxing corn** (husking).

When an animal is found trespassing it is brought down to the yard, and its owner comes to redeem it by a money payment. John Wee-wee was brought in in the same way and according to custom was given something to do while he waited.

faithful. A faithful person is one in whom confidence is reposed.

XXIII. ANNANCY IN CRAB COUNTRY.

ONE day Annancy form himself as a minister, an' was going out an' preaching about. An' Annancy preach an' preach till he get in Crab country. An' Crab them wouldn' hear Annancy at all.

An' Annancy went home back, an' dress himself in a black gown, an' get some red paint an' redden his 'tummy, an' ask a few friend to walk with him.

An the friend was Mr. Toad an' Ratta an' Blackbird.

An' they all start.

An' when Annancy reach to Crab country he beguns to preach.

An' he preach an' preach till they wouldn' hear him again.

An' Annancy hire a house from Crab to stop in the night

An' Annancy, seeing he couldn' catch them with his preaching, made a drum an' a fiddle an' give Blackbird the fiddle to play. An Ratta was playing the drum. An' Annancy see that the music didn't sufficient. He wait, until the next day he made a flute an' give to Toad.

An' when he done he put up the music them an' got in friendship with Crab, an' begun to do the same as Crab them are doing.

An' poor Crab didn' know what Mr. Annancy mean.

An' Annancy go on go on until they got used to Annancy.

An' when they got used to Annancy, Annancy write out plat-card and put it out an' tell his friend Mr. Crab that he is going to have a nice baptism at his house, an' tell them that he will have a bands of music playing in going home, an' how the music will be so sweet they won't tired walking.

An' when Annancy start with his three friend he tell Ratta to roll the drum, an' Blackbird is to rub the fiddle 'tring till it catch fire, an' Toad is to blow the flute as hard as he can, an' he will be reading the tune.

An' he start like this:—

The bands a roll, the bands a roll, the bands a
roll, a go to Mount Si-ney. Sa - lem is Zakki-
low, Some a we da go to Mount Si-ney.

An' when Annancy get home he made a bargain with his t'ree friend that he is going to baptize them an' let Crab see.

An' when he baptize them, Crab they were very glad to see this treat which Annancy do to his t'ree friend, an' they say that they want Annancy to do them the very same.

An' Annancy tell them that they must wait till to-morrow.

An' Crab them agree.

An' Annancy made a bargain with his t'ree friend an' is going to baptize Brother Crab with boiling water.

An' he get a deep barril an' order Crab them that they must go in the barril, an' Crab they do so.

At that time Annancy have a good pot of boiling water an' as Crab a settle theirself in the barril Annancy tilt the pot of boiling water on them an' the whole of Crab body get red.

An' Annancy was very glad an' said:—"T'ank God I have got some of the clever man them for me break-fus'."

An' from that day Annancy was going about an' fool all his friend.

Jack Mantora me no choose none.

NOTES.

The black land-crab is a much-esteemed delicacy. Formerly every property had its crabber, whose duty it was to provide crabs for the house. Since the introduction of the mongoose they have become scarcer.

form himself as, pretends to be.

stop in the night, stop in for the night.

put up, put away.

do the same, etc., live in the same way as the Crabs.

plat-card, placard; a rough written advertisement affixed to the trunk of a tree. When there is a public gathering the musicians play as they walk to the place of entertainment and again as they leave it.

XXIV. GAULIN.

ONE day there was an India woman who have a daughter, an' when the gal born she born with a gold ring on her finger. An' everybody hear about it but they never see it.

An' Mr. Annancy was very crave to got the gal to be his wife.

An' Annancy study a plan an' take up his bands of music an' go down to the gal yard, an' when him go down they admit Mr. Annancy.

An' when they admit him Annancy beguns to play all different tune just to see if the gal would laugh with him. But the gal was very sad, neither would laugh nor smile, until Annancy see there was no good, an' tell good bye an' go home back.

Annancy when him goes home back, met his friend Mr. Rabbit in the road.

Rabbit ask him :—" Brother Annancy, where you is comin' from ? "

An' Annancy begun to tell Rabbit.

So Rabbit make a bargain with Annancy that he is going to try his luck.

So Annancy say :—" As you being such a clean an' white gentleman I think you will succeed. So if you succeed, when you coming home back you must make me know ; then you can take me to be your servant."

That time Rabbit didn' know what Annancy study. Annancy mean was to take away the gal from Rabbit.

So Rabbit start to the yard, an' when him go they admit him in.

An' the mumma ask Rabbit what he come about.

Rabbit says he is looking for a courtier.

An' the mumma say to Rabbit :—" Oh, my dear Mr.

Rabbit, I am very sorry! You is only but a meat,[1] so I can't give you my daughter."

An' Rabbit spend a little time till he tell goodbye.

Meanwhile Annancy wouldn' go home. Him sit in the road till Rabbit coming home back. An' him ask Rabbit if him succeed.

Rabbit say:—"Oh no!"

So they begin to talk. An' by this time Sea-gaulin was passing an' hear what they are saying.

An' when Gaulin go home back, him 'tudy between himself that, if him only get a bus an' dress himself tidy an' drive to the gal yard, she'll sure be his wife.

An' Sea-gaulin goes down, an' the gal was very glad to see him an' invite him inside the house, an' they begun to arrange to be married.

An' there was a old-witch boy which was brother to the gal whisper to her:—"That one is Gaulin."

An' the gal say:—"Oh no, it is my dear love."

So the boy say to then:—"Never mind, one day you will find out if he is not Mr. Gaulin."

So, when Gaulin tell goodbye an' go home to his yard back, the boy follow him an' go to the river side where Gaulin is fishening, an' he climb a tree which hung over the water.

An' when Gaulin come down the river he 'tart a singing:—

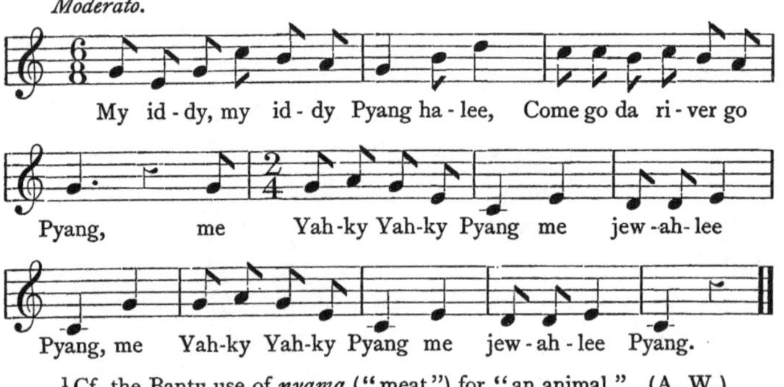
Moderato.
My id-dy, my id-dy Pyang ha-lee, Come go da ri-ver go
Pyang, me Yah-ky Yah-ky Pyang me jew-ah-lee
Pyang, me Yah-ky Yah-ky Pyang me jew-ah-lee Pyang.

[1] Cf. the Bantu use of *nyama* ("meat") for "an animal." (A. W.)

An' that time Gaulin didn' know that the boy was on the tree hearing him.

When he first sing his hat fall off.

An' he sing again his jacket was off.

That time the boy was seeing every bit.

An' he sing again an' his shirt was off.

Sing an' sing till the trousies drop off.

An' as he done he find himself inside the water begun to fishening.

An' as him put him head under a stone-hole the boy come down off the tree an' find himself back to his yard.

An' next Wednesday when Gaulin come to get married, the boy provide for him to sing that very same tune when they are on the cake table.

An the boy say :—" Ladies and gentlemen will you like to hear a song ?,'

An' everybody say " Yes."

An' that time the boy was a fiddler, an' he tune up his violin an' beguns to play " My iddy, my iddy Pyang halee."

Gaulin say :—" Oh no, my brother, stop that tune. That same very tune kill my grandfather, an' when you sing it you let me remember my old grandfather."

An' the boy never stop sing an' play till all Gaulin clothes drop off.

An' Gaulin fly out the door mouth an' find himself right up in the air.

An' from that day that's what make Gaulin fly so high.

Jack Mantora me no choose none.

NOTES.

Gaulin, the Egret. In stormy weather the egrets leave the sea-side and fly up into the country to fish in the streams. They are especially fond of the small crabs which abound in the mountain rivulets. The words of the song have been spelt so as to convey as nearly as possible their right sound. **Halee** rhymes in both syllables to the **stali** of the Venetian gondolier. **Jewahlee** is **Jubilee** with a different middle syllable. **Pyang** with French **a** made as short as possible is the Egret's cry. It should be accented and brought out strongly.

When him goes home back, as he was going home.

white gentleman. This counts many points in the estimation of the Negro.

Rabbit spend a little time. Most characteristic. After the rebuff one would have expected him to go away at once, but that is not the Negro's way. He is never abashed, and after the curtest refusal of any favour he has come to ask, will sit on and talk of other things, finally taking his leave as if nothing had happened.

bus, the buggies which ply for hire in Kingston are so called.

Wednesday, the favourite day for weddings. The bridegroom is accompanied to church by a godmother, not the baptismal one but another specially appointed for the occasion.[1] They ride to church, which is usually at some distance from the yard. The bride also rides from her yard, accompanied by a godfather and two bridesmaids between the ages of eight and eleven. The ceremony and signing of the register over, the newly-wedded couple mount and gallop to the wife's yard, the rest of the company following more leisurely. Arrived there, the bride proceeds to put on her wedding-clothes and the guests are received by the godfather and given sugar-water and bread. When the bride has donned her satin gown and veil (she was married in her riding-habit) and with much sorrow pinched her feet into white shoes too small for them, the company sit down to the cake table. This has upon it two cakes, two fantastically fashioned loaves of shewbread, triumphs of the baker's art with their doves and true lovers' knots, and three vases of cut flowers. The bread is not eaten then but is distributed (*distribbled*, as they have it,) to friends on the days following the wedding. One cake is cut. A knife and fork being handed to a bridesmaid she takes off the cake-head, which is a small top tier or addition to the cake proper. This is put aside and afterwards sent to the officiating minister. The godfather then proceeds to the more serious work of cutting up the cake, giving pieces first to the bride and bridegroom and then to the guests. The second cake is left intact. Wine is poured out, and there are speeches and toasts and hymns. Then follows dinner, which is over about five o'clock. They then begin to play *Sally Water* (see introduction to the Ring tunes) which goes on for an hour or two, and as night falls dancing is started. This goes on all night and does not end, at the earliest, till dusk on the following day, Thursday. It is often kept up until Friday evening or even until Saturday, the dancers and musicians appearing to require no rest. The latter are well supplied with rum and when they get sleepy they beg for an extra tot to rub their eyes, which burns them and keeps them awake. The whole of this time refreshments are supplied to the guests, and as long as these hold out they do not disperse, or as they put it:—"till hungry bite them they no go 'way."

[1] Is this a survival of the African institution of "sureties" (Yao, *ngoswe*, see Duff Macdonald, I. 118), or "sponsors," who arrange the marriage? I am not sure whether the custom exists among Negro as well as Bantu tribes. (A. W.)

The Sunday after the wedding is 'turn t'anks (return thanks). The married couple and their friends get all the beasts, *i.e.* horses and mules, they can muster, and ride to church dressed in their best. The bride and bridegroom, attended by the godfather and godmother, sit in "couple bench," the rest of the party going to their own pews. After service the whole cavalcade gallops as hard as it can, regardless of the precipices which skirt all Jamaica mountain paths, up hill and down hill to the husband's yard. There wine is provided, and the second cake is cut and eaten. Dinner follows at three, and then *Sally Water* is again played until midnight, when dancing recommences and goes on till four or five o'clock on Monday afternoon. This is the end of the festivities, which sometimes cost twenty pounds or more.

provide for him, prepared himself.

door mouth includes not only the opening, but also the whole space just outside the door.

XXV. ANNANCY, MONKEY AND TIGER.

ONE day Annancy an' Tiger get in a rum-shop, drink an' drink, an' then Monkey commence to boast. Monkey was a great boaster.

Annancy say:—"You boast well; I wonder if you have sense as how you boast."

Monkey say:—"Get 'way you foolish fellah you, can come an' ask me if me have sense. You go t'rough de whole world you never see a man again have the sense I have."

Annancy say:—"Bro'er Monkey, how many sense you have, tell me?"

Monkey say:—"I have dem so till I can't count dem to you, for dem dé all over me body."

Annancy say:—"Me no have much, only two, one fe me an' one fe me friend."

One day Monkey was travelling an' was going to pass where Tiger live. Annancy was working on that same road.

As Monkey passing, Tiger was into a stone-hole an' jump out on the fellah an' catch him. All his sense was gone, no sense to let him get 'way. Tiger was so glad, have him before him well ready to kill.

Here come the clever man Mr. Annancy.

When he saw his friend Monkey in the hand of such a wicked man he was frighten, but he is going to use his sense.

He said:—"Marnin', Bro'er Tiger, I see you catch dat fellah; I was so glad to see you hold him so close in hand. You must eat him now. But before you eat him take you two hand an' cover you face an' kneel down with you face up to Massa God an' say, 'T'ank God fe what I goin' to receive.'"

An' so Tiger do.

An' by the time Tiger open his eyes Monkey an' Annancy was gone.

When they get to a distant Annancy said to Monkey:—"T'ink you say you have sense all over you 'kin, why you no been get 'way when Bro'er Tiger catch you?"

Monkey don't have nothing to say.

Annancy say:—"Me no tell you say me have two sense, one fe me an' one fe me friend? Well! a him me use to-day."

From that day Tiger hate Annancy up to now.

Jack Mantora me no choose any.

NOTES.

can come and ask me, that can come. The ellipsis is best explained by giving the sentence another turn: "Get away you man who are so foolish that you can come," etc.

into a stone-hole, in a cave.

Tiger was so glad, etc., Tiger was well pleased and held him in his paws all ready for killing.

why you no been, why didn't you.

a him me use, that is the one I used.

XXVI. THE THREE PIGS.

ONE day a Hog have three Pig an' the three of them was boy. When they were about two month the father died, so the mother grow them up herself. When the Pig them come to big young man the mother said to the first son :—" Me son, a time fe you go an' look you own living."

The day come when he was to start. The mother tie up his clothes an' give him, an' said :—" If you get work sen' an' tell me."

The Pig start.

As he was going he meet a man with a cart of hay.

He said :—" Please, sir, you can give me that hay that I may go an' build a house ? "

The man give him.

Pig go an' make up a house with his hay, an' find it very warm an' comfortable.

One day Wolf come, call :—" Little Pig, little Pig, let me come in."

Pig say :—" No, no, by the hair of my chinnychin-chin.

Wolf said :—" I will huff an' I will cuff an' blow you house down."

Wolf huff an' cuff an' blow down the house, an' go in an' eat Pig.

The mother wait an' can't get no letter from the first son.

She send the other one, second to the first, an' that one travel until he meet a man with a cart of kindling.

He say :—" Please, sir, you can give me that kindling that I may go an' build a house ? "

The man give him.

He make up his house, an' one day Wolf was passing, see that it was pig house, call to him:—"Little Pig, little Pig, let me come in."

Pig say:—"No, no, no! by the hair of my chinnychin-chin."

Wolf say:—"I will huff an' cuff an' will blow you house down.

An' he do so an' go in an' eat Pig.

The mother wait six months an' don't get no letter.

She said:—"Those boy must be get good work an' can't get to write."

The last son she said:—"Me own little son, time fe you go look you living."

Pig say:—"Yes, mumma me wi' go now."

She tie up his bundle give him some money an' kiss him, say:—"You must try write me."

The boy start.

He travel an' travel till night take him. He has to sleep under a stone-hole. When he was sleeping he get a dream that he see his two brother was in a frying-pan. He was so frighten he wake an' start away the same hour. He travel till day clean. At about nine o'clock he get to a big road. He travel on that road till he meet a man with a cart of brick.

He said:—"Please, sir, you can give me that brick that I may go an' build a house?"

The man give him.

He go an' make up a grand house with the brick.

When his house finish Wolf hear, an' come one day, call to Pig:—"Little Pig, little Pig, let me come in."

Pig say:—"No, no, no! by the hair of my chinnychin-chin."

So wolf think that this house was like the rest.

He said:—"I will huff an' cuff an' will blow you house down."

He try for one whole day an' never succeed, so he lef' an' go home an' 'tudy upon Pig.

One evening he come an' call Pig an' tell him he know where there is a garden of all sort a t'ing, so Pig must come an' let them take a walk.

Pig ask him:—"What time you will be going?"

He said:—"A two in the morning."

Pig 'tart eleven, go an' come back with all good food.

At two Wolf come an' call:—"Little Pig, you ready?"

Pig say:—"You lated; I go an' come back already."

Wolf was so vex he go home back. He didn' want nothing but to eat Pig.

He said a next day:—"Little Pig, I know where there is a apple tree a Mr. Simmit garden, make we go an' get some."

Pig ask:—"What the time?" Wolf say "T'ree."

Pig go two.

By Pig was on the tree fulling up his basket here come Wolf. Pig was so frighten he was on the tree trimbling. Wolf was quite glad to think he was going to catch Pig. He couldn' stand his ground, but dance about with joy.

Pig say:—"The apple is so sweet that I have fe take a good load. Mr. Wolf, you would like to taste one?"

Wolf say "Yes."

Pig say:—"Let me see if you can run as that apple?"

Pig throw one of the apple far an' Wolf run after it. By the time he is come back Pig get down off a the tree, leave him baskit an' everyt'ing, an' run nearly reach home.

Wolf was so sorry when he come, left the apple an' gone home,

Next night he call to Pig an' tell him that he know where there will be a met, so they must take a walk.

Pig say:—"What hour?" Wolf said "T'ree."

Pig start twelve an' go dance till two. He was the best dancer an' they give him a butter-churn as a reward. As he walking home he see Wolf at a distant coming.

He said :—" My goodness King! What I going to do?"

Nevertheless he get in the churn a roll down the hill.

Wolf see the thing. He run for his home.

The next day he go an' ask Pig if he did go to the ball.

Pig said :—" Yes, an' as I was coming home I see you, an' was so frighten I get in me churn an' roll down to see if you don't run. An' so you did run, Ha! Ha!"

Wolf get vex. He huff an' cuff all day again to see if he could broke down the building, but all he do he has to lef' it.

So one rain night he send his wife with a young baby to see if Pig would take her in by changing her voice.

She went an' call ;—" Mr. Pig, please Sir, if you can give a night rest, Sir; for rain, an' I am from far."

Pig said :—" No, I don't take in no stranger whatever, especially you, Mrs. Wolf. You husban' try an' try an' can't manage, an' now him send you to see if you can kill me."

Mrs. Wolf commence to climb the chimley.

Pig put a big copper of water on the fire an', by the time she reach the top an' was coming down the chimley, she drop in the water an' dead, she an' the child.

Wolf come again an' call Pig.

An' Pig take up this song :—

Allegretto.
Wolf, Wolf, Wolf! no use you try fe come in, You

wife dere da ready; Ha! Ha! Ha! You wanta try fe
come in, Come Wolf, Me will put you both to-gether.

Wolf get worser vex, commence to beat Pig house with all his might an' couldn' get in. He climb up the chimley, an', by he fe get to the top, the pot of boiling water was long time ready waiting for him, an' he going down in a haste make a slip, drop in the water.

Pig salt them an' put them in his cask to soak, an' write to invite his mother to help him eat them for he find out it was them eat his two brother.[1]

Jack Mantora me no choose none.

NOTES.

Pig them. Read these words together, not, Pig—them come.

you can give, can you give.

huff, scratch with the hoof.

kindling, small wood to light fires with.

day clean. Day is clean when you can see to walk.

big road, one that is what the Italians call *carozzabile,* carriageable. In the hills of Jamaica the roads are for the most part mere mule tracks.

Simmit, Smith.

make we go, let us go.

What the time? at what time?

By Pig, as Pig.

fulling, trimbling, always so.

when he come, etc., when he came back to the tree, that he left the apples and went home.

met, meeting, ball.

da ready, already.

by he fe get, by the time he got.

cask to soak. Salt meat is kept in a tub of brine.

[1] Cf. Joseph Jacobs, *English Fairy Tales,* No. xiv., and note, p. 233. (C. S. B.)

XXVII. DUMMY.

THERE was a man couldn' talk, called Dummy.

One day Annancy bet the King he going to make Dummy talk.

So the King say:—"If you make Dummy talk I will give you one of my daughter fe marry."

Well, Annancy went to Hog, ask him:—"Bro'er Hog if I carry you fe Dummy, whé you wi' say?"

Hog say:—"Me wi' say ugh! ugh!"

Annancy say:—"You won't do."

He went to Goat:—"Bro'er Goat, if I carry you fe Dummy, whé wi' you say?"

"Me wi' say Meh—eh—eh!"

"You won't do."

So he went to fowl.

Fowl say:—"Me wi' say Clk! Clk! Clk!"

"You won't do."

So he went to Bro'er Peafowl an' ask him:—"What you will say if me carry you fe Dummy?"

Peafowl say:—"Me wi' say:—

Andante.
Chirry - way, Chirry - way, Chir - ry -
way dem dé, Chirry-way, Constan' dead to-day, Chirry-way.

Then Annancy say:—"A you me wanty."[1]

[1] See the story of Tangalomlibo in Torrend, *Comparative Grammar of S. African Bantu Languages*, p. 319, where the cock is chosen as messenger, when the ox and goat are rejected. (A. W.)

So Annancy beg Bro'er Peafowl he must come with him to Dummy.

An' when Dummy hear the tune it sweet him so, he commence to shake him head an' hum.

So them went to the King yard, Peafowl before, Dummy in the middle, Annancy dé a back.

An' as they reach up Annancy say "Wheugh!" being him breat' gone an' him tired, but peafowl never cease with the song.

When Annancy got him breat' he say to the King:—"Master me a come, me a go make Dummy talk."

Then the King say:—"I will like to hear Dummy talk."

An' Peafowl sing an' sing, an' make all sort of figure before Dummy.

Dummy commence to shake him head two t'ree time de way de song sweet him.

At last Dummy begin to hum.

As Peafowl see him commence to hum, Peafowl make a sudden spring, went up to Dummy with a great flourish, an' at last Dummy sing right out the same as Peafowl:—

Chirry-way, Chirry-way, Chir-ry-
way dem dé, Chirry-way, Constan' dead to-day, Chirry-way.

An' Annancy get the bet an' the King marry him off.

An' Annancy give Peafowl gold all over his body an' six quarts of corn. From that Peafowl cover all over with gold.

NOTES.

Whé you wi' say, what will you say?

sweet him so, pleased him so much.

Constan', Constance.

XXVIII. ANNANCY AND CANDLEFLY.

ONE day Annancy go to Brother Candlefly yard fe fire.

When him go Candlefly give him fire an' tell him to wait an' he will go give him a few eggs.

When Annancy get the eggs he go home with the fire.

The next day he go back fe fire an' Candlefly give him more eggs.

Annancy go till him get halfway, out the fire an' turn back.

When him come him say:—"Bro'er Candlefly, the fire out; give me some more."

When Candlefly give him the fire, him wait an' wait to see if him can get more eggs. Candlefly never give him one.

Annancy say:—"Bro'er Candlefly, the fire a burn me, please give me one egg make me wet me han', fe make it better."

Candlefly give him one an' tell him to come an' he will carry him where any amount of egg da, "But you must not come till close a night."

Annancy don't wait till night, go about midday. When him go him get a long bag ready. Every minute him come out of the house an' look on sun. Annancy couldn' tarry but only praying to see if night can come.

When night come Candlefly get ready an' tell Annancy to stay aback. Them travel till at last them get. (Annancy going to play out Candlefly.)

Every gash Candlefly gash an' see a egg going to pick it up, Annancy say:—"A me first see ahm."

Candlefly gash again: Annancy take away every one till him bag full. Candlefly don't get one. So as Annancy such a strong man Candlefly compel was to lef' without say a word.

But Annancy going to feel the blow.

After Candlefly gone with the light Annancy couldn' find nowhere to put his foot.

Annancy say :—" Poor me boy, I mus' try see if I can fin' the way."

Annancy start.

Him travel till him go an' buck on a house. The way the night was so dark he never see the house, he just buck on it.

He don't know whose house it was but him call "Godfather!"

The person answer :—" Who is that calling?"

Him say :—" Annancy, you godson, bring some eggs fe you."

During this time Annancy never know that it was Tiger who him hate so much.

When the door open there come Brother Tiger.

Annancy say :—" Marnin', Godfather Tiger."

Tiger say :—" Come in."

Same time Tiger send his wife to go an' put on the copper on the fire.

So them boil the whole barrel-bag of eggs.

When the eggs boil Tiger ask Annancy if him want any.

The frighten in him, him say " No."

So Tiger eat the whole bag of eggs, he an' his wife an' children.

To find out if Annancy want any of the eggs Tiger tell him wife fe lef' two of the good shell. So Tiger get a lobters an' put with the egg shell.

When Annancy go in to sleep, Annancy see these two eggs, don't know that it was shell. Tiger know how the fellah love eggs.

When lamp out Annancy 'tretch him hand to catch the eggs.

Lobters paw give him a good bite. Him jump. Then Tiger know that it was the egg the fellah want.

Tiger ask:—"What the matter Mr. Annancy?"

"No dog-flea a bit me up so, sir? Me never see place have dog-flea like a you yard."

Tiger gone back to sleep.

Five minute more Annancy cry out:—"Lahd! me never see place have dog-flea like a you yard."

During this time he was trying to get the egg-shell. So he try an' try the whole night an' never get.

When day light Tiger say:—"Me son, me sorry to see dog-flea bit you so last night. You is the first man come here a me house say dog-flea bit you."

Annancy say:—"Godfather, I don't get a rest from I go to bed till now."

Tiger wife get tea an' give him, so he get ready.

Tiger say:—"Go a me goat-pen, you see one goat, fetch him ya fe me before you go."

Annancy go. When him go he see a big he-goat, him beard was a yard long. Annancy catch the beard, lift him up t'row him a ground, take a big stick begin to beat him, give bup! bup! say:—"You b'ute! a you master nyam all me egg never give me so so one self."

Him beat him so till the goat form 'tiff dead. Now this was Tiger all the time. Annancy leave him gone to see if he can get any knife to cut him up.

By Annancy come back him don't see no goat, only a big old man standing up. Him put after him. Annancy run back to Tiger yard. The man was after him. Annancy see a gourdy, run right in it. Tiger lost the fellah.

Well! Tiger take his gourdy going fe water.

Annancy, knowing that Tiger mother was sick, as Tiger get half way with the gourdy on his head Annancy call out of the gourdy mouth:—"Bro'er Tiger, you mumma dead a house from yeshterday."

Tiger stop, him listen, him can't hear.

He make a move.

Annancy bawl out again:—"Bro'er Tiger, you mumma dead a house from yeshterday."

Tiger stop, him listen, him can't hear.

He go on again, he hear the voice again.

He throw down the gourdy.

Annancy get out, said to Tiger:—"You b'ute! if you been broke me foot you wouldn' min' me wife and picny."

Tiger hear the voice but never see a soul.

Him run gone home to see if his mother dead. When he go his mother was still alive.

Annancy go home an' go to Candlefly yard tell him say:—"I never will be cravin' again, ya, Bro'er? you fe carry me again. An' Candlefly say "Yes."

Every day Annancy come. Candlefly wife say:—"Him gone long time."

Annancy never get to go with Candlefly again, an' he don't know the place.

Jack Mantora me no choose any.

NOTES.

Candlefly. Among the smaller fire-flies which twinkle all the year rushes, in the summer months, the great Candlefly. It makes a roaring sound with its strong, swift flight, and is a strange and splendid object. It has three lights, two looking like eyes, and a larger and much more brilliant one underneath the thorax. When at rest only the eye lights shine, but with the spread of its wings a shutter is drawn back and discloses the abdominal light. The insect, which is the size of a cockchafer but rather longer, is commonly called Big Winky or Peeny.

da, is pronounced like Italian.

look on sun, looks at the sun to see if it is sinking.

a back, behind.

get, get to the place.

gash, flash. Lightning is said to gash. As explained above, this gashing of the great light of the Candlefly is continuous while it is in flight, but ceases as soon as it rests.

buck on, run against. A horse **bucks**, here, when he stumbles. A man **bucks**

his toe when he knocks his naked foot against a stone, and women fight (**men** too for that matter) by **bucking** with their heads.

Marnin'. Good morning and good evening are used as salutations without reference to the actual time of day.

barrel-bag, a bag of the capacity of a flour barrel.

the frighten, etc., owing to the fright which was in him he said "No."

fe lef', to leave.

lobters. This transposition of letters has a ludicrous effect on the word.

paw, pronounced **pah** very broadly.

Fleas are always called dog-fleas, or rather dahg-fleas.

tea, the morning sugar-water, is the signal that it is time for the guest to be soon moving on. Generally, however, he is given something to do before he goes.

ya, here.

so so one self, even one.

form, pretended.

Him put after him. The old man put (ran) after Annancy.

You couldn' mind, etc. This piece of pleasantry is common. When two men are doing anything that requires care to avoid accident, such as moving a heavy stone, one says to the other :—"No kill me ya, you couldn' min' me wife an' picny," you can't support my wife and children.

ya, do you hear? Which is also its meaning in the preceding note. Just now **ya** meant 'here.'

XXIX. PARSON PUSS AND PARSON DOG.

ONE day Toad was courting for a long time to a very pretty India gal, an' Toad didn' want marry the gal. An' him didn' want the gal was to leave him but to live without married.

An' Puss was Toad parson. An' the mother send an' call Puss, an' when Parson Puss come, the mother lay the matter before Parson Puss.

An' Parson Puss call Toad one of his lovely member in the church, an' him didn' want Toad was to leave his church. An' Parson Puss talk until Toad agree to married the gal.

An' Dog himself was a parson.

So Toad send out a invitation to all his countrywoman an' countryman, an' invite Tacoma an' his families, an' likewise invite his friend Mr. Annancy an' his families. An' when him done Toad invite Parson Dog.

An' the day when Toad is to married Parson Puss come to married Toad.

An' Parson Dog come with his gown was to take away the business from Parson Puss.

But Toad say:—"Oh no! he will like to give his Parson the preference."

An' Dog say:—"Yes, I must have it. If not will be mossiful fight to-day."

Puss wife, was the organ-player, say:—"What a man fe swear!"

An' Parson Puss say to Toad mother-in-law:—"You don't mustn't listen what that fellah Parson Dog is saying. He so tief, as soon as they 'tick the hog he will soon forget all this for he has to go an' lick blood, so when he gone I will marry my member Toad."

An' so Dog did go away.

Until he come back Parson Puss marry off Toad.

An' when they eat cake done, then Parson Puss ask the young ladies them to let them go an' play in the ring, an' so they did do.

That time Parson Dog didn' know what was doning, but soon he hear this sing:—

Allegretto.
When you see a hug-ly man, When you see a hug-ly man,

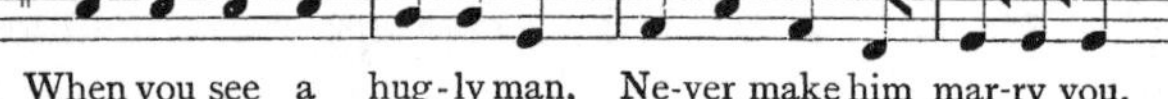
When you see a hug-ly man, Ne-ver make him mar-ry you.

An' as him hear him hold up one of him foot an' listen.

An' he come nearer an' hear again:—

Par-son Dog won't married me, Par-son Dog won't married me,

Par-son Dog won't married me, Cut your eye an' pass him.

Then Parson Dog shake him head, run come.

An' as he run come he meet Parson Puss was wheeling all the gal.

Parson Dog get very vex an' he bear an' bear.

But as he hear plain how the sing go, an' see that some of the gal Puss was wheeling began to laugh after him, say:—"No see how him mout' long," Parson Dog get fairly upstarted till him run in the ring an' palm Puss an begin to fight him.

An', as Parson Puss feel Parson Dog 'trength more than fe him, him look for a very tall tree an' run right upon it to save his life.

An' from that day that why Dog an' Puss can't 'gree until now.

Jack Mantora me no choose any.

NOTES.

lovely member. A certain amount of blarney is supposed to be admissible to keep your sheep from straying to a rival's flock.

to married Toad. Though they sometimes say **marry** (see the first song) they prefer **married.** The **d** before the **T** of Toad is very awkward to pronounce, yet the reciter, whose normal speech is of the laziest, like that of all his kindred, got it out quite plainly.

mossiful, unmerciful. Dog really used a bad word here, which is always put in his mouth. He uses the same word in "Finger Quashy." So much does it belong to him that it occurs as a descriptive adjective to the dog in the tune for the third Quadrille figure, which will be found among the dance tunes. The word is not really very bad, but it was not considered appropriate to a book which may find its way into the nursery, so in every case another one is substituted.

'tick, stick. The pig was killed for the wedding festivities, which were only just beginning. See note on weddings in "Gaulin."

play in the ring, play Sally Water, see Ring Tunes.

doning, being done.

never make him marry you, never let him, etc.

cut your eye, turn your eye aside. Where we use transitive **cut** they put intransitive **cut eye.**

wheeling, turning them in the dance.

run come, came running up.

bear an' bear, was patient for a while. A picturesque way of describing Dog's self-restraint. He bears it and he bears it again.

no see, etc., don't you see how long his mouth is. This is always the joke about Dog. About Puss it is :—"You face too (very) short. Cut off half inch you don't have nose."

upstarted, angry.

palm, touch or hold with the hand.

fe him, his.

XXX. CHICKEN-HAWK.

ONCE a lady have t'ree daughter. One of the daughter, the youngest one, born with a gold teet'. The other sisters h'ard of the teet' an' ask their sister to show them the teet', but she never would show them.

One day they get Monkey an' Goat to come an' dance to let the sister laugh. They make all sort of mechanic. She never laugh all the dance Monkey an' Goat was dancing.

Those other two pay her so much to see the teet'. She won't show them.

So the second sister tell the big one say :— " Sister, let we go make bargain with Chicken-hawk to try if we can see the teet'."

So they did go an' see Chicken-hawk about it an' pay Chicken-hawk so much.

The day come when they fix up to go to the river.

Chicken-hawk was on a tree.

So they gone to swim for a long time, the big sister them swimming an' laughing in the water for the little one to laugh for them to see the teet', but she never laugh.

During that time Chicken-hawk took up all three of them clothes an' gone on a high tree where them can see him.

When the sister know that Chicken-hawk took the clothes they came out of the water all t'ree of them.

All the clothes was gone.

The first sister commence fe sing :—

Chicken-hahk oh! Chicken-hahk oh! give me me
frock. Chicken-hahk oh! Chicken-hahk oh! Chicken-hahk!

An' Chicken-hawk bring come.

The next sister do the same an' get her frock.

Here comes the youngest one. She shut up her mouth an' was calling from her t'roat :—

Hm— - - hm— - - - hm—
- hm— - - hm— - - hm— .

Chicken-hawk never give her.

When the big sister see that she won't call for them to see the teet' they leave her, an' she become 'fraid an' call out :—

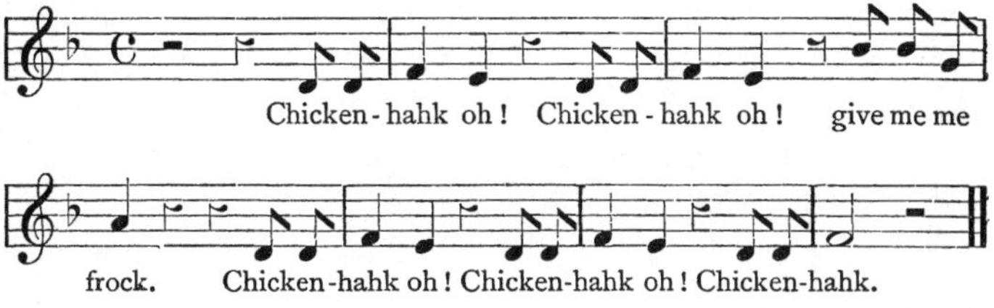
Chicken-hahk oh! Chicken-hahk oh! give me me
frock. Chicken-hahk oh! Chicken-hahk oh! Chicken-hahk.

An' the big sister run come an see the golden teet' an' was so glad.

They go home an' tell their mother that we have gain the battle an' have seen the gold teet'.

From that day we see gold teet' until now.

NOTES.

mechanic, antics.

so much, a sum of money.

XXXI. PRETTY POLL.

ONCE a Duke have a sarvant. So this sarvant was courting to a young man for a long time.

So one day another friend come to see the Duke. So he love the Duke sarvant an' the Duke sarvant love him. So this man ask the Duke for her.

The Duke say :— "No, she is courting already."

So the friend was sorry.

The gal tell the young man say:— "Me love you, an' if you going to marry me I will lef' my lover an' come."

The young man say :— "How you will manage that the Duke not going to allow it?"

The gal say :— "You look out."

So one evening, when the gal lover come home, she ask him to let them go for a walk far away. "I am going to show you a very pretty place."

During this time the gal know where a well was, so she is going to shub him into the well.

As they reach to the place they see a pretty flowers in the well.

So they was looking at the flowers.

As she see that her lover was gazing at the flowers she just shub him right in the well an' said :— "T'ank God! me going to get that pretty young man."

During this time there was a Parrot on a tree seeing all that was going on, cry out :—

Allegretto.
Ha ha! Ha ha! I have a news to take to the Duke at
home; you have your dearest lover an' cast him down to the well.

The gal look up an' see the Parrot.
She get frighten, call to Poll :—

Allegretto.
Come, Pret-ty Poll, come! There is a house of
gold an' sil - ver be-fore you sit 'pon tree.

Poll sing :—

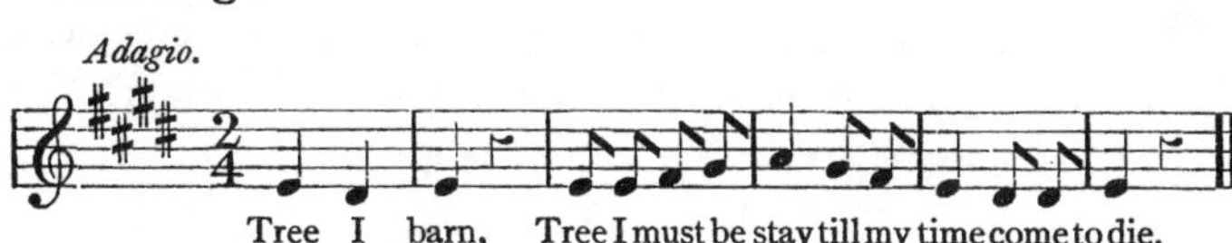
Adagio.
Tree I barn, Tree I must be stay till my time come to die.

An' Poll commence to fly from tree to tree an' she was following him till they get out to a village. Poll was still singing an' she was begging.

Poll fly from house to house till he get on the Duke house an' sing.

The gal was crying.

The Duke hear, send out man an' they listen until them hear what Poll said, an' them catch the gal an' chop off her head.

An' Poll get good care.

Jack Mantora me no choose any.

NOTES.

This is another version of the "King Daniel" story.

before you sit, instead of your sitting.

Tree I barn, etc. On a tree I was born, on a tree I must stay.

XXXII. ANNANCY AND HOG.

ONE day Annancy an' him grandmamma go to a ground.

Annancy left him fife.

When him coming home, he an' his grandmamma, he said:—"Gran'mumma you know I leave my fife at groun'."

Him grandmamma say:—"Me son a know you well. You is a very bad boy. Go for it but don't play."

When Annancy coming home he play:—

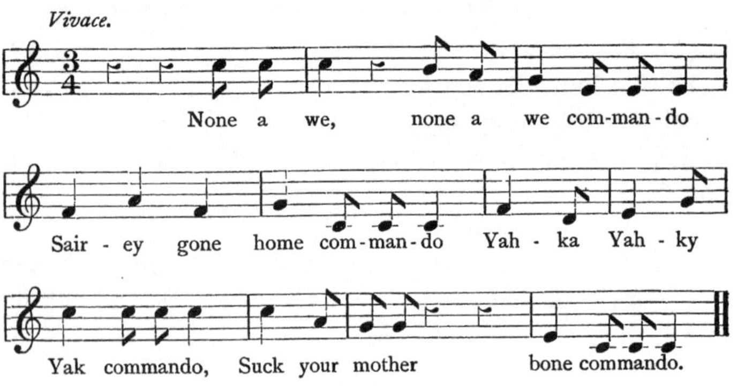
Vivace.
None a we, none a we com-man-do
Sair - ey gone home com-man-do Yah - ka Yah - ky
Yak commando, Suck your mother bone commando.

An' as he play he meet Hog.

Hog say:—"Brother, a you a play da sweet sweet tune."

Annancy say:—"No, Bro'er."

Hog say:—"Play, make me hear."

Annancy play twee, twee, twee, all wrong note.

Hog say:—"Tche! you can't play."

Hog gone round short pass.

As Hog go round short pass, him buck the boy was playing the tune.

Hog say:—"Bro'er Annancy I think a you a play, you beggar, you light fe me dinner, you libber fe me dog."

An' Hog carry home Annancy an' goin' to do him up for him dinner.

An' when Hog think him done up Annancy him done up him own mother.

An' that made Hog nasty feeder up to to-day.

Jack Mantora me no choose none.

NOTES.

ground, a provision ground where yams, etc., are grown. They often pronounce it **grun,** rhyming to run but even shorter.

a leave, I leave.

This tune has a bobbin, see *Digging sings.* Nonsense words of course.

commando, pronounced common doe.

yah, with French **a.**

pass, path. It no doubt should be **gone down short pass.** The paths circle round the steep mountain sides and short cuts connect the loops.

buck, stumbles on, meet.

you light, etc. Your lights for my dinner, your liver for my dog.

XXXIII. DRY RIVER.

ONCE a man have t'ree daughter. Dem go go pick wacky.

When dem a come, dem come to a river having no water.

Dem meet a old man beg dem a wacky.

The two biggest one give the old man two wacky, one each, an' the little one wouldn' give any.

An' the old man sing:—

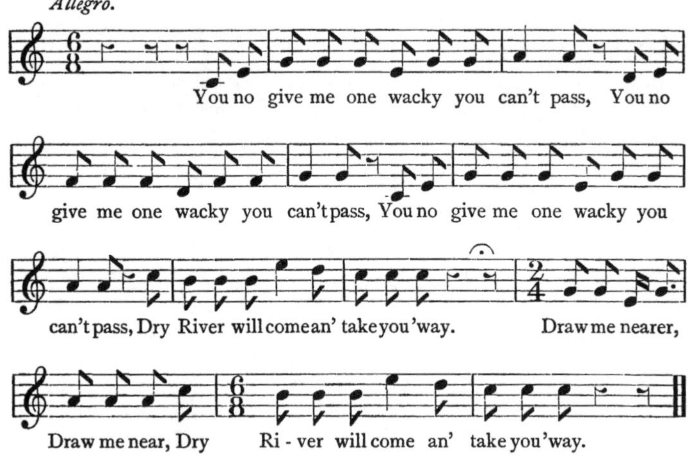
Allegro.
You no give me one wacky you can't pass, You no give me one wacky you can't pass, You no give me one wacky you can't pass, Dry River will come an' take you 'way. Draw me nearer, Draw me near, Dry Ri - ver will come an' take you 'way.

An' the little one won't give.

An' the two big sister want to give two more of their wacky to the old man; but the old man say:—"No, the little one must give me one of fe her wacky."

An' she won't give.

So the old man sing the sing again.

An' still the little one won't give, until at last the river come down carry him gone.

From that day people drowning.

Jack Mantora me no choose none.

NOTES.

In the heavy rains of October and May the rivers rise suddenly, and an insignificant stream or dry river-bed becomes a raging torrent. Travellers are delayed in the Seasons, as these rainy times are called, owing to the fords becoming impassable. This happens now less frequently than formerly, not because the rivers do not 'come down' but because many of them are bridged.

wacky (French **a** with a turn to **o**, almost "wocky"), guava. This fruit which makes the well-known jelly is wild. It is the size of a small apple, and has a delicious scent when ripe and yellow. Raw, however, it is not a good fruit. The flavour is coarse and the pulp is full of very hard seeds, which must be swallowed whole.

when dem a come, when they reach the place where the wackies are they come to a river.

old man beg, etc., old man who asks them for a wacky. Much of the conciseness of negro speech is due to the suppression of relatives and prepositions.

you no give, if you do not give.

XXXIV. YELLOW SNAKE.

ONCE a woman, name Miss Winky, have four children, three son an' one daughter. The son them was hunter-man and the youngest son was old-witch. This sister never can find her fancy. Everybody come she say: "Lard, this one hugly, me no like him at all!"

Till one day she an' the mother an' old-witch boy was at home.

Snake was on a journey, get to a rum-shop. Talking an' talking they bring up some talk about this gal, that everybody go for her she refuse.

Snake say:—"Is she a pretty gal?"

They say:—"Yes, man, she is a beauty to look at."

Snake said:—"I bet anything I get that gal."

Snake change an' fix up himself an' go to the yard.

When he go he said:—"Good day, Miss Winky, I come to ask you for your daughter."

The gal, was in the room, run out to see if it is a pretty man.

As she come out she said:—"Mamma, this is my love, no one else."

So Snake was invite in the house.

The mother said:—"Well, as you get your fancy I am going to married you."

So the next day they go an' get marry.

After dinner Snake get ready, an' the gal mother tie up all her clothes an' they start.

They travel the whole night until daylight an' never could get, till about midday they reach the place. It was a big stone-hole.

Snake carry her under, put her to sit down.

An' after Snake get a good rest he commence to swallow her.

On the meantime the old-witch boy, name of Cawly, know all what was going on in the wood, tell his two elder brother to come "an' let us go hunting for I hear the voice of my dear beloved sister crying for me in the wood."

The two brother said:—"You always goin' on with your foolishness."

He said:—"Never mind, come let us go an' see."

So they start an' they walk like beast, till at last they nearly reach where they could hear the sister.

They hear a voice:—

Andante.
Fe me Caw-ly Caw-ly oh! - If no
hunterman no come here oh! - Yalla Snake will swallow me.

Snake, fe all him mout' full, get to say:—"Me will swallow you till you mumma no fin' piece of you bone."

The brother come close to the place, climb upon the stone.

They hear the voice plainer, come down off the stone an' see that Snake leave but the head of their sister.

They go down on Snake an' kill him an' split him an' take out their sister an' carry her home.

From that day she never marry again for she feel the hand of marry.

So everybody that pick too much will come off the same way.

Jack Mantora me no choose none.

NOTES.

Snake, pronounced in two syllables, Se-nake with the exact value of vowels in the French words *ce n'est que*, and of course stopping at the *k* sound of the *q*.

Tie up all her clothes, in a bundle which she would carry on her head.

get, get to Snake's home.

beast. This is the generic name for a beast of burden, horse, mule, or donkey.

fe all, although.

get to say, managed to say.

fe me, my.

feel the hand of marry, a biblical expression. She felt the hand of matrimony, and behold it was heavy.

XXXV. COW AND ANNANCY.

ONE day Annancy was passing Cow pastur', saw the whole of them was cleaning their teeth with chewstick.

He was so frighten for Cow, he stay outside the pastur' on a tree an' call to Cow, telling them howdy.

Cow never answer him, so he get worser frighten.

He said to himself:—"If I give them piece of cane, fool them say it is my chewstick, they might a come friend with me."

So Cow them go out in the night to feed.

An' when them gone Annancy go an' get his side-bag full with cane as quick as he can. An' when him come Cow them gone away for the whole night, so he climb the tree an' sleep on the tree until daylight.

An' when the sun begin to hot the Cow come under the tree fe throw up their food fe eat it back. Same time Cow cleaning him teeth with the chewstick.

Presently the papa Cow see a big piece of something drop out of the tree.

He look up see Annancy, call to him :—"What you doing dé?"

Annancy say :—"Me bring piesh a chewshtick fe you."

Cow take up the cane begin to chew. Instead of cleaning teeth he was swallowing both juice an' trash.

Cow say :—"Him sweet; you no hab no more dé now?"

Annancy say "Yes."

Cow call him down from the tree.

When he come down he give everybody piece of the cane, tell them that it is fe him chewstick.

During this time he have a big bottle of cane-juice, ask Cow if him want a taste.

Cow take a taste, he done the whole bottle of it.

So they all get in friend with Annancy.

An' Annancy invite Cow to go home with him, an' he will show him where he get such good chewstick.

Cow say :—"You no have nobody a you yard."

Annancy say "Yes."

Cow say :—"Me shame fe go."

Annancy say :—"Make me go home an' sen' dem 'way."

Annancy go home, tell all his friend them must look out, him going to fetch Cow, ya.

Them say :—"If you bring Cow you we will never trust you the longest day we live.

Annancy say :—"Look out."

He take a rope. When he go back he tell Cow that him no see nobody a yard, so Cow must come make dem go.

Cow say, "Yes."

Them 'tart.

Annancy tell Cow that as he is such a coward man him have a piece of rope, Cow must make him put it on his neck, afraid a when him a go the picny them go see him, go make noise, you go turn back.

Annancy say: "Bro'er Cow, when you go near me yard, if you yerry them picny a make noise no frighten, fan you tail with strength."

When them get to where all the friend an' children could see him, him call to them:—"A da come, no see me frien' a come tell you howdy." He turn to Cow said:—"Fan you tail, no min' dem people.

At last them reach the yard.

Annancy have a big tree at the front of his house. He tell Cow:—"Bro'er Cow, stay ya, make me go look after the house; me wife no know, say me a bring 'tranger ya, so we can't carry you in so, so you can fan you tail as much."

During this time Annancy gone to get all his tool sharpen to kill Cow. He left his biggest son to watch Cow but he can't trust the boy. Every minute he come to look if Cow is there.

The first time he come an' look he say to Cow:—"Fan you tail."

When the thing them nearly done sharp he come back, see Cow was fanning his tail.

He said to Cow:—"You Cow, you no yerry me say 'No fan you tail a me yard?'"

Cow fan fe the better.

He come with his bill, said to Cow:—"If you no 'top fan you tail either you kill me or me kill you."

Cow won't stop.

He say to one of the friend:—"Now, now, sir, you see how that man a frighten me picny a me yard, him mout' so hugly."

Him come up nearer to Cow say:—"If you no 'top fan you tail somet'ing mus' done."

Cow won't stop, seeing the fly a trouble him.

Annancy set a run with his bill chop at Cow neck.

Cow draw back his head, the bill catch the rope, set Cow free, so he run for his life.

Annancy say:—" Come back, Bro'er Cow, a fun me a make wi' you, simple little fun, you run gone home." But Cow was flying for his home an' never stop. Annancy take up this song:—

Allegro.
Lard! Lard! has - ty kill me dead oh!
Poor me boy oh! a whe me a go do? Me put me pot a
fire fe boil Cow liver, but has-ty kill me dead.

From that day Annancy never can go where Cow is. Anywhere Cow see him he reach him down with his mouth.

Jack Mantora me no choose any.

NOTES.

We have had this story already in another form (Annancy and Cow, No. 20).

chewstick, a common climber. A piece of the stem about the thickness of a pencil is cut and makes a sort of soapy froth as it is chewed. It has an agreeable bitter taste and is used to clean the teeth.

howdy, how do you do?

cane, sugar-cane.

fool them, take them in, delude.

side-bag. Everybody has his side-bag or namsack (knapsack).

papa, pronunciation something between puppa and poppa, with slight accent on the first syllable. Cows in Jamaica are of both sexes.

dé there; the *e* is that of "debt" lengthened. French "est" gives it exactly. Whé has the same *e*.

trash, the fibre. Trash is any kind of refuse, such as shells of peas, husks of maize, the remains of Cassada after the starch is washed out, withered banana leaves, the outside pulp which encloses the coffee beans, etc., etc.

ya sometimes means *here*, sometimes *do you hear?*

rope, pronounced ro-up. So gate becomes gé-ut (French *é*), goat, go-ut (Italian *o*), much as in some provincial districts in England.

a da come, I am coming.

carry, lead.

as much, as much as you like.

a fun me a make, I was pretending. A man is said to make fun when he is only pretending to work, what schoolboys call "sugaring."

hasty, haste, *i.e.* your hurrying away.

hungry kill me is a common expression meaning "I am very hungry." Here *hasty* is substituted for *hungry*. Your hasting away will leave me without food, and hunger will kill me.

XXXVI. LEAH AND TIGER.

THERE was a man an' his wife got one daughter, only the one picny they got. An' many a people come for her to courten to her, an' she refuse, an' she would stay a world without marry.

An' the father said to the wife:—"Them people usual trouble me with my own daughter; we must do something to get her out of them sight."

An' the both of them agree to make up a very big house in the wood to lef' the daughter there where nobody wouldn' see him.

An' the father said to the wife:—"When the house done you mus' carry him breakfas' every twelve o'clock an' dinner at four."

An mumma say:—"Yes, me dear, I think so better."

An' they take Leah an' walk with her all night an' lodge her into the house before daylight.

An' at the meantime Leah got a very valuable ring on one of her finger, a very pretty young woman too, though me never see him.

Mumma tell him that when him going to bed he must always say him prayers. An' she tell her that, when she re'ch the hillside she sing the song, she must know a him honey a come. An' this the song:—

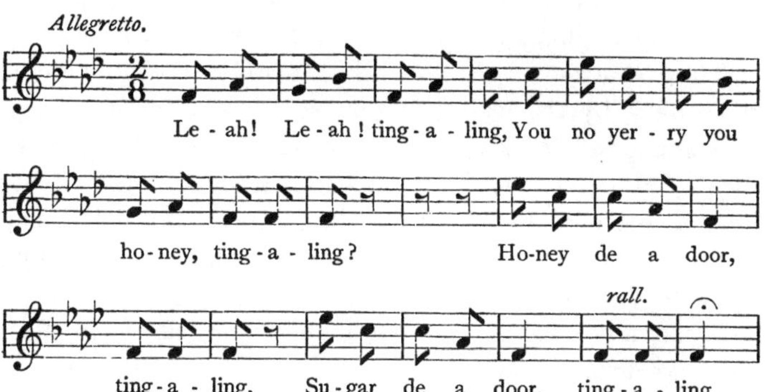
Allegretto.
Le - ah! Le - ah! ting - a - ling, You no yer - ry you
ho - ney, ting - a - ling? Ho-ney de a door,
rall.
ting - a - ling, Su - gar de a door, ting - a - ling.

An' this time Tiger was under the house hear all the bargain.

An' Tiger lie down very 'teady. (Some days to come he must get meat fe eat a this bush.)

Then mumma go away, next day come back with him daughter breakfas', an' 'tart the tune from hillside to the spot of place where the house is. An' the door was double double double latch. An' the tune 'tarted.

An' the gal open the door an' mumma come in give her her breakfast, an' make very much of each others, an' eat done an' tell goodbye.

When the mumma gone Tiger creep out of the house with a great rolling of voice, can't 'tan' him heel. He go down to see Brother Blacksmit' if he would do a kind favour for him.

An' Brother Blacksmit' say:—"What sort of favour I can do for you?"

An' Tiger say him see a very nice meat a bush, him want go eat it then, so me want sweet voice fe sing like a him mumma.

Then Brother Blacksmit' put the iron a fire, make him red hot, so tell him open him mout'. Blacksmit' poke ahm down his t'roat, heap of smoke come out a him 'tomach.

When him finish he tell him mus' sing make him hear.

So Tiger sing, an' true him voice sound so good.

Then Blacksmit' say:—" Min' mustn' eat no duckanoo nor guava by the way, else you voice turn rough again."

Tiger gone making his way fe go eat the gal fe meat. He was very hard on his journey going on. As he get halfway he see guava an' duckanoo, an' being him so thirsty he say:—" Make me nyam ahm, nothing goin' to do me voice."

He nyam until he unrestful an' come his voice after was like groun' t'under.

" Well," he say, " never min'; by the time me re'ch up me voice will come good."

So he lay down under the floor waiting for twelve o'clock when the mother usual come.

An' when it nearly come 'pon twelve Tiger creep out under the floor commence to sing:—

Leah! Leah! tingaling,
You no yerry you honey, tingaling?
You sugar de a door, tingaling,
You honey de a door, tingaling.

An' Leah say: —" Hé! Hé! it is not my mother dat."

An' Tiger shame, gone under the house back, voice too coarse.

Presently his mother is up, sing with a very sweet voice:—

Leah! Leah! tingaling,
You no yerry you honey, tingaling?
Honey de a door, tingaling,
Sugar de a door, tingaling.

An' the door open, an' she go in give her daughter him breakfas'.

An' her daughter hug her up an' kiss her, an' he commence to tell her mother that him hear a great rolling like groun' shaking while ago outside, an' it make her frighten to deat'. She tell her mumma she would like to go home with her back.

The mother refuse from do so, an' lef' an gone home, tell the father what happen with Leah in the bush.

An' puppa say:—"What make you lef' me daughter a bush? Go back for him to-night."

Mamma say:—"No danger wi' me daughter, me wi' carry him dinner four o'clock, lef' him come back."

Next day Tiger 'tart to Blacksmit' fe run iron down him t'roat back. Blacksmit' get vex, tell him he going to lick him down with the iron, for his ears hard.

Tiger said:—"Do Bro'er Blacksmit', me yerry all whé you tell me this time."

An' Blacksmit' put the iron two hour a fire an' shub him down Tiger t'roat. Tiger can't take him ground, iron too hot.

When he done with him he tell him to sing make him hear, an' beg him anything that him see in the way must make him yeye pass it.

An' Tiger say:—"Yes, so me going do."

Him shut him yeye now, take the whole a road for himself, say:—"Me boy never would a nyam nothing more a pass: sweet, sweet meat like a that so a bush me could a lef' ahm so?"

He was very hurry to the house, an' just before twelve o'clock he commence to sing, an' this time his voice sound well.

Leah open the door, t'ought it was her mother, an' Tiger jump right in an' eat the whole of Leah, lef' one finger with the ring.

Him eat done, half shut the door an' go back a him bed under the house.

Leah mumma come fe sing now:—

Leah! Leah! tingaling,
Yo no yerry you honey, tingaling?
You sugar de a door, tingaling,
You honey de a door, tingaling.

An' nobody answer her.

She sing two time more: nobody answer.

An' she shub the door an' go inside to find only one finger of her daughter.

An' him put him hand on him head, bahl, then go home to him husband, tell him husband him daughter dead, something eat every bit.

Him say:—"Me no min tell you fe bring home me daughter: you will have fe find ahm gi' me. Then if you know whé good fe you just bring him go," catch up one big junka 'tick an' lick down the wife.

An' after the wife dead the man take to heart an' dead.

That make you see woman ears hard up to to-day. They want mus' man fe carry them anywhere they told fe go. A him make them something a happen a this world up to to-day day.

Jack Mantora me no choose none.

NOTES.

usual, are wont.

when she re'ch, when she (the mother) reaches the hillside and she sings the song, she (the girl) will know that his (her) honey has come.

tingaling. Some tellers of this story have it **tindalinda.**

'teady, steady, with a peculiar vowel like a dull French *eu*.

him daughter breakfas', came back with her daughter's breakfast and began to sing when she reached the hillside overlooking the house, and went on singing till she got to the house.

An' the tune 'tarted. The reciter sings it here.

out of the house, out from under the house. See note to "Yung-kyum-pyung."

rolling, roaring.

can't 'tan' him heel, can't stand on his heel. See, further on, **can't take him ground.** Both mean that Tiger cannot stand still.

a bush, in the bush.

ahm, him, it.

true him voice, really his voice sounds very well. Only, **true** means what it says, **truly,** and does not imply the reservation at which it *really* hints. Tiger's voice did sound very well.

duckanoo, a kind of mango.

going to do; eating the fruit is not going to do my voice any harm.

until he unrestful. He ate too much.

groun' t'under, ground thunder. It is often difficult to distinguish between distant thunder and an earthquake.

Tiger growls on a low note, and says the words very fast.

Hé! Hé! French é as in whé and dé.

groun'shaking, earthquake.

from do so, refuses to do what she asks.

down him t'roat back, down his throat again.

Blacksmith was vexed because Tiger had eaten fruit on the previous occasion. His ears had been hard, *i.e.* he had acted against orders.

make him yeye pass it, let his eye run over it without desiring to eat it.

take the whole a road, staggering along, first to one side and then to the other.

a pass, in the path, on the journey.

put him hand on him head, an expressive action indicating horror and bewilderment.

bahl, bawl, cry out.

me no min tell, me no been tell, didn't I tell you?

you will have fe find ahm gi' me; when anything is lost, they say:—You will have to find it and give it to me.

a him, etc., it is that (their ears being so hard) that makes this sort of thing happen.

XXXVII. TIMMOLIMMO.

ONCE there was a Bull live in a pastur'. He make a law that every young Cow born, if it is a Bull, they must kill it. So the Cow them hear what the master said. The Bull name was Timmolimmo.

So one day one of the Cow have baby an' find out that this child was a boy. She take him an' go to a deep bush an' hide her child in a stone-hole, an' feed him till him was growing an' begun to talk.

The place where the mother was taking water when she was at the pastur' was a mile from the hiding hole, an' she has nowhere to take water but there.

So every day she go an' fetch water to her son.

One day when the boy was six months old she carry him to the place where she taking water, an' hide till the master come drink an' gone. Then she give her son water, and after she take him home back.

An' when another six month come she take him back to the place an' show him the father footprint, an' commence to tell the son why him have to hide in the bush is because the father would kill you if he see you.

The boy said to his mother:—"A so all right, when me come big man I going to go an' have a fight with him."

The mumma say:—"No, me son, nobody can't fight him."

So the mother take the boy home back till another six months when the boy catch a year an' a half.

Then they go again an' the boy ask if he no can fight.

The mother say:—"Come, make me measure you foot."

When he go put his foot in his father footprint it was about two inch short.

He go home.

After six month more he come back, he alone, measure his foot in his father one. It want half inch to catch.

Him gone home back for six more month.

So one day him get up, tell his mumma that I am going to fight me puppa.

The mother say "No," but him rist an' go.

When him go to the place he measure his foot. It was one inch wider.

Him say:—"I am going fe the battle."

Him come back, tell his mumma that him going to fight puppa. So him go on till him get where his father can hear him, an' sing out:—

Maestoso.
Timmo - limmo, man dere, Timmo - limmo, man
dere, Come down make we bat - tle, man dere.

One of the Cow call say:—"Master, Master, I hear some one calling your name."

"No, no, not a man can call my name."

The son give out again:—

"Timmolimmo, man dere,
Timmolimmo, man dere,
Come down, make we battle,
Man dere."

Timmolimmo yerry.

Him make one jump, him jump half mile.

The son make one, him go one mile.

So they meet at a cross-pass.

As the father come him lift the son with his horn, send him half mile in the air.

The son drop on his four leg.

The son lift the puppa, send him three quarter mile.

As him drop, one foot gone.

The puppa stand on the t'ree foot send the son up again in the air.

The son drop on four foot.

The son send him up again, him come down on two.

Him stand on the two, send the son.

Him come down on four.

The son send him up again, an' him come down on one.

The puppa stand on the one foot an' send the son, an' the son come down on four.

An' the son send him up, an' him come down on him side an' broke him neck.

The son go home to his mother an' tell him that he has gain the battle, so they must come go in the pastur' an' him reign.

From that two Bull never 'gree in one pastur'.

Jack Mantora me no choose none.

NOTES.

rist, risks it.

dere, pronounced day-er, the French vowel quite abandoned.

cross-pass, cross-path.

foot, leg.

XXXVIII. CALCUTTA MONKEY AND ANNANCY.

ONE day Calcutta Monkey work a very large field of corn, an' when the corn commence to ripe Monkey beguns to miss the corn, an' him couldn' find out who was tiefing the corn, an' the robbing continually going on.

Till one day Monkey went to Annancy yard an' suspish upon Annancy. An' Annancy get very short an' ready to fight Calcutta Monkey.

An' Monkey say to Annancy he won't fight him but he will soon know who is tiefing the corn.

An' same time Annancy say to Monkey :—"I bet it is that big-voice Mr. Tiger."

An' Monkey say he won't judge no one again but will find out.

An' him went home back to his yard an' cut his card. An' when he cut the card he sees no man on the card but Mr. Annancy, an' Monkey think it very hard to himself that Annancy wouldn' own it.

An' the next day he went to the ground an' he find the robbing was going on. An' he met Annancy on the road an' he said to Annancy he well know who tiefing the corn.

An' Monkey send a challis to Annancy an' tell him that if him cut the card again an' find him in the card he going to give him a terrible flogging.

An' when Annancy hear about the flogging he get a little frighten, an' him stop off the robbing for about two days. The day to make t'ree Annancy couldn' bear no longer an' he beguns again to tief the corn.

An' Monkey made up a drum an' got a hunting-whip.

An' next day when Monkey go back to the ground an'

find the corn tiefing he goes home to his yard, an' take up his drum an' his hunting-whip an' start looking for Annancy.

An' when he going he beguns to knock the drum ribbim-bim-bim, "Annancy no dere," ribbim-bim-bim, "Annancy no dere."

An' that time Annancy went an' climb a cullabunka tree.

Annancy hide himself in the heart, an' as Monkey get to the tree he sound the drum say:—ribbim-bim-bim, "Annancy dere."

An' he put down the drum an' wrap the whip round his neck an' climb the tree an' give Annancy a good flogging, an' Annancy run off the tree an' say that he wont do it again.

Till a few days after Annancy broke in the corn-piece again, begun to tief the corn like witch.

An' Monkey go into the ground an' see the tiefing. An' he went home an' look over his card.

He sees no one again but Mr. Annancy, an' he took up his drum an' his whip to look for Annancy again to flog him.

An' this time Tiger have a very large banana-walk.

Annancy wented there an' look for one very large bunch of banana an' go in the heart of the bunch an' hide himself,

An' as Monkey 'tart playing the drum again he get to the banana-walk. An' as he get to the spot he sound the drum say:—ribbim-bim-bim, "Annancy here."

But this time Monkey an' Tiger can't agree, an' this banana is for Tiger.

Monkey has to leave Annancy an' goes home back.

An' Tacoma says to Monkey, if him want to catch Mr. Annancy he can catch him for him. An' Monkey was very glad.

An' Tacoma made a dance an' send an' invite Mr. Annancy.

An' when Annancy come to the gate Annancy mind tell him that Calcutta Monkey is there, an' he only 'tand to the gate an' wave his hand to the ladies inside, say :—" Good evening, ladies all" ; an' he turn right back an' go in the banana heart an' take it for his own dwelling.

An' from that day Annancy live in banana bunch up to now.

Jack Mantora me no choose any.

NOTES.

suspish upon, suspect. They also use **suspish** alone, a delightful word.

cut his card. Monkey is clearly an Obeah-man, a dealer in the black art.

ribbim-bim-bim, etc., half sung, with strong even rhythm.

cullabunka, a kind of Palm.

banana-walk, technical name for a banana plantation.

is for Tiger, belongs to Tiger.

XXXIX. OPEN SESAME.

ONE day there was a very hard time, an' Annancy an' his family was dying for hungry.

An' there was a regiment of soldier find out a silver mine.

An' when they find it out they made a very large house.

An' they move the money an' put it in the house, an' when they are moving it they t'ought that nobody see them.

What that smart fellah Mr. Tacoma does.

He hide himself on a tree, seeing them when they passing with the money.

An' when they reach to the house, the house work with no key, an' they has a certain word to use when they want the door to open. They say "Open Sesame."

An' they go in an' t'row in the money, an' when they coming out of the house they say "Shut Sesame," and the door lock.

An' Tacoma hear what they say.

An' he go home an' harness up his cart with his mule an' drive to the house.

An' when he go him use the same word an' the door open. An' he go in an' load the cart, an, when he load done he drive home.

When he come home he want to measure the money an' he couldn' get no quart pot, an' he sent to his neighbour Mr. Annancy an' borrow his quart pot.

An' continually so he go an' come back, him still borrowing Annancy quart pot.

An' Annancy think it very hard, say:—"Somet'ing

Bro'er Tacoma is measuring." An' Annancy want to know what it is.

A second day when Tacoma sent for the quart pot again Annancy 'tudy a plan.

When Tacoma come him give it to him, an' as Tacoma reach his yard don't begin measure yet, Annancy tell one of his picny that they must go a Bro'er Tacoma yard an' tell him that him really want the quart pot, must make haste make haste send it at once.

An' when the picny go he tell him must look an' see what Bro'er Tacoma measuring. An' he couldn' find out.

An' a third day him sent to the shop an' buy penny half-penny white flour, an' when him gone home he make it to paste an' piecen the quart pot bottom inside, an' said to himself:—"Anyt'ing Bro'er Tacoma measure, whether fe rice or gungo or flour, or either money, one must fasten in the flour."

An' when Tacoma come back he sent for the quart pot.

An' when Tacoma measure done he send it back. An' as he send it a very large two an' sixpence piece fasten in the flour.

An' Annancy say:—"T'ank God I find out what Bro'er Tacoma doing with my quart pot."

An' same time he goes to Tacoma yard an' begins to cry upon Tacoma that Bro'er Tacoma must carry him an' show him where he get the money.

Tacoma didn' agree.

Annancy cry an' cry till him tell him that he must get a cart an' a mule to-morrow evening, an' when him passing he will call to him.

An' Annancy couldn' wait, an' him harness up his cart from morning an' watching out for Brother Tacoma.

An' he watch an' watch till Tacoma come.

When Tacoma was coming he lash him whip, an' as he lash, Annancy lash his own too.

An' they started.

An' when they get to the house Tacoma say "Open Sesame," an' the door open.

An' they run the cart up to the door mout' an' load it, an' they come out an' drive home.

An' by the time Tacoma get home to his yard Annancy t'row out his money an' turn back again.

An' when he go he use the same very word an' the door open.

Annancy load his cart an' when him coming home he meet Tacoma on the road an' through his strongy yeye an' his ungratefulness he want to shoot Tacoma cart a gully an' to kill his mule, that him one may be the master of the bank.

An' Annancy made a sing when he is coming home;—

Andante.
Right t'rough, right t'rough de rocky road, oh Charley Marley call you, Mid a
rock, mid a rock, mid a rock, me Char-ley, Char-ley Mar-ley call you; Oh de
han'-some gal are no fe you one; Oh Charley Mar - ley call you.

NOTES.

Here is another story founded on Ali Baba, which differs considerably from the previous one of "Blackbird and Woss-woss." The chief peculiarity of this version is that the entrapping through forgetfulness of the password is altogether lost.

Hard time. This refers to the months of June and July when provisions are scarce. The old yams are done and the new ones are not in yet. Subsistence has to be eked out with a few sweet potatoes and the mangoes, which are abundant in these months, and go on till the October rains bring back a season of plenty.

so he go, as he goes.

piecen, a nice word. They use it also in speaking of the patching of old clothes.

lash him whip, crack his whip as a signal.

strongy yeye, covetousness. To give the pronunciation a *y* has to be tacked on to strong.

him one, he alone.

The exact application of the song is doubtful. The end is pretty clear, meaning:—all the good things are not for you alone, Tacoma. It will be observed in this and some other stories that Jack Mantora, etc., is omitted. That is because they have no tragic termination.

XL. SEA-MAHMY.

ONE day, height a hungry time, Blackbird have a feedin' tree in a sea. An' every day Blackbird go an' feed.

Annancy say unto Blackbird:—"Please, Bro'er Blackbird, please carry me over a you feedin' tree."

Blackbird say unto Annancy:—"Bro'er Annancy, you so cravin' you goin' to eat every bit from me."

He say:—"No, Bro'er Blackbird I won' do it."

Brother Blackbird say unto Annancy:—"A you no have no wing, how you a go?"

Well! Blackbird take out two of him tail feather, 'tick upon Annancy. He pick out two of him wing feather, 'tick upon Annancy. He take two feather out of him back again, 'tick upon Annancy; two feather out of him belly feather, 'tick upon Annancy.

Well! Blackbird an' Annancy fly in a the sea upon the feedin' tree.

Every feedin' Blackbird go fe pick, Annancy say that one a fe him.

Blackbird go upon the next limb, Annancy say a fe him.

Blackbird go upon the t'ird limb, Annancy say a fe him.

Till Annancy eat a good tummy-full.

Annancy drop asleep upon the tree.

Well! Blackbird take time, pick out all the feather back, an' Blackbird fly away.

When Annancy wake out of sleep he say:—"Make me fly."

He can't fly.

He broke a branch off a the tree, t'row in the sea. The branch swim.

Annancy say if the branch swim him will swim, an' he jump off a the tree, drop in the sea an' sink.

An' when he go down a sea bottom he meet Sea-mahmy.

He said to Sea-mahmy:—"Mumma, mother tell me me have a cousin down a sea bottom, ya."

Sea-mahmy say:—"I going to see if me and you are cousin."

Sea-mahmy put a pan of sand in the fire for well hot. When him get hot he take it off a the fire, give to Brother Annancy for drink it off.

Brother Annancy say:—"Cousin Sea-mahmy, it don' hot enough. Put it out a de sun fe make it hot more."

After him put it out a the sun then he say:—"Cousin Sea-mahmy, I think it hot now."

An' Sea-mahmy say:—"Well you must drink it off an' make I see if you an' me are cousin."

An' Annancy do drink it off.

Annancy spend t'ree day down a sea bottom.

Well! the next day Sea-mahmy said to him:—"Whé you going to come out."

Him said :—" Cousin Sea-mahmy, sen' one of you son fe carry me out a lan'."

Sea-mahmy give him one of him son, the name of that son call Trapong.

Well! Trapong an' Annancy travel, make middle in a sea.

Sea-mahmy call :—

Adagio.
Tra-pong, Tra-pong, fetch back 'tranger man, come back.

An' Trapong say :—" 'Top, Brother Annancy, I think I hear my mother calling me back."

Annancy say :—" No, make way! War de 'pon sea!"

An' Trapong sail with Annancy on him back till they reach shore.

When they go to shore he say :—" Bro'er Trapong, take dis bag weigh me, see whé me weigh."

Trapong lift him up, say :—" Yes, Brother Annancy you heavy."

So Annancy come back out of the bag.

He say :—" Bro'er Trapong, you come in make I weigh you see."

Trapong went into the bag.

He tie Trapong, tie tight.

Trapong say :—" Brother Annancy you a tie me too 'trong."

He say :—" Me no a tie you fe see if you heavy?"

Trapong say to Brother Annancy :—" Me heavy?"

Annancy say :—" You heavy oh! You light oh! You heavy enough fe me wife pot." An' for all the bahl Trapong a bahl he gone back to him house an' Annancy eat him.

Jack Mantora me no choose none.

NOTES.

height, in the height of, at the worst of.

Sea-mahmy, Mermaid.

feedin' tree. It was a duckanoo mango according to some accounts.

Annancy behaves just as he did with Candlefly and the eggs.

The connecting **wells** of this story, which take the place of the **ands** and **sos** of other narrators are said with a little upward turn of the voice.

Whé you going. Whé (what) seems to be doing duty for **how** here.

Trapong, tarpon, the famous sporting fish of Florida and Santa Catalina, common also in Jamaica.

make middle in a sea, get to the middle of the sea.

No, make way! Annancy shouts this out.

The outrageous confidence trick which follows necessitates a Jack Mantora.

XLI. CRAB AND HIS CORN-PIECE.

ONE day Brother Crab work a lovely field of corn.

An' when the corns beguns to ripe Crab begin to lose the corn, an' he couldn' find out who was tiefing it.

An' he get Annancy to be a watchman for tief.

An' this arrangement make between Annancy. Crab tell him that he will come in the night and see if he is watching. An' Annancy wasn' agree at first.

Him stand for a good time an' study: an when he study he tell Crab yes that he can come.

An' when Crab gone he sent an' call his friend Mr. Tacoma an' tell him that Bro'er Crab leave him here to watch over the corn, an' say that he is going to come back in the night to see if he is watching. An' as Crab being 'fraid of Tacoma Annancy tell him that he must set a watch in the road for Crab an' catch him.

That time Ratta was hearing Annancy bargain which

he is making with Tacoma. An' he went home an' tell Crab that he mustn' go to the corn-piece in the night for Tacoma going to catch him.

An' so Crab did hear Ratta.

An' him send an' discharge Annancy.

An' Annancy was very sorry, an' same time he goes to Crab an' he ask Crab what he done.

Crab tell him that he mustn' mind, he must leave the work, he is going to get another man to watch.

An' Annancy did leave, an' Crab give the job to Ratta.

An', as that wicked man Mr. Annancy know that Ratta frighten for Puss, he sent an' tell Puss that he must go in Bro'er Crab corn-piece an' keep a good watch for Ratta an' catch him an' eat him.

An' that time Candlefly was hearing Annancy what he is telling Puss to do Ratta, an' he went an' tell Ratta that he must leave the work, an' if he don't leave it he going to lose his life.

At that time Ratta get very 'fraid an' send an' give up his discharge to Crab.

When Ratta gone Crab couldn' get no one to watch the corn again, an' he consider to himself that he knows two friend very love corn an' the meal likewise.

An' the two friend was Mr. Dog an' Mr. Cock.

An' he sent an' call them an' they did come.

When they come he tell them that he have a piece of corn an' he can't get none, tief is eating out the whole.

An' he says to Dog that him know he is a very good watchman, an' same time Cock say to Crab that him watch as any soldier.

An' Crab was very glad, say:—"You is the two man that I want."

An' they says to Crab that they won't charge no money, but when the corn came in Cock is to get his share of dry corn an' Dog get his share of meal.

An' Cock ask Crab to give him a gun.

An' Crab didn' have a gun, an' he give Cock a flute an' give Dog a drum, an' tell them that anyone catch a tief they must play an' let him hear.

An' Cock tell Crab that he can't sleep on the ground, an' he wants to know if there is any tree in the corn-piece, an' Crab say "Yes."

So Cock an' Dog started.

An' when they go Cock fly upon the tree an' Dog pick up the corn trash which they cut already an' make a very soft bed an' get into it, an' Dog lie down until he fall asleep.

An' Cock sing:—

Allegretto.
Brether Dog oh! Brether Dog oh! Brether Dog a-sleep oh! Brether Dog oh! Tief come an' gone oh, Brether Dog oh! Tief come an' gone oh, Brether Dog oh!

When the tief come Dog didn' know. An' Cock, as he being a brave soldier, he caught the tief. An' when he catch the tief he start a tune in his flute:—

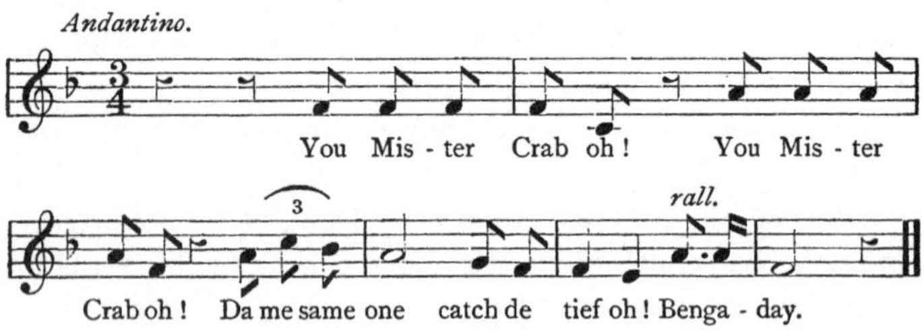
Andantino.
You Mis-ter Crab oh! You Mis-ter Crab oh! Da me same one catch de tief oh! Benga-day.
rall.

An' as Dog being love sleep an' don't watch to the end he lose his reward.

An' Cock by him catch the tief takes the corn.

NOTES.

arrangement between Annancy; no misprint. **Between** may stand for **with**, or there may be an ellipsis of the words **and Crab.**

he mustn' mind. This is likely to convey a wrong idea. Crab was not trying to soothe his feelings, but was speaking angrily. What he said was:—"Never you mind, etc."

XLII. DRY-GRASS AND FIRE.

ONE day Brother Dry-grass an' Fire get in confusion.

So Fire tell his frien' Annancy (not knowing that Annancy an' Dry-grass was better friend):—"Brother Annancy I going to burn that fellah Dry-grass to-morrow."

Annancy say:—"When you a go you fe call me a yard. I goin' to make one shell. When we nearly get to the place we blow, make the fellah know that man a come."

During this time Annancy make bargain with Water that any time he hear the shell blow him must come down like rain.

So Fire reach up an' as the shell blow he see rain coming down.

So Fire has to go home.

Water tell him say that Annancy tell him that you are going to fight Dry-grass, so I must come an' help to see if we can manage you.

Fire say:—"A so! That fellah Annancy I going at his yard."

So Fire walk at Annancy yard an' tell him:—"Brother Annancy I going to come an' see you next week."

Annancy say:—"Yes, Bro'er Fire, with all pleasure."

Fire tell him that he must put all his clothes a door to make him find out the yard for I don't want to lost the way.

So Fire gone.

Annancy wife said:—"Me husband, send go stop Fire from come a you place."

Annancy say:—"No, me wife, a me best frien' so him have free come."

Just before the time Fire was appoint to come, Annancy go to Brother Tiger, an' as him walk into the house he saw some clothes.

An' he pick up the clothes an' say:—"See, Bro'er Tiger, how you clothes damp, you must have fe put dem a sun."

So Tiger hang out all his clothes on a line before the door mout'.

An' presently Fire was coming like a lion bringing Breeze with him.

When Fire see all the clothes he say to Breeze:—"See that fellah Annancy yard."

So Breeze blow harder an' come with a speed. An' Fire make a jump till he nearly got to the yard.

Tiger hear the speed Fire was coming, call to him:—"Turn back, you red-face fellah, me no want you company."

Fire was coming down more and more.

Tiger bawl fe Fire a stop, but Fire coming for the better.

So Fire get in the yard an' burn all Tiger clothes an' house, an' turn right home back.

Annancy laugh, an' sing:—

Allegretto.
Me wife say me no fe in-vite Fire, Brether Fire bring
Breeze oh! Fire de 'pon lan' Fire, Fire de 'pon lan' Fire.
He burn up all Tiger yard, ha ha! Brether Fire an'
Breeze oh! Fire de 'pon lan' Fire, Fire de 'pon lan' Fire.

Jack Mantora me no choose any.

NOTE.

The shell looks like a very small cowhorn and gives a similar sound when blown. It is used as a signal for a variety of purposes. It summons to work and marks the hour of release. When a train of mules is nearing a sharp turn in the road, the head muleman blows a fanfare to give warning of his approach. The shell is in fact to the mule-track what the whistle is to the railroad. Imitation shells are sometimes made of bamboo. It was perhaps one of these that Annancy made.

XLIII. JOHN CROW.

ONE day there was a lady who have but only one daughter, an' Mr. Tacoma hear about the gal an' he went to court the gal.

An' when Tacoma go the gal wouldn' receive Tacoma.

An' the mother was really vex.

As the mother being a old lady, when Tacoma going Tacoma carry a brass mortar to made it a present to the old lady to beat her fee-fee. An' when the old lady see the brass mortar he really want the mortar.

But Tacoma said to her if him don't get the gal he not going to leave the mortar.

An' the gal 'treat away himself inside the room an' hide.

An' Tacoma feel very sorry an' he return home back.

When he goes home he tell Annancy about the gal, an' Annancy get a concentina he going to carry down make a present to the gal.

An' Annancy say if the gal can only take the concentina from him the gal must be his wife.

An' when Annancy go down Annancy was playing.

The gal wouldn' receive Annancy in.

An' when the mumma hear, the music was so sweet she commence to dance; an' said to the daughter, this is the son-in-law him want, for he can get him own dance any time him ready.

Not for all Mr. Annancy playing the gal wouldn' receive Annancy, until Annancy has to go home back.

When that ugly fellah Mr. John Crow hear it he study between himself an' get a carriage with his pair of horses an' his coachman, an' the carpet in the carriage was a gold carpet.

An' John Crow said between himself when him put on him watch an' chain an' his coat an' shoes, if him don't bring that gal home believe him no Mr. Goldman.

An' John Crow drive away.

An' when him get to a distant to a look-out, the gal was at his window sitting down, an' as him look, him see Mr. Goldman was driving coming.

An' him holloa to him mumma :— "Mumma, mumma, my dear love is coming."

An' as John Crow reach the yard the gal was out an' sling Mr. Goldman out the carriage an' escort him right into the house.

An' after John Crow introduce himself to the gal that his name is Mr. Goldman.

An' when John Crow tell the gal so, the gal have a old-witch brother an' says to his sister that that man is John Crow.

An' the gal get vex an' say :— "Oh no, don't use a word like that ; it is my dear Mr. Goldman."

An' when the mumma come the gal introduce him to Mr. Goldman, an' tell him that his dear love just come now.

An' Mr. Goldman fix a time when to come back an' get married, and the mother was agree, an' the gal was very glad too.

An', when they settle that, John Crow drive back to his yard.

An' when he is coming back the next night he brought a old-witch boy with him an' hide him half part of the road near the yard, an' tell him that as he see day clearing, he must call him that he may got home before day clear.

An' he reach the yard an' spend the night in a very joyful dance.

So it getting near day an' the boy sing:—

Allegro.

Mis-ter Gold-man oh! Gold-man oh! Day da clean oh!

An' when the boy sing out the people them inside the house hear.

An' when they hear they say:— "Stop! Stop! Stop! some one is calling Mr. Goldman."

An' the dance so sweet Mr. Goldman he wouldn' stop to listen. He only says:— "Oh don't listen to that foolish boy." An' when him use the word him one in the ring wheeling all the gal them.

An' that time him hear a sing:—

Allegro.

Poor mir - ry - bim - bim rib - bim - by - bim - bim, Gold -
man a wheel him gal, Gold - man a wheel dem.

An' when him wheel all the gal him look outside the door an' see that day catch him; so him cry excuse an' went up'tairs.

An' when he go up he take a piece of meat an' look for a broken sash an' 'queeze himself t'rough.

An' as him go t'rough, the sash 'crape off the whole of him back head, an' from that day every John Crow born with a peel head.

Jack Mantora me no choose none.

NOTES.

fee-fee, food.

'treat away himself, retreats, retires.

concentina, always with this **n**.

him ready, she is ready for it, wants it.

a look-out, a place visible from the house.

sling, hand, with a notion of vigorous action.

an' says, who says.

a word, often a sentence of several words.

tell him, tell her mother.

sweet, pleased.

when him use the word, as he said this.

excuse, to be excused; pronounce the **s** like **z**.

John Crow is the vulture-like scavenger bird of Jamaica, and has a peeled (bald) head.

XLIV. TIGER'S DEATH.

ONE day Mr. Annancy an' Monkey made a bargain to kill Tiger, an' they didn' know how to make the confusion for Tiger was Monkey godfather.

An' being Monkey have more strength than Annancy, Annancy try to keep close Monkey an' wouldn' leave Monkey company at all by he afraid for Tiger.

Until one day Annancy went to river an' catch some fish, an' send an' call Brother Monkey to come an' help him enjoy the fish.

An' when the breakfast ready, instead of Mr. Monkey come, it was that cravin' man Mr. Tiger who Annancy really hate, an' to every piece of the fish Annancy take up to put in his mouth, Tiger take away every bit an' never cease till him finish the whole.

An' when Mr. Annancy friend who he invite come, there was none of the fish to give him.

An' as Monkey being love fish he began to cuss his godfather Tiger.

An' that time Puss was passing when the confusion occurred.

An' they go on an' go on till Puss laugh. An' as Puss laugh Tiger get worser vex an' begun to cuss Puss, an' Puss said to Monkey:—"Come, make we beat him off to deat'."

An' Monkey wasn' agree to beat his godfather, but Annancy an' Puss force him.

An' Tiger get cross begun to lick, an' the first man him lick was his godson. An' then as him lick him godson Puss catch a fire 'tick, an' Annancy catch up a mortar 'tick, an' they never cease murder Tiger till they kill him.

An' they 'kin Tiger an' just going to share.

An' there comes a singing from the tree:—

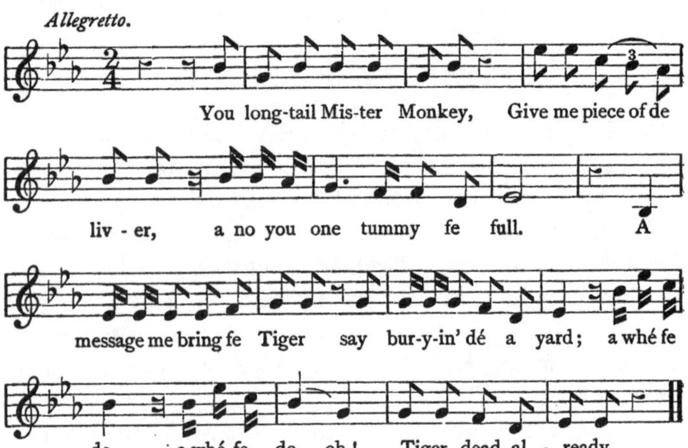
Allegretto.
You long-tail Mis-ter Monkey, Give me piece of de
liv - er, a no you one tummy fe full. A
message me bring fe Tiger say bur-y-in' dé a yard; a whé fe
do, a whé fe do oh! Tiger dead al - ready.

An' all the look Monkey an' Annancy look, they never find the person that was singing.

So they salt Tiger.

Then Peafowl come down in the yard say:—"Good evening Mr. Annancy an' Mr. Monkey, I am very hungry. I was on a long journey bring a message to Tiger that him wife dead, but Tiger dead already."

So the whole of them stop an' eat of Tiger.

Peafowl never go back with no answer to report, for Puss an' Monkey an' Annancy give Peafowl gold not to talk that they kill Tiger.

So Peafowl never can be a poor man for he keep the t'ree friend secret.

Jack Mantora me no choose any.

NOTES.

confusion, quarrel, which was to be made the pretext for killing Tiger.

whé fe do, what to do? what is to be done? To this question the implied answer is "Nothing." So the phrase means:—"It can't be helped.

XLV. THE OLD LADY AND THE JAR.

A OLD lady have two son, one name Dory Dunn an' one name Tumpa Toe, an' Tumpa Toe an' Dory Dunn is a hunterman.

Well, they give them mumma enough things an' say:—"Mumma, I am going a wood, don' interfere with that Jar in my room."

When them gone old lady say:—"I wonder what my son have in that Jar say me no fe touch."

Old lady go an' shub him hand inside in the Jar.

The Jar hold old lady.

Old Lady say:—

Andantino.
Tumpa Toe, Lord! Dory Dunn oh, Lord!

An' the Jar say:—

Allegro.

Mum-ma longu - be - lo, tum tul -la - lul - la-lum tum.

An' the Jar fire him from the room to the hall.
An' when him reach to the hall him say:—

"Tumpa Toe, Lord!
Dory Dunn oh, Lord!"

Jar say:—

"Mumma longubelo
Tum tullalullalum tum."

An' all this time the Jar holding him by the hand an' can't let him go.

An' the Jar t'row him outside a door.

When him get out a door old lady say:—

"Tumpa Toe, Lord!
Dory Dunn oh, Lord!"

Jar say:—

"Mumma longubelo
Tum tullalullalum tum."

Jar hold him 'till.
Jar fire him to seaside now.
An' he got one daughter a seaside.
The daughter say:—

Larghetto.

Do my Jar, Do my Jar, will you save, will you save my mother life!

Jar say:—

Maestoso.

Old la-dy touch me, old la - dy touch me, you never will see him no more.

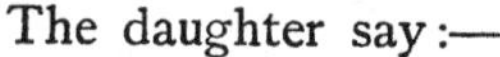
The daughter say :—

Larghetto.

Do my Jar, Do my Jar! I will
give you some sil - ver fe save my mo-ther life.

Jar say :—

Andante.

No, my gal, No, my gal, I got sil-ver al -
read - y ; You ne - ver will see him no more.

The Jar fire him in a sea.
Jack Mantora me no choose none.

NOTES.

Tumpa, stump. A man who has lost his arm is called a tumpa-hand man.

enough things, plenty of things to eat.

In these curiously simple tunes, if tunes they can be called, it is most important to mark the time and to pay great attention to the lengths of the notes. To hear them sing, or rather say, "Lord!" is the most laughable thing. The first one begins on a note rather below the **C** of **Toe,** and slides downwards ending with an expiring grunt on a very low note of the voice. The second one is done in the same way, but is, all the way through, a little lower than the first. The point is to let the breath go with the sliding note instead of holding it as in singing.

longubelo. The first syllable is pronounced as in English, and the rest of the vowels are Italian, the **e** being rather more narrowed, but never quite reaching to the sound of **bale.**

tum tullalullalum tum. Strong accent on the **tull** and clean neatly cut syllables. Italian vowels.

mumma. The **u** between Italian **u** and Italian **o.**

fire him, throws her. Yet not quite "throws," for the Jar never lets her hand go. **Fire 'tone** is the usual expression for throwing stones. The Jar fires her first from the bedroom to the living-room (hall), next from the hall to the yard, then from the yard to the seaside, and all the time it holds her by the hand.

XLVI. JOHN CROW AND FOWL-HAWK.

ONE day Fowl-hawk go to John Crow yard an' tell him that him fe come have a walk with me to a country for something promise there to me.

"One day I go out an' in my way I pass a river. As I come to the river I meet Fowl. Him ask me to help him up, an' the baby any time him born I must come for it. Well my dear sir, the baby born; an' when I go, Fowl say him never make a promise with me. Look you, sir, if you see the picny, nice fresh fe we mouth, an' a no the one, but him hab more. So you will get a good bag of fresh, but the country danger home."

John Crow say:—"Me yerry dat place hab bad name, me no want go."

Hawk say:—"You too fool, we a man! we'll get 'way, me son, if them want to catch we. When me go dé the first time me go slam in a Fowl yard. Me an' him stay a whole day a quarrel, an' me no dead. Come, me good friend, make we go."

Them start.

Them fly an' fly till them get over the country.

Hawk say:—"Brother John, we get over the place. Look down yonder, look fresh!"

John Crow say:—"Me no go down dé."

Hawk say:—"A so! you too fool! Come make we go down little more."

Them go down till them pitch on a tree.

Hawk say:—"Brother, you see them better. I da go sing make them know say me a come."

John Crow say:—"If them yerry you, dem no will kill we!"

"No, all time me go down me an' Fowl a good friend, no mo' the little quarrel we have."

Hawk call out:—"See me ya me da come, me da come to the bargain, me da come, come; twillinky twing ping ya, me da come."

Fowl hear, tell him picny dem fe go hide.

So Dog was a gunner man, an' him an' Fowl a good friend, for Fowl always give him good treatment.

So Fowl go an' tell Dog say:—"Danger! hawk a come fe me daughter, so me a beg you fe come a yard an' shot him fe me when him come."

Dog come, an' him an' Fowl hide.

Hawk said to John Crow:—"Come make we go down."

John Crow say "No."

Hawk say:—"Hungry will burn you back."

John Crow say:—"Me no trust, me wi' wait 'pon God leisure."

Hawk say:—"All time you wait 'pon God fe give you you will never get; no see me a man no wait 'pon no man? Me go look what me know me want, but me if I get anyt'ing I never give you little piece self, you foolish fellow you! I gone."

Hawk start the singing again going down:—"See me ya, me da come, twillinky twing ping ya."

By Hawk get down Dog hit him *bam.*

Hawk dead.

John Crow laugh "Ha ha! let me pull me rusty bosom shirt an' put on me gown an' go down to see what do that fellah."

John Crow go down.

As him get on Fowl-hawk find that him was dead him say:—"T'ank God, ha, ha!"

John Crow dig out the two eye and say:—"A this eye the fellah take a see," an' put it in his pocket an' turn on eating.

Dog look, an' say to Fowl:—"You finish with that one, so, sister, any time them come you send an' call me. I can't stop, I am very vex. I send out my son yesterday an' Puss meet him on the road an' beat him an' take 'way the money that I give him to give Brother Monkey. Him tell me son say him have a old grudge fe me an' him can't get to beat me, so him will beat all me picny. So, sister, I ha da go home, will be blue fire when I catch Puss."

When Dog go to Puss yard an' call him, Dog ask Puss for a drink of water an' a piece of fire.

Puss say:—"Go 'way from me gate, I know whé you come about."

Dog say:—"Ah, me man, will be blue fire!"

Puss gate was lock, for Puss have company the day. This company was Rabbit.

Dog say:—"I want to see you."

Puss say:—"Go 'way I tell you, you mout' long like a devil fork."

Dog broke the gate an' go in.

Puss lock up his house, an' stay inside an' cuss Dog till Dog has to go home.

An' Monkey say him will get the money from Puss for them is good friend.

So Dog go home to his yard an' have a hatred for Puss till death.

Jack Mantora me no choose any.

NOTES.

help him up, with his head-load.

fresh, fresh meat.

a no the one, etc., he has not only one, he has several.

danger home, is very dangerous.

over the country, over the place.

see me ya, etc., see me here, I am coming.

twillingky twing ping ya, a good imitation of the Hawk's vengeful shriek. Strong accent on the **ya.**

bam, French **a,** English **m,** imitating the discharge of the gun.

what do that fellah, what has befallen that fellow.

XLVII. FINGER QUASHY.

ONE day Dog invite four Puss to dinner. They were good friend. One of the Puss name was Tatafelo, one name Finger Quashy, one name Jack-no-me-touch. The last one was Tumpy John because he has no tail.

When them come, all the Puss was in long coat an' burn-pan hat. Dog was in trousies an' shirt.

An' Dog tell them all howdy very friendly, for he didn' know what Finger Quashy doing him.

An' Finger Quashy quite glad fe see how Dog look friendly an' please, an' didn' have no t'ought that him was tiefing fe him pear.

So the whole of them sit down, Dog making a complain to them that, so he get a pear an put it to ripe, by the time he ready for it him don't see none.

An' Finger Quashy was doing it.

An' Finger Quashy jump up tell Dog:—"Mr. Dog, me no tell you all time say you want one watchman? a da' fellow Ratta a tief you pear. Last night me dream say me see you put me fe watchman an' me catch the fellah, so you better put me fe guard you house from that tiefing Mr. Ratta."

Dog was quite agree.

Dog said:—"After dinner I will tell you better."

Quashy said "Yes."

So Dog lef' them gone to get dinner.

By Dog gone, Quashy come out of the house, go into Dog buttery, see two green pear, take them out go hide them.

Ratta see him go over the kitchen cry out :—"Why, why, why! Quashy take you pear; you no yerry? Quashy take ahm gone."

By Dog get in the house Quashy was in already sitting down look quite meek an' christianable.

Dog lef' them go see if his pear was there.

When he go there was none, an' Dog don't like nothing as his pear an' bone, an' he get vex, take all the dinner t'row it 'way, go in the house take down his 'tick.

By the time Dog fe lick one of the Puss everybody was on a tree on the far side of Dog yard.

Dog swear all sort of bad word fe the one that take him green pear.

Everybody say :—"Thank God me no eat green pear."

Finger Quashy said :—"Lard! what a man fe swear!"

Dog see that he couldn' manage to catch Puss, leave and go away.

An' as Dog turn round, his son playing with fire burn his house an' all his clothes.

From that day Dog hate Puss till now, for it is Puss cause him to have one suit till him dead.

Jack Mantora me no choose none.

NOTES.

Tatafelo, Italian **a,** the other vowels English.

Pear, *i.e.* the West Indian pear, a delicious vegetable.

tell you better, make the final arrangement.

Why, why, why! squeaked like a rat.

by the time Dog fe lick, as Dog was going to strike.

everybody, used also of inanimate objects. They say :—"I going to water cabbage, tomato, everybody."

T'ank God, etc., a favourite form of exculpation, which, however, does not necessarily imply innocence.

XLVIII. ANNANCY AND HIS FISH-POT.

ONE day Brother Annancy always set him fish-pot in a river ober a fallin' fe catch jonga. Tacoma usual to go an' knock it.

An' Annancy set watch into a river corner, an' Tacoma come fe knock it; he didn' know Brother Annancy hide there fe watchin' him.

As Tacoma go over de fish-pot Brother Annancy chuck him down, an' Tacoma catch in de fish-pot.

Annancy go beg Brother Rabbit say:—"Bro'er Yabbit, me fish-pot catch a big fish, come an' help me knock it, me one can't manage it, Bro'er Yabbit."

Brother Annancy an' Brother Rabbit went to the river.

Annancy say:—"Bro'er Yabbit, me feel me tummy hurt me dis marnin', no able fe put me foot in de cold water, see if you one can manage fe take out de fish-pot."

Brother Rabbit go an' take it out till he nearly make shore with the fish-pot.

Annancy say:—"Bery well, you kill Brother Tacoma! Bery well, you kill Brother Tacoma!"

Then Brother Rabbit commence to cry now, an' the frettenation in a Rabbit he say he kill somebody an' he know they going to hang him, an' next day Rabbit dead.

Then the case didn' try again.

Jack Mantora me no choose none.

NOTES.

fish-pot, made of bamboo strips and looking like a lobster-pot.

jonga, the smallest of the three kinds of crawfish which abound in the streams and rivers of Jamaica.

knock, empty.

tummy; a less pretty word is really used. Annancy squeaks his words more than usual here.

Bery well, etc., in $\frac{6}{8}$ rhythm ♪♪ | ♩ ♪♪♪♪ | ♪♪♪ and he claps his hands to the measure twice in the bar.

frettenation, probably fright, but may have something to do with fretting. Owing to Rabbit's fright, he says that he has killed a man. Rabbit, through fright, says that he has killed a man. These elliptical expressions are hard to understand until one has heard them often.

try again, try after all.

XLIX. HOG AND DOG.

ONE day Hog was going out to look work, an' Hog name was Cuddy.

An' he got out an' walk all about an' couldn' get no work.

An' when he come home Ratta employ him to keep watch for him when Broder Puss is coming.

An' Hog ask Rat how much is his pay.

An' Rat tell him that he will give him t'ree an' six-pence a week but he must find himself every t'ing to eat an' drink.

An' Hog didn' agree. But as the time being so hard he says he will bear with Ratta till the week out.

An' when the week done Ratta pay Hog, an' Ratta t'ought that Hog was still keeping watch for him.

So Ratta go out, an' when he come back he didn' fin' Hog.

An' him say:—Wasn' God, Puss would broke in on him.

An' him cuss Hog that Hog would walk an' never get no work, an' some which worse than Hog will laugh after him.

An' Hog start one morning to look work.

What that fellah Mr. Dog done Hog.

As he, being a market-keeper, he set down at the market gate an' see Hog was passing, an' he ask Hog where he is going.

Hog tell him that he is going to look a little work.

Same time Dog burst out a laugh. An' as he burst out a laugh he ask Hog t'ought he was working with Ratta.

An' Hog feel so shame to himself till he wouldn' answer Dog.

An' Dog laugh after Hog with this sing:—

Allegro.
Time get so hard Hog an' all a look work, Dog sit down a
market gate an' go laugh at a Hog distress; me ra-rabum Cuddy dé da
door, me rarabum Cud-dy dé da door, me rarabum Cud-dy dé da door.

An' Dog sing an' sing an' sing till Hog get vex an' come home back.

An' from that day that's why Hog must always hate Dog until now.

Jack Mantora me no choose none.

NOTES.

Cuddy, short for Cordelia.

wasn' God, if it wasn't for God.

rarabum, nonsense word, Italian vowels.

dé da door, is at door, is out of doors.

L. DEVIL AND THE PRINCESS.

ONCE a King has a daughter, an' that gal was a pet to her father.

So one day a Prince come to ask for her.

The father love the young man, but the gal say:—"Puppa, me don't like him." So the father promise her that anybody she see she like he will agree to it.

So one night a good friend of the King made a dance an' invite the young Princess to the ball.

This man who made the dance invite all classes of people. So he invite Devil too, but they don't know that it was Devil.

When all the guests come everybody give their name. Devil give his name Mr. Winkler. So the ball commenced.

Devil see the gal. He went an' ask her if she wish to dance with him.

The gal was so glad say:—"Yes, sir, for I love you the most."

When they dance till daylight the gal don't want to lef' Devil.

She say to Devil:—"Come have a walk home with me."

Devil say:—"Yes, I would go, but I am a man have such a great business, I has to go home very soon to seek after it."

The gal say:—"Come go home with me you will get me to marry, for my father is a King."

An' as Devil hear about marry he go home with the gal.

When she get to the house she call to her father:—"Puppa, here come my lover, I have found him at last."

So the servant-boy was an old-witch, said:—"Young mistress, you know that man is Devil?"

The gal get vex, begin to cry.

She go to her father crying, tell him "the servant-boy cuss me most shameful."

The father get upstarted, come out to the boy, don't ask the boy nothing, catch the boy an' put him in prison.

They take Mr Winkler in the palace, an' the father fix up an' they get marry.

After Mr. Winkler get marry he said:—"I am ready to go."

The King say:—"No, I can't send away my one daughter. You must stay and I will make you a King too."

Mr. Winkler say "No."

During this time they don't know that it was Devil, for when the boy tell them they get vex.

Devil marry ten time an' he eat all his wife, so he was going to eat this Princess too.

So, as he was so anxious to go, the gal have to go with him.

When they ready to start the father give them a long bag full with money. Devil get a boatman an' they start.

They sail four days before they get to their home.

When the gal get there she go meet a old lady in the house. This lady was Devil cook.

As he got in he said to the cook:—"I have got a good fat meat for the party."

So Devil go an' lock up the gal in a bar, an' lef' the old lady to watch if the gal is going to get 'way. He lef' a Cock that any time the old lady say that the gal get 'way he must call, an' him lef' a bag of corn to feed the Cock that he may keep good watch.

The old lady say "Yes."

Devil ready to start, order his t'ree-foot horse saddle, for he is going to invite his friend to come an' help him eat the gal.

He start, deeble-a-bup, deeble-a-bup.

As he get about a mile the old lady go in to the gal, take her out an' tell her that her husband is Devil an' he is going to eat you.

The gal begin to cry.

The old lady say:—"Don't cry, I love you an' I going to let you go, but the Cock is a watchman; he will see you, an' if he see you he will call for his master, but never min' I will try."

The old lady get ten quart of the corn an' a gallon of rum, soak the corn in it for about a hour, an' after give it to the Cock.

An' the Cock eat the whole evening till night, an', after him finish eat, him drop asleep.

The old lady get a boatman an' pay him an' he take the gal over the sea.

When day nearly light the Cock wake an' go to look if he see the gal through a hole. When he look the gal was gone. Him go to the cook an' ask.

The lady said:—"Him gone, an' I was calling you an' you never wake."

Then Cock sing out:—

Allegro.
Mister Wink - ler Wink - ler oh— coo-coo-ri -
co— the gal is gone. A - wake me
wake go look a hole— the gal was gone.

Mr. Winkler hear an' was coming like lighten with his t'ree-foot horse, deeble-a-bup, deeble-a-bup.

He call out:—"Me coming", deeble-a-bup, "Me coming", deeble-a-bup.

At last he reach the yard an' see the gal gone. He get a canoe an' start after her, an' by next day light he see the gal boat was far away.

He call out:—"Sairey dé 'pon sea, Sairey dé 'pon sea, come back darling, you husband dé come fe you."

When the gal look he say:—"Shub ahead, boatman, do, to save me life!"

An' by the time they get a land Devil was near them.

An' the boatman shot off a piece of Devil canoe an' water get in, so Devil has to go home back.

An' when the gal go home, tell her father what was her life, the father say:—"Don't marry again to nobody, not if even the King."

An' the father take her in an' give her servant to look after her.

Jack Mantora me no choose any.

NOTES.

cuss, abuse. It does not imply swearing. To swear is to **cuss bad word.**

in a bar, a barred-up room.

deeble-a-bup, the sound of the three-legged horse's step. Compare the itty-itty-hap of "Mr. Bluebeard."

The Cook adopts Annancy's device in "Annancy and Screech-owl."

coocoorico. The Cock's crow is excellent. The Negro is very clever in his imitation of animals.

a hole, at the hole, through the hole.

canoe, pronounced with accent on the first syllable and French **a.**

LI. WHEELER.

ONE day Puss was going out on a journey, an' he travel till he reach to a river mouth. An' as Puss being afraid for water he couldn' cross the river.

An' Puss has to stop for two day an' one night, an' Puss climb a tree which hang over the water.

An' Mr. Annancy was fishening.

An' Annancy fishening till him come where Puss was, an' Puss didn' call to Annancy.

An' same time Annancy meet up a licking 'tump a river side. Annancy lick, him lick, him lick, him lick outside till him sen' him han' inside.

An' when Annancy shub him hand him feel something hold him.

An' Annancy get very frighten an' pull fe get him hand out, an' him couldn' get 'way.

An' Annancy ask the question :—"Who hold me?"

An' a voice in a the 'tump said :—"Me, Wheeler."

An' Annancy said to him must wheel him make him see.

An' him wheel Mr. Annancy mile an' distant.

An' when Annancy drop he didn' dead, an' he said :—"T'ank God! I met with a little accident, but I see it going to be a living for me an' me family."

An' Mr. Annancy went home an' get some lovely iron peg, an' when him come he plant them in the river course to the very spot which him did drop.

That time Puss seeing all what Mr Annancy is doing.

Annancy leave, an' come where Wheeler is, an' keep himself very quiet, an' presently Peafowl was passing.

An' Annancy call upon him say :—"Bro'er Peafowl, a living is here for me an' you."

An' Peafowl ask him what is it.

An' he take Peafowl an' carry him where Wheeler is, and he says:—"Bro'er Peafowl, you see that hole. As you hand is so long, don't be afraid, just shub you hand in there now an' you will find something grand."

An' as Peafowl shub in him hand Wheeler hold him.

An' Annancy tell him that he must pull.

An' when him pull he couldn' get 'way.

An' Mr. Annancy feel very proud an' happy till he laugh with joy in his heart.

An' when him done laugh him tell Peafowl to say:—"Who hold me here?"

An' Wheeler say:—"Me, Wheeler."

Annancy tell him to say:—"Wheel me mile an' distant."

An' him wheel Peafowl an' dash him on the iron peg, an' Mr. Annancy went an' pick him up an' put him in his bag.

An' him went back to his old place a bush an' sat quiet.

That time Puss was seeing all this.

Ratta was passing, an' as Annancy see him Annancy said to him:—"I's all you deeshent man I like to see.

An' Ratta ask him:—"What for?"

An' Annancy say:—"Don't be afraid; a living is here for you an' me."

An' he carry Ratta an' show him the 'tump.

An' when him show Ratta, Ratta ask him if this is the living.

Annancy say:—"No shub you han', man, in the hole, an' you will fin' a living."

An' as Ratta shub him hand Wheeler hold him.

An' Annancy tell him that he must pull.

Him say he can't get 'way.

Annancy tell him to ask:—"Who hold me?"

"Me, Wheeler."

Annancy tell him must say:—"Wheel me mile an' distant."

An' he wheel Ratta an' dash him on the iron peg again.

Annancy went an' pick him up an' put him in his bag, an' go back same place.

After, Puss come down off the tree an' walk through the bush an' go down the river a little ways an' then turn up back, coming up very meek an' poorly.

Annancy so glad to see Bro'er Puss him say:—"Walk up my bold friend Mr. Puss. Come an' see the living which is here for me an' you."

An' Puss playing as to say that he didn' know nothing at all about it.

An' Mr. Annancy begin to show Puss the 'tump, an' he tell Puss to shub him hand in the hole.

When Annancy show Puss the hole, Puss say that him don' see it.

Annancy get vex and say:—"Shub you han' you so, man! Shub you han' you so, man! There, there!

An' Puss put him hand another way, playing to say he don' see it. An' he go on, go on, till Annancy make a flourish with him own hand, an' Annancy hand slip in the hole an' Wheeler catch him.

An' Annancy begin to cry as him know the danger which is down below.

An' him cry out:—"Do, me good Bro'er Push, jus' run a river course; you will see some iron peg, pull them up for me."

An' Puss begin fe walk in him sinnicky way, an' hide a bush where Annancy can't see.

When Puss come, him say him pull them.

Annancy wouldn' believe, an' crying still say:—"Bro'er Push, mus' go an' fetch one come make me see."

Puss go, an' when him come back him come without it.

Annancy ask him where is it.

Him tell Annancy that it too heavy, an' him roll it 'way.

An' Annancy, still crying, wouldn' believe. An' he begin to call Puss Godfather Push, an' beg him hard:—"Do, me good Godfather Push, just you jump pull dem."

An' him go on, go on, till him believe Puss, an' him ask the question:—"Who hold me?"

"Me, Wheeler."

"Wheel me mile an' distant."

An' Annancy fly by the air an' drop slam on his own trap.

An' Puss walk down an' pick up Annancy, an' put him in the bag with Peafowl an' Ratta an' carry off all the living with a jolly song:—

Allegretto.
Poor me lit - tle Cub-ba boy, barn day no Cub-ba?
Me da go da Vay - lum, barn day no Cub-ba?

Jack Mantora me no choose none.

NOTES.

licking 'tump, a tree stump with bees in it. The honey trickling out makes a licking-stump of it.

lick, him lick, him lick. These words are run closely together, then a pause, and then **him lick outside.** Pause again, after which the sentence finishes.

wheel, to cause to turn or spin. I have no clue to **Mr. Wheeler.**

mile an' distant, to the distance of a mile.

I's all you, etc., it's all you decent men.

What for? Ratta was suspicious of Annancy's flattery.

poorly, poor in spirit, meek.

sinnicky, sneaky.

Bro'er Push, must go, you must go.

barn day no Cubba? is not my born-day (birthday) Cubba. Children used to be named according to the day of the week on which they were born.

Day.	Boys.	Girls.
Sunday.	Quashy.	Quashiba.
Monday.	Cudjo.	Jubba.
Tuesday.	Cubbenna.	Cubba.
Wednesday.	Quaco.	Memba.
Thursday.	Qua.	Abba.
Friday.	Cuffy.	Fibba.
Saturday.	Quamin.	Beniba.

According to this list, Cubba is a girl's name, but it is perhaps short for Cubbenna.

me da go da Vaylum, I am going to Vaylum.

PART II. DIGGING-SINGS.

THE Negroes when they get together never stop chattering and laughing. They have a keen sense of the ludicrous, and give a funny turn to their stories as they relate the common incidents of daily life. The doings of their neighbours form the chief topic of conversation here as in most places, and any local event of special importance is told over and over. Presently, after repeated telling, the story, or part of it, is set to one of their dance tunes, and tune and words henceforth belong to one another. This is the origin of the songs which follow. With the explanatory notes attached to them it is hoped that they will afford some insight into the peasant life of Jamaica.

The tunes fall into two main divisions, "dancing-tunes" and "digging-sings," and besides the formal dances, whose steps are thoroughly known, there is an informal kind called "playing in de ring." It may be described as dancing mixed with horse-play. It was in this kind of romping that Parson Puss took part in the Annancy story (No. XXIX.), and perhaps it was hardly the thing for the cloth! Ring tunes begin anywhere and anyhow, and do not necessarily conform to the eight-bar rhythm of the more regular dance tunes.

To the other class of songs belong the "digging-sings" used, together with rum, as an accompaniment to field labour. In March it is time to think of getting the land ready for planting. So, having rented a piece of hillside from a neighbour, if he has none of his own, the Jamaican begins to clear the ground. The biggest of the trees fall to the axe, and the brushwood, or bush, as it is called, is chopped down with the cutlass, a few rod-like saplings being left here and there to serve as supports for the yams, which will by and by climb them like hops. After a few days' exposure to the sun, he burns all the top and lop that lies on the ground, which is then ready for digging. He now calls in some of his friends to help him dig yam-hills—so the phrase runs. What they dig is, of course, holes, to begin with. The loose soil is then piled up into small mounds in which the yam heads will be placed. The object of the mound is to enable the proprietor to see easily at any time how the tuber is getting on, by just "gravelling" it with his hand. As the hills are being dug, the rum bottle circulates, and the digging-sings, which began quietly enough, get more and more lively. The Negro is cheery at all times, but when well primed with liquor he is hilarious. Nothing more joyous can be imagined than a good "digging-sing" from twenty throats, with the pickers—so they call their pickaxes—falling in regular beat. The pickers work faster and faster to the strains of a rousing "Oh, Samwel, oh!" or "The one shirt I have ratta cut ahm." One man starts or "raises" the tune and the others come in with the "bobbin," the short refrain of one or two words which does duty for chorus. The chief singer is usually the wag of the party, and his improvised sallies are greeted with laughter and an occasional "hi," which begins on a falsetto note and slides downwards, expressing amusement and delight very plainly.

LII.

Here is a specimen:—

Allegro.
Oh Miss Nancy Ray, Oh hur-rah boys! Oh Miss Nancy Ray,

Oh hur-rah boys! Nancy Banana da broke man heart, Oh hurrah boys!

Nancy Banana da broke man heart, Oh hurrah boys! O Miss Nancy Ray,

Oh hur - rah boys! Oh Miss Nan-cy Ray, Oh hur - rah boys!

The bobbin is "Oh hurrah boys!" and a good swinging one it is. If the bobbin is well taken up each sing lasts for about five minutes, and the raiser of the tune prides himself on the number of "turnings" or slight variations he can give it. He also improvises words as he goes on. Such a sally as changing Miss Rag's name to Banana would be met with laughter when it was first heard.

("Da broke man heart" means "has broken a man's heart.")

LIII.

The next example is a type of many of the sings. It turns on a piece of local gossip. The "at last" is significant and points to Catherine being an old offender. The proffered sympathy is hardly sincere.

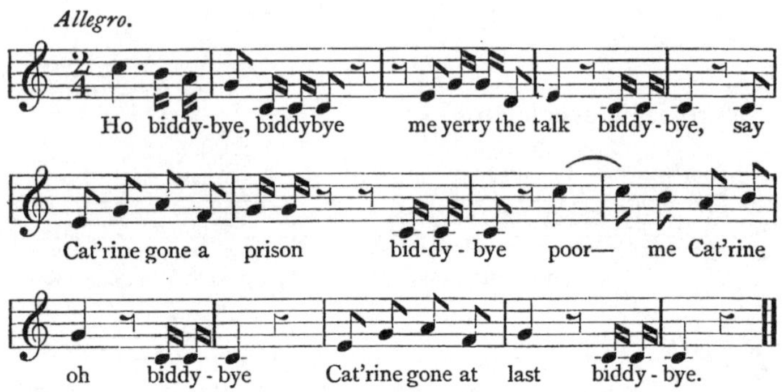
Allegro.
Ho biddy-bye, biddybye me yerry the talk biddy-bye, say
Cat'rine gone a prison bid-dy-bye poor— me Cat'rine
oh biddy-bye Cat'rine gone at last biddy-bye.

Here is the story in plain English, "deep English" as the Negro calls it, not understanding it well:—"Oh by the bye I hear a report that Catherine has gone to prison. My poor Catherine!"

(For "say" read "which says." "Biddybye" is the bobbin.

LIV.

We come now to one which refers to labouring life:—

Allegro.
Tell Mis-ter Link-y me want go, hm! hm! oh— — —
Ben-ji-man! Bar-ra-rap Bar-ra-rap Bar-ra-rap me Ben-ji-
man oh— — — Ben-ji-man!

The men are in the field watching the sun which is getting low. They begin to think the head-man, Mr.

Linky, is forgetting how time goes. He should be giving the signal to "knock off work." So one of the gang, meaning Mr. Linky to hear, says to his neighbour:— "Benjamin, tell Mr. Linky I want to go." "Hm, hm!" with closed lips, means a great deal. It is a sort of good-natured remonstrance. Always *Benjiman* for Benjamin and the *Barraraps* culminate in a sharp final staccato *rap*. This has a longer bobbin "Oh Benjiman!"

LV.

The next might easily be mistaken for something of the same sort:—

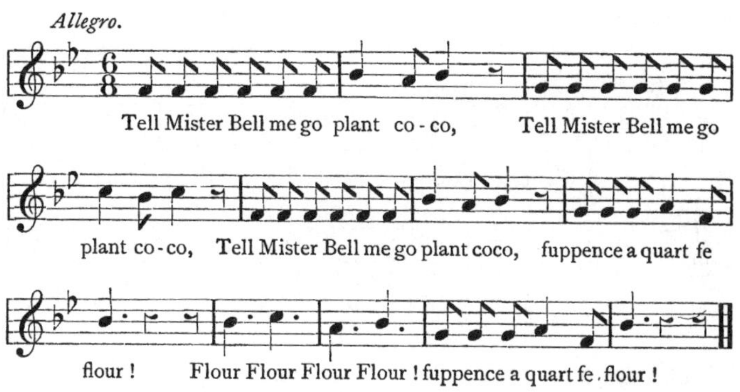
Allegro.
Tell Mister Bell me go plant co - co, Tell Mister Bell me go
plant co - co, Tell Mister Bell me go plant coco, fuppence a quart fe
flour! Flour Flour Flour Flour! fuppence a quart fe flour!

Mr. Bell is, however, the keeper of a country shop. "Tell Mr. Bell I am going to plant cocoes. Threepence a quart for shop flour! No, it's too much expense." ("Too much expense" is a favourite phrase.)

The accent which the music gives to the word *coco* is not the right one. It should be on the first syllable.

"Fuppence" is fivepence, but means threepence. This is the survival of an old coinage in which sixpence was called tenpence. The *u* in "fuppence" is an Italian *u* with a turn towards an open *o*. It sounds more like fourpence than fippence.

"Plant coco" is the bobbin, but a gang who were inspired not to leave too much to the raiser of the tune, would take upon themselves to add "Fuppence a quart fe flour." ("Fe," sounded "fy," with short *y* as in "very.")

LVI.

The next has again a well-defined bobbin in "nyam an' cry," and hereafter no reference will be made to this feature, which by now must be thoroughly understood. Where it appears to be wanting, the whole sing is sung in chorus.

Allegretto.
Bad homan oh! — — bad homan oh! nyam an' cry, me
co - co no ripe, nyam an' cry, me ha-foo no ripe, nyam an' cry.

The man is "working his provision ground," and his wife is always saying she has not got enough to eat. She is a bad woman, who does nothing but "nyam an' cry," eat and call for more, and my cocoes are not ready to dig and my Afoo (Italian *a*, ahfoo) yam is not ready either. (There are as many different kinds of yams as there are of potatoes.)

LVII.

Continuing with subjects connected with field-work, we come now to a sing which must have originated in old slavery days, when ringing a bell was the signal for beginning and knocking-off work:—

Andante.
Bell oh, Bell oh, Bell a ring a yard oh! oh— De-
gay, Bell a ring a yard oh! Baboon roll de drum oh,
Monkey rub de fid - dle, oh— — — Bell a ring a yard oh!

The bell is ringing up at the house, says one of the slaves to Degay the head-man, and we want our breakfast; and another, seeing Degay look cross at anybody presuming to make suggestions to him, tries to make him laugh with the piece of nonsense that follows. We shall meet with Degay or Deggy, for there is some doubt about his name, again. It will be thought that either the word Baboon is misplaced or the barring is wrong, but it is not so. The negro is careless of accent, as of many things. Here he likes to have it on the first syllable, which he lengthens to "bah." "Rubbing" a fiddle conveys the exact idea of the way they play it. Holding it not up to the chin but resting on the biceps, they rub a short bow backwards and forwards across the strings. If one of these is tuned it is considered quite satisfactory, and the rest make a sort of mild bagpipe accompaniment. Time is no object.

("Bell a ring" may mean either "The bell is ringing" or "The bell has rung." "A yard," in the yard. The immediate surroundings of the house are called the yard. They seldom speak of going to a friend's house. They say they are going to his yard.)

LVIII.

Breakfast is at twelve o'clock, and after a short rest work goes on again. A shower starts a new train of thought:—

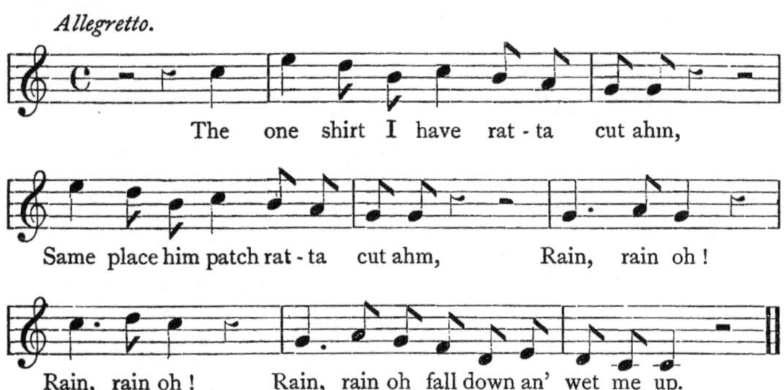
Allegretto.
The one shirt I have rat - ta cut ahm,
Same place him patch rat - ta cut ahm, Rain, rain oh!
Rain, rain oh! Rain, rain oh fall down an' wet me up.

"The rats have cut my only shirt with their teeth. I put in a patch and they bit it through again in the same place, so when the rain came down it made me very wet."

(The broad "ahm" (for him, it), is more used now by the Coolies than the Negroes. "Ratta" is both singular and plural. When I first heard the word I thought it referred to a terrier. "Same place him patch"—in the same place where it was patched, just where it was patched.)

LIX.

The kindly sun comes out, the shirts are dry, and an amorous youth, with that absence of self-consciousness which is characteristic of the race, begins:—

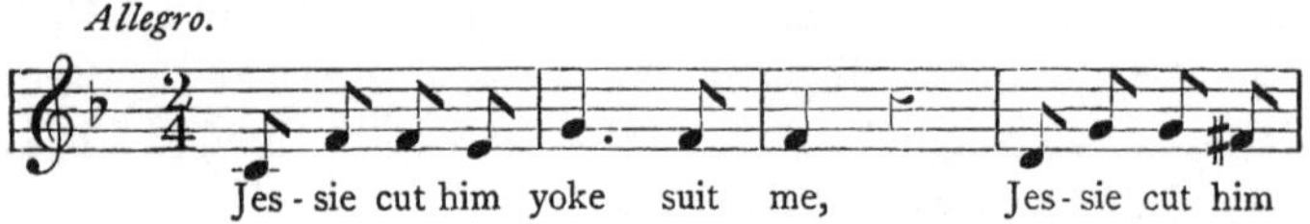
Allegro.
Jes - sie cut him yoke suit me, Jes - sie cut him

yoke suit me, So - so wahk him wahk suit me,
Jes - sie cut him yoke suit me, oh — — suit
me, oh — — suit me, oh —
— suit me, Jes - sie cut him yoke suit me.

Broadly this means:—"all that Jessie does is right in my eyes. She dresses perfectly, but it is enough for me to see her walk to adore her. Jessie cuts her yoke" —technical term of modistes and tailors I am told—"to suit my taste."

("So-so walk him walk," is literally:—"the mere walk that she walks with suits me." They are fond of this repetition of a word, first as noun and then as verb. Thus they will say:—Me like the play him play:—It sweet me to see the dance him dance:—The talk him talk was foolishness:—The ride him ride, him boast about it.)

LX.

"Three acres of Coffee" which follows, is more interesting musically.

Andante.
T'ree a - cre of Cahffee, Four a - cre of bare lan',
T'ree a - cre of Cahffee, Why you no come come ask fe me? Mum-

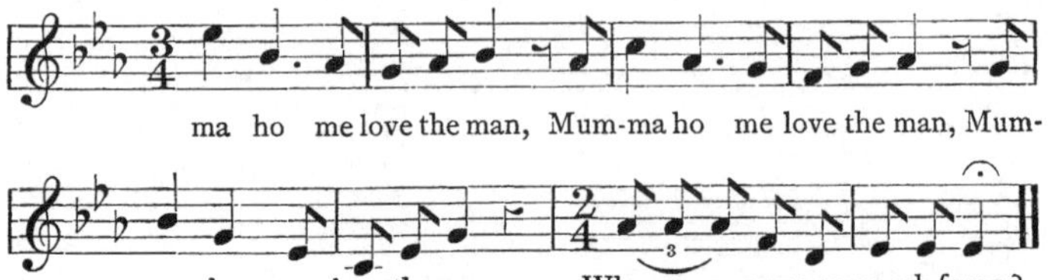
ma ho me love the man, Mum-ma ho me love the man, Mum-
ma ho me love the man, Why you no come come ask fe me ?

The boy has been telling the girl of his worldly possessions, but has not made any offer of marriage. She is thinking it all over. "So you have got three acres of coffee and four acres of bare land, then why don't you come and ask for me?"

"Bare" land is good land which has not yet been taken into cultivation. The first money a poor boy earns he spends in boots, which are the outward and visible sign of being well-to-do. They hurt him, "burn him" as he says, but no matter. Next he buys a piece of land. This is probably in bush, covered that is with the rough growth of grass, bushes and trees that so quickly springs up in the tropics. He clears and plants it piece by piece, as opportunity offers and inclination suggests.

LXI.

They are clever at inventing nonsense words to run easily off the tongue. For instance:—

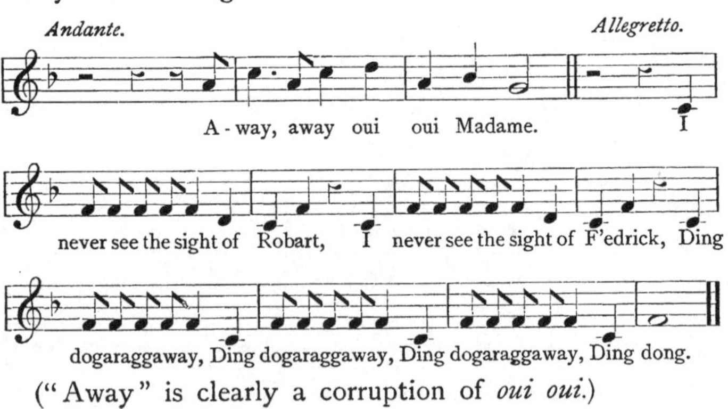
Andante.
Allegretto.
A-way, away oui oui Madame. I
never see the sight of Robart, I never see the sight of F'edrick, Ding
dogaraggaway, Ding dogaraggaway, Ding dogaraggaway, Ding dong.

("Away" is clearly a corruption of *oui oui.*)

LXII.

They like to complain of their little ailments, as thus:

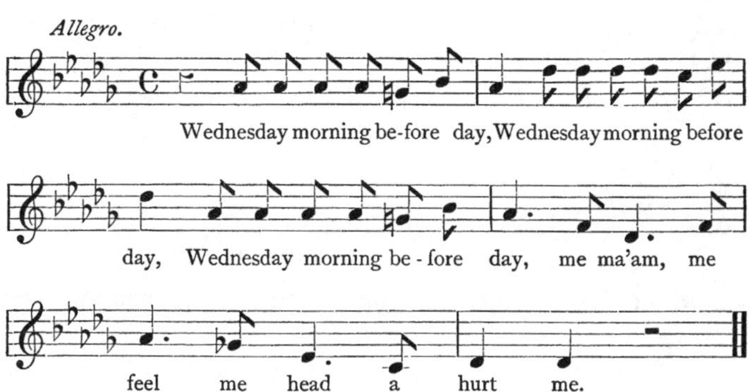
Allegro.
Wednesday morning be-fore day, Wednesday morning before
day, Wednesday morning be - fore day, me ma'am, me
feel me head a hurt me.

If a man happens to hurt himself, he sends or brings the most exaggerated account of the accident. If it is a cut on the hand, he "nearly chop him hand off." If there is a trickle of blood, "the whole place running in blood." In my early days in Jamaica my boy Robert came rushing up with gestures expressing the utmost consternation, and gasped out "Rufus hang!" Rufus was the pony. "He dead?" I asked. "'Tiff dead!" was the reply. We were doing a piece of important planting in the garden, and I said "Well! as he's dead there's nothing to be done, and we'll go on with this job." Two or three hours later, to my surprise, I saw Robert carrying grass towards the stable. "What are you doing with the grass, Robert?"

"It for Rufus."

"But Rufus dead."

"No! he don't dead again," which meant that he was still alive. When I went to see, I found him rather exhausted with his struggling—he had fallen on the hill-side and got entangled in the rope—but not very bad, and by next day he had quite recovered.

This kind of exaggeration enters into all their talk. Once, travelling in a tram-car, there was a slight accident. The car just touched the shaft of a passing carriage and broke it. One man said to his neighbour, "See dat? de buggy 'mash to pieces."

"All gone to snuff," replied the other.

LXIII.

Here are two different versions of the same sing. The chord of the seventh held on by the voices sounds well.

Allegro.
Oh Sam - wel oh! Oh Sam - wel oh!
Oh Sam-wel oh! Oh Sam-wel oh! Samwel, the
lie you tell 'pon me turn whole house a me door.

(They never tell lies *about* people here, but always *upon* people. "Turn whole house a me door," turns the whole house out of doors, upside down as we should say.)

LXIV.

Allegro.
Oh 'li - za oh! Oh 'li - za oh!

Oh 'li - za oh! Oh 'li - za oh! 'li - za
'pread you coat make I lie down dé under the Bu - sha - tahl.

"Coat" is petticoat. I am told that 'liza could take off a petticoat and still be quite properly dressed.

"Make I lie down," etc., *i.e.*, let me lie down under the Butcher's Stall. This is the name of a precipice just below my house. Horses have several times fallen over it and been killed. They then become butcher's meat for the John Crows, the vulture-like birds which are so useful as scavengers.

LXV.

We do not get many songs of the American plantation type like the following:—

Allegro.
Aunt - y Ma - ry oh! Aunt - y Ma - ry oh!
Aunt - y Ma - ry oh! Aunt - y Ma - ry oh!
Aunt - y Ma - ry oh! Aunt - y Ma - ry oh!
Aunt - y Ma - ry Thomas, O meet me a cross road.

(Cross roads are always a favourite place of meeting, and a rum shop is generally to be found there.)

This is a monotonous form, and I am glad the musical bent of our people turns in another direction.

LXVI.

See how superior this truly Jamaican form is:—

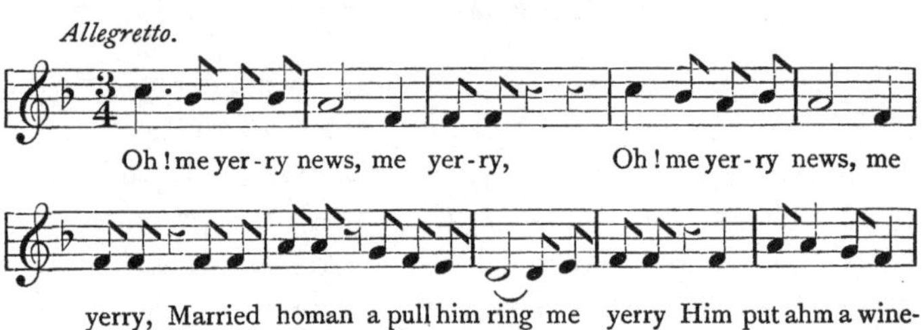
Allegretto.
Oh! me yer-ry news, me yer-ry, Oh! me yer-ry news, me
yerry, Married homan a pull him ring me yerry Him put ahm a wine-

glass—me yerry Oh! me yerry news—me yerry.

Local scandal again. "I hear news; a married woman has pulled off her wedding ring and put it in a wine-glass," the first convenient receptacle she saw.

LXVII.

It was some time before an explanation was forthcoming for the next:

Allegretto.
Jes' so me barn, jes' so me barn, you can
wear - y long boot, jes' so me barn.

The words mean:—"I was born just so; you can wear long boots, boots that come high up the leg." A girl, who has not money enough to buy boots, is envious of a companion who is wearing them. She says:—"I was born, just as you were, poor. Yet you have got long boots, while I must put up with 'bulldogs,' rope-soled slippers. Where did you get the money to pay for your boots? Did you tief it, or what?"

LXVIII.

In the example that follows, a girl has been left to look after her little brother, and somebody reports that she has been "ill-treating," *i.e.* beating him. So the message is sent back:—

Andante.
Tell Mary say, no do Johnny so. Oh!
Tell Mary say, no do John-ny so.

"Tell Mary she is not to do Johnny so." "To do a person something" is to do them an injury. "He so crahss" (cross), a boy will say of his master, "and I done him nothing," or "I never do him one def ting," a single thing. "Def" is emphatic, but is not a "swear-word."

"Say" is often added in places where it is not at all wanted. It occurs again in:—

LXIX.

Allegro.
Me tell them gal a Portlan' Gap Min' Dallas man oh! me amber
hé! me amber hé! me amber ho! tell them say.

"I tell the girls at Portland Gap 'Mind Dallas men.'" Portland Gap is in the Blue Mountains; Dallas in the Port Royal Mountains between the Blue Mountains and the sea.

(The exclamatory "hé" has the Italian vowel, hard for some English ears to catch. It is nearly but not quite "hay.")

The significance of "amber" is lost. This word occurs again in the pleasant flowing melody which stands next, and the boy who gave it me explained its meaning quite correctly, saying it "stood for yellow."

LXX.

Allegro.
Gold oh! Gold oh! Gold am-ber gold oh! Gold dé a me
yard oh! Gold am - ber gold oh! Sell doubloon a joint oh!
Gold am-ber gold oh! fe me gold a sunlight gold! Gold am-ber
gold oh! fe me gold no copper gold! Gold am -ber gold oh!

"Gold is in my yard," perhaps buried, but also perhaps in the house, yard often including it. "My gold is sunlight gold, none of your rascally copper stuff."

The doubloon is a large gold piece worth sixty-four shillings. It has long been out of use and few people in Jamaica have seen one.

("Fe me," for me, often does duty for "my." "This a fe me hoe," this is my hoe; "take fe you panicle," take your panicle, the tin mug out of which the morning sugar-water is drunk.)

LXXI.

No. 71, "Gee oh John Tom" is a brisk and vigorous sing till it gets to "a me lassie gone" where the little tinge of sadness is given by simple means, again the right thing in the right place, good art.

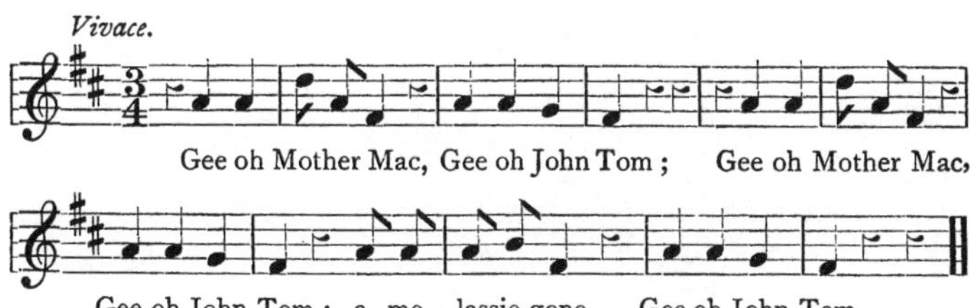
Vivace.
Gee oh Mother Mac, Gee oh John Tom; Gee oh Mother Mac,
Gee oh John Tom; a me lassie gone, Gee oh John Tom.

LXXII.

Here is something very short:—

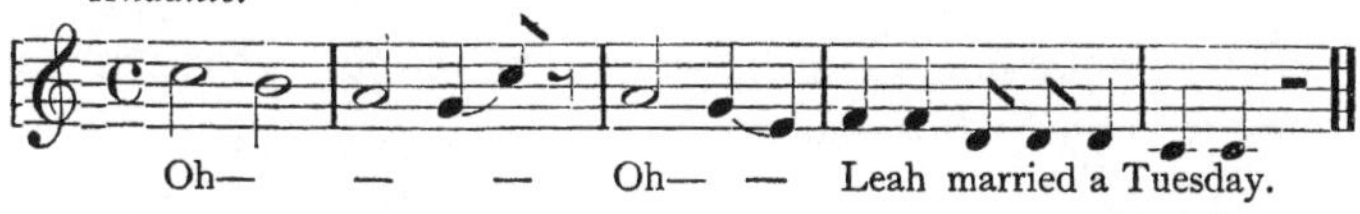
Andante.
Oh— — — Oh— — Leah married a Tuesday.

On asking if that was all, Levi, the contributor, said:— "It no have no more corner," it hasn't any more corners, or "turnings" as they generally say, what we call variations. Levi likes to cut everything short and rattle it through with lightning speed. He it was who gave me that little gem of an Annancy story about the rats and their trousers (No. XI.), and this is his:—

LXXIII.

Allegro.
Cheer me oh! Cheer me oh! Cheer me oh! My will fight fe you.

LXXIV.

In imitating animals the negro is clever. He moos like a cow, grunts like a pig, whinnies like a horse, besides the minor accomplishments of miauling and barking. Even trammelled by music this cock's crow is good:—

Allegro.
Me cock a crow— coo-coo - ri - co, before day him a
crow— coo -coo-ri-co, him a crow fe me wake—coo-coo - ri-co.

(Sound the *i* short as in rich.)

LXXV.

Now we come to a tragedy. Selina is drowned, and they sing smoothly and flowingly:—

Allegretto.
Oh— Se - li - na! Oh— Se - li - na!
John Crow de a riv - er side a call fe Se - li - na! Oh poor Se-
li-na! Duppy an' all a call fe Se-li-na! Oh poor Se-li-na.

Everybody in Jamaica believes in Duppy, and many women and children will not go out at night for fear of meeting one.

A man, they say, has two spirits, one from God and the other not from God. The one from God is good, and the one not from God may be either good or bad. During sleep, these spirits leave the body and go to other people's houses in search of food. Being shadows themselves, they feed on the shadow of food and on the smell of food. They are seldom far apart, and the heavenly spirit can always prevent the earthly spirit from doing harm. At death the God-given spirit flies up upon a tree, and goes to heaven the third day. The other spirit remains on earth as Duppy. Its abiding place is the grave of the dead man, but it wanders about at night as it did when he was alive. A good Duppy will watch over and protect the living. A bad Duppy tries to frighten and harm people, which it is able to do now that it has lost the restraining influence of its former companion, the heavenly spirit. It can assume any sort of shape, appearing sometimes as a man, sometimes as an animal. If it is a very bad Duppy, it makes the place where it is unbearably hot. The Negro believes that he can put a bad Duppy upon another person.[1] He proceeds as follows:—Going to the grave at midnight, he scoops a small hollow in the ground and puts in some rice, sprinkling it with sugar-water, a mixture of water and moist cane-sugar. He then directs Duppy to visit the person whose name he mentions, and goes away without looking behind him. The person on whom Duppy is put becomes "tearing mad," and it requires a ten-pound fee to "take the shadow off." How to do this is the Obeah-man's secret. A Duppy of one's own family is worse than a stranger's, and the "baddest" of all is Coolie Duppy. One of the most dreaded Duppies is "Rolling (*i.e.* roaring) Calf." It goes about making a hideous noise, and clanking a chain. "If Rolling Calf catch you, give

[1] [Cf. Miss Kingsley, *The Fetish View of the Human Soul*, in *Folk-Lore*, vol. viii., p. 138; also R. E. Dennett, *Bavili Notes*, *ibid.*, vol. xvi., p. 371.]

you one lick, you dead." Your only chance is to run, and you must keep on "cutting ten" (making the sign of the cross), and the pursuing monster has to go round that place ten times. "Shop-keeper and butcher," so goes local tradition, "tief too much (rob their customers very much) and when they dead they turn Rolling Calf."

Those who are born with a caul can see Duppy. So can those who rub their faces with the rheum from the eye of a horse or dog, and those who cut their eyelashes. Every Duppy walks two feet above the ground, floating in the air. If a child is not christened before it is six months old, Duppy will carry it away into the bush. To avoid this, a Bible and pair of scissors are laid on the child's pillow. The scissors are a protection, owing to their cross-like form.

Such are the main beliefs with regard to this remarkable superstition of Duppy on earth.[1]

This, however, is not all. At the day of judgment the two spirits will be reunited to the body, and in many cases the God-given spirit will go to hell after all. I often ask my boys which of these three is themselves? Is it the body? Is it the heavenly spirit? Is it the earthly spirit? But they do not understand the question and have no sort of reply. When I ask if it is not hard that the heavenly spirit after its sojourn in heaven should go to hell, they laugh.

LXXVI.

Leaving the religious, we come now to, what Jamaica considers more important, the colour question:—

Allegretto.

Sam - bo la - dy ho! Sam - bo, Sam - bo la - dy

[1] [See *Folk-Lore of the Negroes of Jamaica*, in *Folk-Lore*, vol. xv., pp. 87, 206, 450, and vol. xvi., p. 68.]

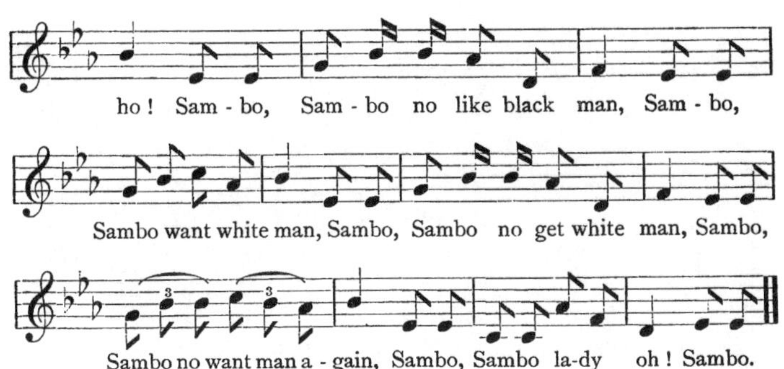
ho! Sam - bo, Sam - bo no like black man, Sam - bo,
Sambo want white man, Sambo, Sambo no get white man, Sambo,
Sambo no want man a - gain, Sambo, Sambo la-dy oh! Sambo.

A Sambo is the child of a brown mother and a black father, brown being a cross between black and white. The Sambo lady, very proud of the strain of white in her blood, turns up her nose at the black man. She wants a white man for a husband. Failing to find one, she will not marry at all.

LXXVII.

"Oh John Thomas!" is a favourite digging-sing at Goatridge, twenty-two miles from Kingston:—

Allegro.
Oh! John Thomas, Oh! John Thomas, Oh! John Thomas,
Oh! John Thomas, We all a combo - low, John Thomas, Me
go da 'lev - en mile, John Thomas, Me see one gal me
love, John Thomas, Me court her all the way, John

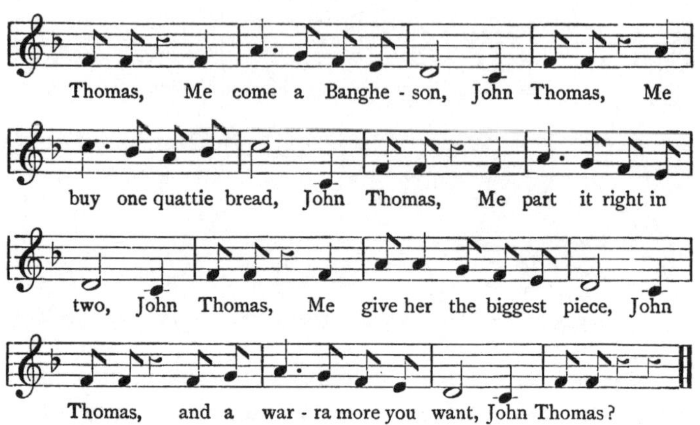
Thomas, Me come a Banghe - son, John Thomas, Me
buy one quattie bread, John Thomas, Me part it right in
two, John Thomas, Me give her the biggest piece, John
Thomas, and a war - ra more you want, John Thomas?

"Combolow" is comrade oh!

"Da 'leven mile," to Eleven-miles, the half-way halting place between Goatridge and Kingston.

When he gets to Bangheson's shop he buys a quattie (pronounce quotty, penny halfpenny, quarter of sixpence) loaf, and what more do you want, John Thomas?

The quattie bread weighs eight ounces only. It is therefore a dear and much esteemed luxury.

LXXVIII.

Sambo, that we had just now, is the shortest of bobbins. Here we have a long one of four bars.

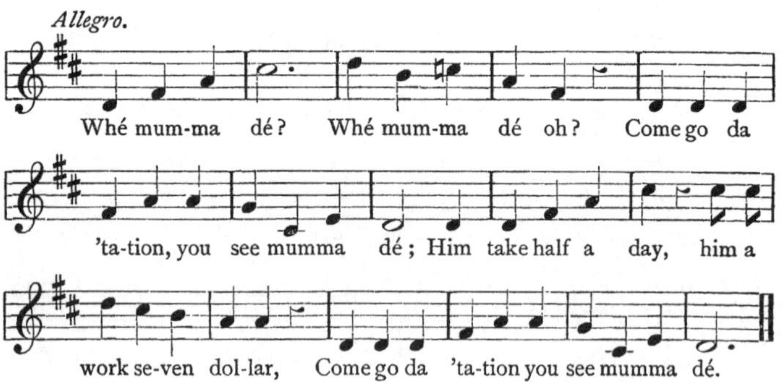
Allegro.
Whé mum-ma dé? Whé mum-ma dé oh? Come go da
'ta-tion, you see mumma dé; Him take half a day, him a
work se-ven dol-lar, Come go da 'ta-tion you see mumma dé.

Mamma has got into trouble, owing to a failing unhappily too common in Jamaica, inability to distinguish between what is mine and what is yours. Her pay for half a day was a "bit" (fourpence halfpenny) and she has managed to "work" (sarcastic use of the word, for it means to get by working) seven dollars—twenty-eight shillings—and has been taken to the police station.

"Whé mumma dé," literally, "where mamma is?" This has been already noted as the usual form of question. The vowel in whé, dé, is the French *é*. We have the sound in English in the words, *debt, west* and many others, but we always make it very short, and when it is lengthened, as it should be here, it generally changes in English mouths to the *a* of *date, waste,* which is wrong.

The C sharp on the word "dé" is peculiar and striking.

The second "dé" stands for "there."

LXXIX.

There is something pleasantly simple and naïve about the planting-sing:—

Vivace.
Toa - dy, Toa - dy, min' you - 'self, min' you - 'self make I
plant me corn; plant me corn fe go plant me peas,
plant me peas fe go court me gal, court me gal fe go
show mum-ma, mum-ma de one a go tell me yes, pup-

pa de one a go tell me no; Toa - dy, Toa - dy,
min' you - 'self, min' you - 'self make I plant me corn.

"Mind yourself, little Toad, let me plant my corn." So sings the boy as he brings down his digger with a forcible thrust. The digger has been described as an earth-chisel, and a very good description it is. It makes a long slit in the ground into which the maize grains or peas are dropped. Maize is always known as "corn." Peas, which are also called Red Peas, are the "beans" of America, familiar at home under the name of French beans. We eat them not only green in the usual way, but also make excellent soup of the dried ripe beans. The boy is thinking of the reward of his labour. "I am planting my corn. Some will be eaten green, some left to ripen. That will be sold. Then I shall buy peas, plant them, and when they are ready for market get sixpence a quart for them, if I am lucky. Then I shall be rich enough to walk with a girl. I shall pick out a nice one that mamma will approve of. She will be the one to say 'yes, me son,' but puppa always crabbed, and him going to tell me no bodder with it, gal too much expense."

LXXX.

When known details run dry, the following gives full play to the inventive faculty:—

Allegretto.
Me know the man oh! know the man, Name John Wat - son,

know the man; him come from Bread Lane, know the man; him ride one grey mule,
know the man; the mule name Vic oh! know the man; him have one tumpa toe,
know the man; him come a Mister Thomson, know the man, fe go
sell him grey mule, know the man; he no make no sale oh!
know the man, me know the man, know the man.1

Other bars of this air have an inclination to $\frac{2}{4}$ time besides those indicated.

It will be observed that repeat marks have only been put to the first sing. It was not considered necessary to continue them. The various "turnings" of the tunes may be put in any order. The negroes themselves never put them twice in the same sequence.

LXXXI.

Andante.
Min-nie, Min-nie, me los' me boar;

[1] "The" always tends to the pronunciation "de," but it has not been thought advisable to write it so as this might render it liable to confusion with "dé," meaning "is," with its differently sounded vowel. Moreover, it is not quite a true *d*, but has a pretty lisping sound intermediate between *th* and *d*.

Min - nie, Min - nie, me los' me boar;
Minnie, Minnie, him a broke-foot boar; Minnie, Minnie, me
los' me boar; Min-nie, Min-nie, and a blind-eye boar;
Min-nie, Min-nie, go find you boar, Min-nie, Min-nie.

"I have lost my boar, Minnie. He's a broken-legged boar and has got a blind eye," and so on through all the defects or excellences that a boar might, could, should or would have.

There could not be a greater contrast to this sombre "Minnie" than the gay:—

LXXXII.

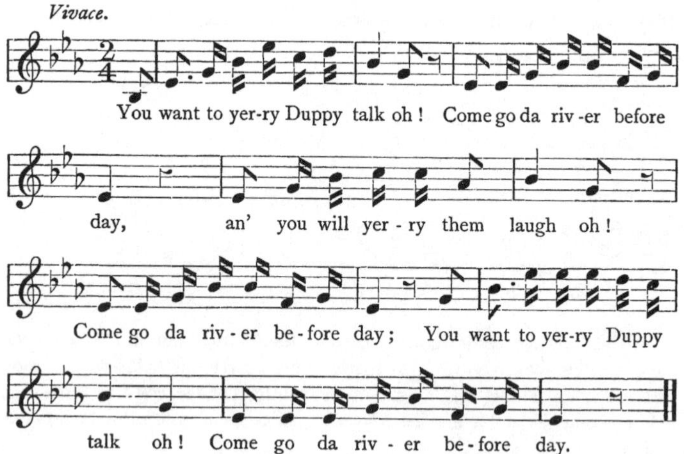
Vivace.
You want to yer-ry Duppy talk oh! Come go da riv -er before
day, an' you will yer - ry them laugh oh!
Come go da riv - er be - fore day; You want to yer-ry Duppy
talk oh! Come go da riv - er be - fore day.

"If you want to hear Duppy talk, go to the river before day."

LXXXIII.

Now the colour question crops up again. The Sambo lady, it may be remembered, wanted a white man and nothing but a white man. Sarah can do with a Sambo man, from which we may infer that Sarah was black.

Allegro.
Oh me know Sa - rah, me know Sa - rah; Sa - rah love white
man, me know Sa - rah; Sa-rah want Sambo man, me know Sarah; Sa - rah no want black man, me know Sa - rah.

LXXXIV.

The pickers fall with slashing strokes to:—

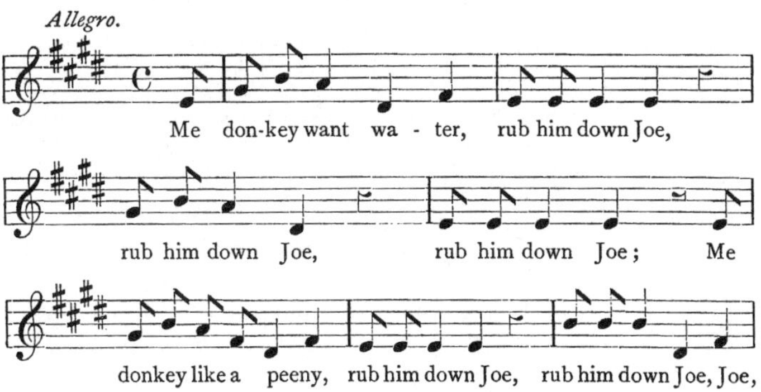
Allegro.
Me don-key want wa - ter, rub him down Joe,
rub him down Joe, rub him down Joe; Me
donkey like a peeny, rub him down Joe, rub him down Joe, Joe,

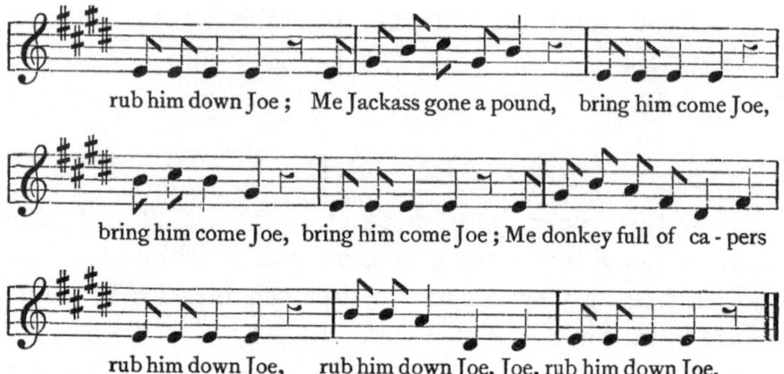
rub him down Joe; Me Jackass gone a pound, bring him come Joe,
bring him come Joe, bring him come Joe; Me donkey full of ca - pers
rub him down Joe, rub him down Joe, Joe, rub him down Joe.

"Peeny" is the Candlefly, which shines like my donkey's coat. "Bring come" for "bring" is very common, and in the same way they say "carry go," the "come" and "go" indicating the direction of motion.

LXXXV.

"Bring dem come" is the title of the next sing. It is in a curious minor mode, almost F minor, but wanting the leading note, which is replaced by E flat.

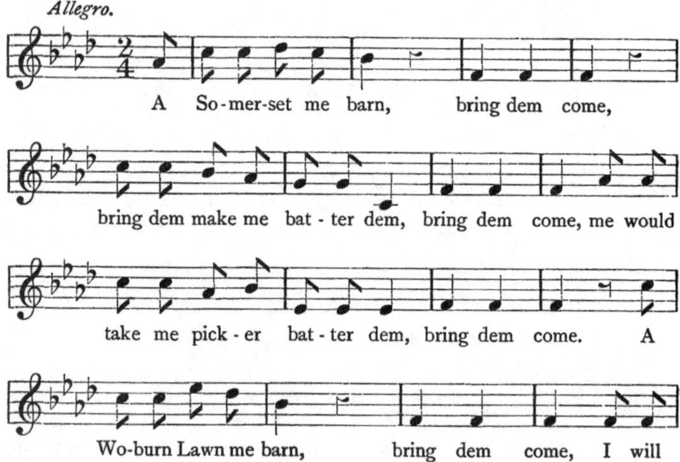
Allegro.
A So-mer-set me barn, bring dem come,
bring dem make me bat - ter dem, bring dem come, me would
take me pick - er bat - ter dem, bring dem come. A
Wo-burn Lawn me barn, bring dem come, I will

like to see dem bat-ter me, bring dem come, A
Goat - ridge me barn, bring dem come, I
want to see dem jos - tle me, bring dem come.

This is a digging contest. The Somerset men challenge their neighbours. Whoever digs most yam-hills in a given time is to be the winner. Every man is confident that he will hold out longer than every other, and boasts like Goliath. "I was born at Somerset; bring the strangers, bring them, let me beat them; I will take my pickaxe and beat them—I was born at Woburn Lawn; I should like to see them beat me." Honour and glory is the sole reward, but that counts for a great deal. It is so gratifying to hear the others say "Lah! that man dig hill, ya."

("Jostle" has the same meaning as "batter." When two ponies race, the riders try to jostle and foul each other.)

LXXXVI.

The next is really a woodcutter's sing, but it is used also for digging:—

Allegro.
Tim - ber lay down 'pon pit, Tim - ber; cut 'im
make we go 'way, Tim-ber; me want go 'way ya soon,

Tim-ber ; tim-ber lay down 'pon pit, Tim-ber ; tim-ber,
tim-ber oh ! Tim-ber ; me wanty go 'way ya soon,
Timber ; me want go home back a yard, Timber ; a
ced-ar tim-ber oh ! Tim-ber ; lash the saw make we
go home, Timber ; tim - ber lay down 'pon pit, Tim-ber.

"Lie down on the pit, timber. Cut it, and let us go away. I want to go away soon, do you hear? Drive (lash) the saw hard."

The pit is not really a pit. The sawing is done where the tree falls. A rough scaffolding is made and the log is rolled up to lie on the top of it. The bottom sawyer stands upon the ground.

The West Indian cedar is not a fir but a deciduous tree (*Cedrela odorata*), which looks like a hickory or walnut. It grows in the hills, and its lightness and durability make it very useful. Most people know it in the shape of cigar-boxes.

The rest bars are sort of pauses for breath. It will be seen that they break the rhythm. Throwing the accent on "go," in "go 'way," is characteristic. We should put it on "'way."

LXXXVII.

Listen how restless and unfinished this sounds:—

Allegretto.
Me want go home a yard oh! me want go home a yard oh! me
want go home a yard oh! me want go home a yard oh! a
Gua - va Ridge me barn oh! me want go home a yard oh! mum-
ma me want come home oh! me want go home a yard oh!
poor me boy me want go home, me want go home a yard oh!
Teach-er Bai - ley crahss 'pon me, me want go home a yard oh!

LXXXVIII.

The last example refers to the rebellion of 1865. Several whites were murdered, and the survivors are of opinion that their lives were saved by the prompt action of Governor Eyre, who proclaimed martial law and restored order by severe measures:—

Andante.
War down a Monk-land, war down a Mor- ant Bay,

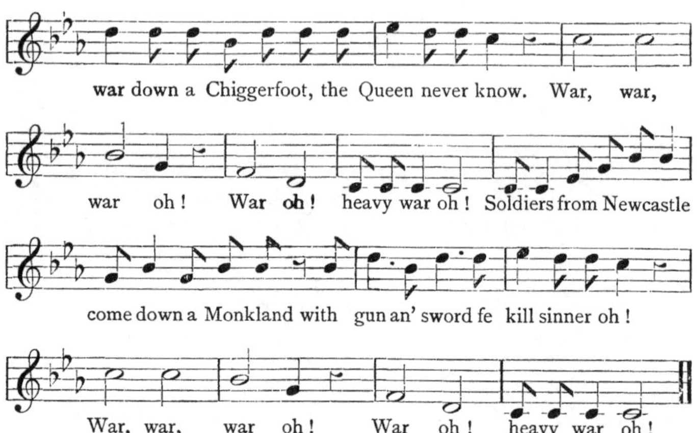
war down a Chiggerfoot, the Queen never know. War, war,
war oh! War oh! heavy war oh! Soldiers from Newcastle
come down a Monkland with gun an' sword fe kill sinner oh!
War, war, war oh! War oh! heavy war oh!

The places mentioned are in the parish (corresponding to English county), of St. Thomas, except Newcastle, the hill cantonment of the white troops, which is in the next parish of St. Andrew. "Chiggerfoot" takes its name from the chigoe, chigger, or jigger, the minute flea which burrows into the foot. It is interesting to see that this contemporary comment by the blacks describes the rebels as sinners. Further on, No. CXXXVII., will be found another view, in which they pose as aggrieved persons. It shows that there was a loyal as well as a disloyal party.

The reader has now had enough examples of digging-sings to show their nature and variety. The Negro is never at a loss for words, and the masters and overseers of the estate on which he generally labours, Bushas as he calls them—a word said to be derived from Pasha—are often satirised. The gangs on private estates are under a head-man, who is responsible to the Busha. The Busha is a white or coloured man as a rule—coloured in Jamaica meaning mixed white and black—and he is responsible to the master or owner. The workers have to be carefully looked after, for like other people the

Negro will not do more work than he can help. Only when he is working for himself will he "let out," as he describes it, the whole of his splendid strength. It is a mistake to suppose that the black man is either stupid or lazy. When he has an incentive to work he is industrious, and will do as much in one day in his own field as he will in two for an employer who pays him. In selecting land for planting his sagacity is remarkable, and he knows just where it will "come," as he says, guinea yam or white yam, and where coffee will succeed and where fail. It is a pleasure to see their provision-grounds, the miscellaneous crop looks so thriving. "Provisions" embrace all eatables, such as yam, sweet potato, coco (*colocasia*), sugar cane, beans of various kinds, maize (or simply "corn," as we call it, having no other), okra (*hibiscus esculentus*), cassada (*manihot utilissima*), plantain, banana, arrowroot, pindar (*arachis hypogœa*, a ground-nut), pumpkin, tomato and cabbage.

PART III. RING TUNES.

THAT informal kind of dancing, referred to in some of the Annancy stories, known as "playing in the ring" or "Sally Water" has its origin in English children's games. Sometimes it is merely a case of hunting the slipper or of finding a key passed from hand to hand, but more often what begins in playing ends in dancing. The nature of this playing in the ring will be best understood from examples.

LXXXIX.

First, as giving its name to the whole, must stand:—

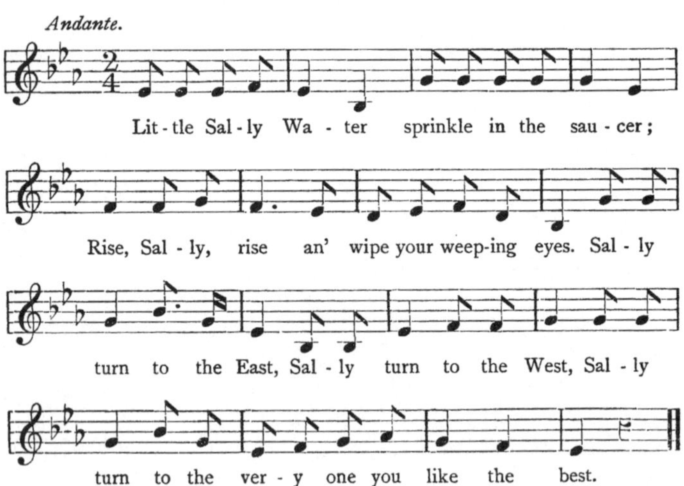

Andante.
Lit-tle Sal-ly Wa - ter sprinkle in the sau - cer;
Rise, Sal - ly, rise an' wipe your weep-ing eyes. Sal - ly
turn to the East, Sal - ly turn to the West, Sal - ly
turn to the ver - y one you like the best.

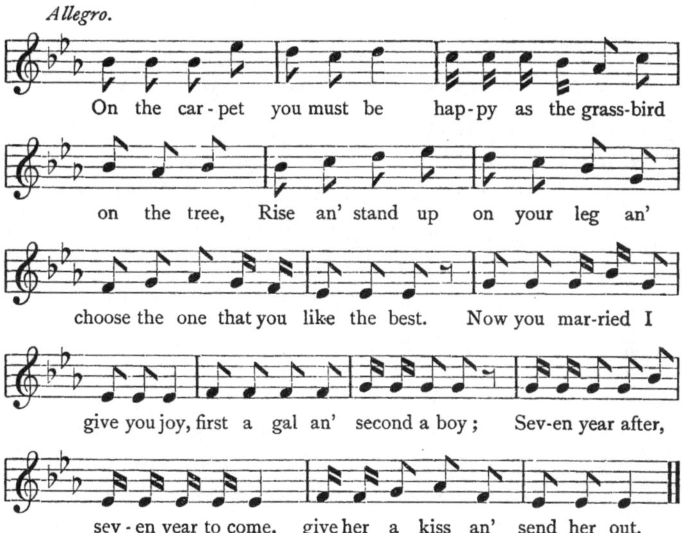
Allegro.
On the car-pet you must be hap-py as the grass-bird
on the tree, Rise an' stand up on your leg an'
choose the one that you like the best. Now you mar-ried I
give you joy, first a gal an' second a boy; Sev-en year after,
sev-en year to come, give her a kiss an' send her out.

The boys and girls join hands and form a ring. One—the sex is immaterial—crouches in the middle and personates Sally Water. At the words "Rise, Sally, rise," he or she slowly rises to an erect position, brushing away imaginary tears, turns first one way and then another, and chooses a partner out of the ring. Where the *tempo* changes, they wheel—a rapid turning dance—and after the wheeling, the partner is left inside the ring and becomes Sally Water.[1]

XC.

Another form of this Ring tune is:—

Andante.
Poor lit-tle Zed-dy they put him in the cor-ner!

[1] For a discussion of this game, perhaps the best-known and most widely-spread of all English singing games, see A. B. Gomme, *Traditional Games*, vol. ii., p. 149.

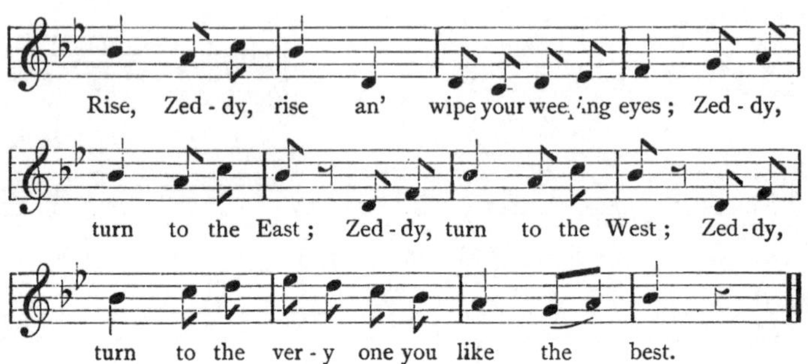
Rise, Zed - dy, rise an' wipe your weeping eyes ; Zed - dy,
turn to the East ; Zed - dy, turn to the West ; Zed - dy,
turn to the ver - y one you like the best.

XCI.

The negro is a born actor, and to give emphasis to his words by appropriate gestures comes naturally to him. The little comedy which follows suits him to perfection :—

Allegretto.
Whé me lov - er dé? See - mya, see - mya. Me
lov-er gone a sea? See - mya, see - mya. Me no see me lov - er
ya. See - mya, see - mya. Him gone a Col-on bay. See-
mya, see - mya. Go fin' you lov-er now. See-mya, see-
mya. No make no 'tu - pid dé. See - mya, see - mya.
Fool dem let dem go. See - mya, see - mya. Me lov - er

come back. See-mya, see-mya. Go take you lov-er
now. See-mya, see-mya. Wheel him make me see. See-
mya, see-mya. Throw a kiss to him. See-mya, see-
mya. Wheel him let him go. See-mya, see-mya.[1]

A ring is formed, and a girl is put in the middle. She asks:—"Where is my lover?" and the ring answers in chorus:—"See him here." "Has my lover gone to sea?" and the answer comes again:—"See him here." The gal goes on:—"I do not see my lover; has he gone to Colon bay?" and then, as though speaking to herself:—"Go, find your lover now. There! don't pretend to be stupid." At this point she takes the hand of a boy in the ring as if she were going to dance with him, but immediately pushes him back, and says, still speaking to herself:—"Fool them, let them go." Then simulating contrition and breaking the hitherto even rhythm:—"My lover, come back!" At "Go take your lover now" she goes again to the same boy, takes him out of the ring-circle and dances with him. They *wheel* at the words "Wheel him make me see," which mean, "Let me see you wheel him." Finally at "Wheel him let him go" they part hands.

Frequent references will be found to Colon. Jamaica labourers used to go there in large numbers to work on the Panama canal.

[1] To avoid the tiresomeness of contraction marks, "see him ya" has been written in one word. It sounds exactly like *senior* with an m instead of an n.

XCII.

To the same class belongs :—

Allegro molto.
Ring a dia - mond, ring a dia - mond, Why oh
ring a diamond. Get in the ring you'll find one Sam-bo boy.
Why oh ring a diamond. Me look me da look me no
find one Sambo boy. Why oh ring a diamond. Me
find me diamond, me find me dia-mond. Why oh
ring a diamond. Wheel you dia-mond, wheel you dia-mond.
Why oh ring a dia-mond. Let go dia - mond,
let go dia-mond. Why oh ring a dia-mond.

This tune has a beautiful swing. In many bars it is almost impossible to distinguish whether the tune is triple or duple. Much license may be allowed in the direction of the latter to a good timist, but the general impression of triple time must be kept. The "Sambo boy" bar must be sung very smoothly. It is neither quite as it is written the first time nor quite as it occurs in the second, but just between the two. Three even crotchets with judicious *tempo rubato* would give it. It will be understood that these tunes are sung antiphonally. In this one the leaders, who know the tune and words well, sing the first four bars and the next four belong to the chorus, after which the leaders take it up again, and so on.

There is an opportunity here for a little harmless "chaff" about colour. The diamond chosen is a *black* diamond, the blacker the better. The ring forms round him joining hands, and one girl is pushed in to look for the Sambo boy. She says:—"I look, I am looking, I don't find a Sambo boy" (*i.e.* a quarter black). At last she finds her diamond, either the boy inside the ring or one of those who circle round him, and they dance together, wheeling and letting go hands at the words "wheel," "let go."

"Why" is an ejaculation, probably the same as Hi!

XCIII.

Another chorus tune of the same kind is:—

Tempo di Valse.
The gal ov-er yon-der car-ry ba-na-na,
gal oh! gal oh! car-ry ba-na-na. A nine-hand ba-
na-na, car-ry ba-na-na, a Chi-ney ba-na-na,

car - ry ba - na - na. You find the ba - na - na? car - ry ba -
na - na. You tief the ba - na - na? car - ry ba - na - na.

The girl is supposed to be carrying a bunch of bananas on her head, and the singers are commenting upon it and asking the girl questions, as they do here at a distance of half-a-mile. "Look! It is a nine-hand banana. No, a China banana. Did you find it? Did you steal it?"

Banana bunches are reckoned by the number of hands they contain, the separate bananas being called fingers. Nine-hand is a convenient market size. The China banana is a stout low kind which withstands wind: the fruit is, however, coarse.

The signal for taking a partner is given by the words "You find the banana?"

XCIV.

In the next there is no dancing. The ring closes up tight, shoulder to shoulder. Hands behind the back pass the ball round and round, and the girl inside the ring tries to find it. The person with whom it is found has to go into the ring and turn seeker.

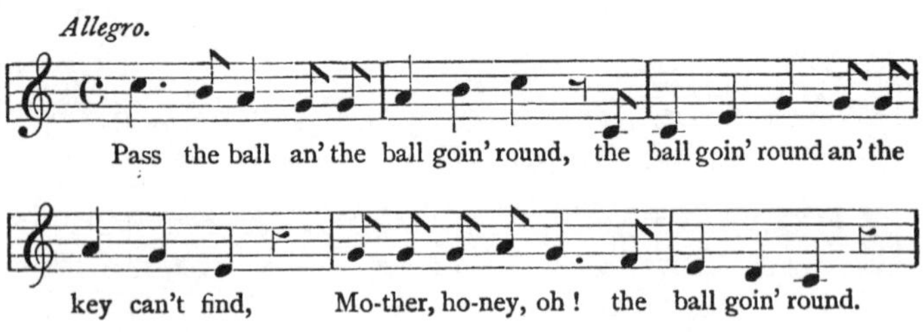
Allegro.
Pass the ball an' the ball goin' round, the ball goin' round an' the
key can't find, Mo-ther, ho-ney, oh! the ball goin' round.

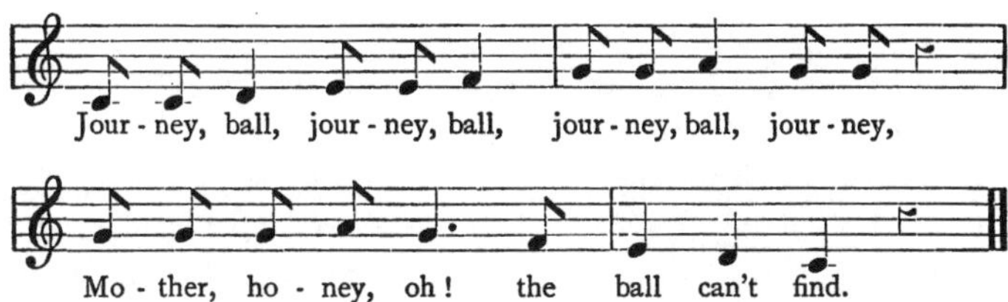
Jour - ney, ball, jour - ney, ball, jour - ney, ball, jour - ney,
Mo - ther, ho - ney, oh! the ball can't find.

The conventional "gwine" for "going" hardly represents it, only the *o* is pronounced so short that the word becomes practically one syllable. In the dance tunes we shall come across the word "dying" shortened in the same way.

XCV.

A variation of this is obtained by putting a ring on a cord and sliding it along. The tune is:—

Allegretto.
Me los' me gold ring fin' an' gi' me, Me
los' me gold ring fin' an' gi' me, Me los' me gold ring
fin' an' gi' me, A me husband gold ring fin' an' gi' me.

XCVI.

In "Mother Phœbe" again there is no dancing:—

Andantino.
Old moder Phœbe, how happy you be When you sit under the

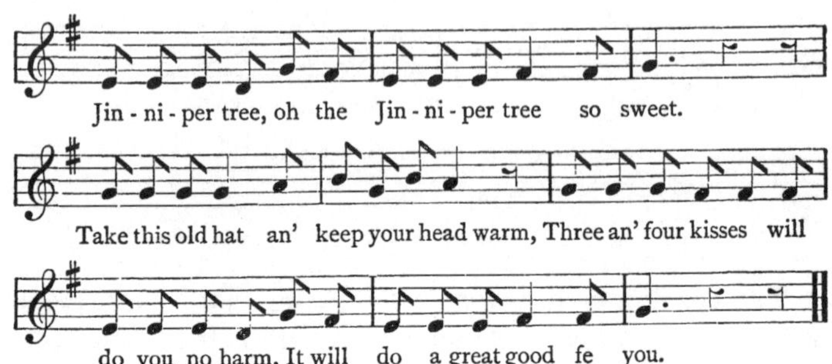
Jin - ni - per tree, oh the Jin - ni - per tree so sweet.
Take this old hat an' keep your head warm, Three an' four kisses will
do you no harm, It will do a great good fe you.

Here the girl inside the ring takes a hat or cap and after several feints puts it on somebody's head, and that person has then to take her place in the ring.

XCVII.

More lively is the joyous :—

Allegro molto.
Do, do, do, do, do, Deg-gy, Deg-gy house a go
burn down, do, De Gay. Deg-gy whé you would a do dé
do, De Gay? Deg-gy dood an' doo - dess do, De
Gay. Deg-gy go roun', Deg - gy do De - gay. An' a
cutch-y fe Deg - gy do De - gay, an' a wheel an' let go
do, De Gay. Deg-gy house a burn down do, De Gay.

The boy inside the ring "makes all sort of flourish," dancing and posturing by himself. The word "cutchy" is accompanied by a deep curtsey, on rising from which he takes a girl out of the ring and wheels her. Deggy or Degay, has occurred already in No. LVII. Whether it is his own house that is burning, or somebody else's, it is impossible to conjecture. Observe the varying accent on the name. In taking down this song I first wrote "doodan doodess," thinking they were nonsense words suggested by the repetition of do, do, do, but on asking further about them was told that "dood" is a "risky beau-man," a smart well-dressed young fellow. So it is the American "dude" and its female counterpart "dudess" which here take the place of the usual "gal and boy."

XCVIII.

The latter we find in:

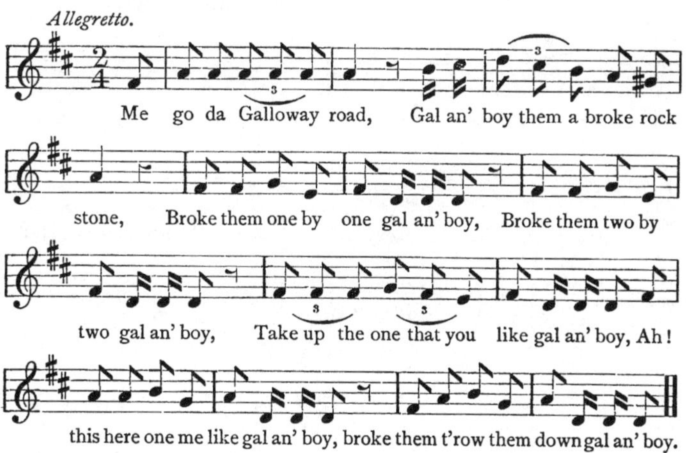
Allegretto.
Me go da Galloway road, Gal an' boy them a broke rock
stone, Broke them one by one gal an' boy, Broke them two by
two gal an' boy, Take up the one that you like gal an' boy, Ah!
this here one me like gal an' boy, broke them t'row them down gal an' boy.

I go to Galloway road (where there is a quarry). Girls and boys are breaking stones. They break them one by one. They break them two by two, etc. Choosing stones suggests choosing partners.

XCIX.

We come across "dude" again in :—

Allegro.
Ros-y-bel oh— why oh! Ros-y-bel oh— why oh!
Ros-y-bel let go Mister Por-ter son, Ros-y-bel oh— why
oh! Ros-y-bel cock cock crow da yard, Ros-y-bel
oh— why oh! Ros-y-bel let go Mister Por-ter son,
Ros-y-bel oh— why oh! Ros-y-bel oh— why oh!
Ros-y-bel oh— why oh— Ros-y-bel wheel him dood jes'
now, Ros-y-bel oh— why oh! Ros-y-bel cock cock
crow you no know, Ros-y-bel oh— why oh! Ros-y-bel
wheel him let him go, Ros-y-bel oh— why oh!

C.

The play in the next is rough, and the holders of hands in the ring must have strong wrists.

Andante.

Me da lé lé lé, me da lé lé lé, Bull a pen

ho! gin-ger-ly! the bull a broke pen! gin-ger-ly! A Mount Siney

bull! ginger-ly! A Galloway bull! ginger-ly! bull a broke pen! gingerly!

Two strong young fellows personate the bulls. One is inside the ring and the other outside. They paw the ground and moo at each other but must not fight unless they can break the ring. When the ring is broken at last by a determined rush, one of the bulls is sometimes seized with panic and jumps back into the pen (ring) where he is safe. The fight, if it does take place, is not a very serious affair, the cowmen soon coming up with their ropes (handkerchiefs) which they throw over the bulls' heads and so draw them apart.[1]

(*Me da dé* would mean Me is there, I am there. Lé is substituted for euphony, being probably suggested by the last syllable of "gingerly.")

CI.

Another rough game is:—

Allegro.

Two man a road, Crom-an-ty boy, Two man a road,

[1] [Cf. "Bull in the Park," Gomme, *Traditional Games*, vol. i. p. 50.]

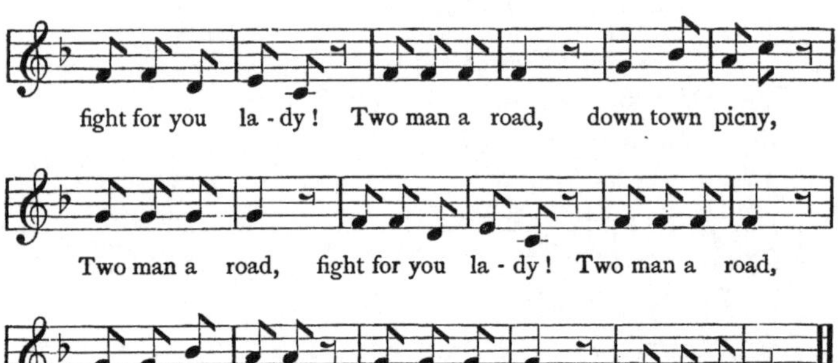
fight for you la - dy! Two man a road, down town picny,
Two man a road, fight for you la - dy! Two man a road,
Crom-an-ty win oh! Two man a road, Crom-an-ty win.

A line of girls stretches along each side of the road and in front of them stand the two combatants armed with sticks. One is a Coromanti (one of the African tribes) and the other a Kingston or down-town boy. "Fight for your ladies" cry the respective lines to their champions. Whoever can disable the other and snatch one of his girls across the road is the winner. A mock doctor comes to bind up the wounds.

CII.

"Adina Mona," with its Italian-sounding words, is noisy, but not so rough:—

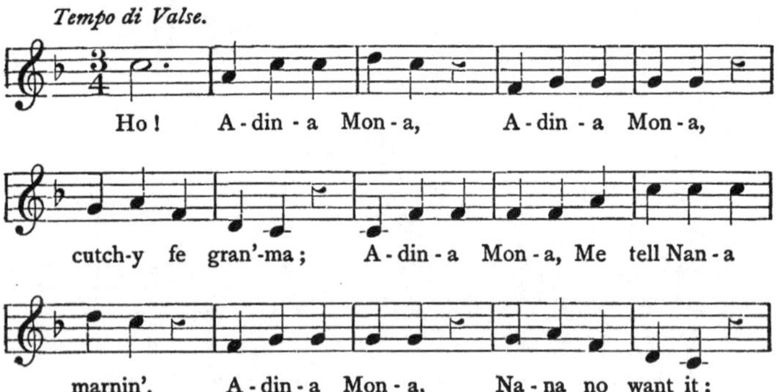
Tempo di Valse.
Ho! A-din-a Mon-a, A-din-a Mon-a,
cutch-y fe gran'-ma; A-din-a Mon-a, Me tell Nan-a
marnin'. A-din-a Mon-a, Na-na no want it;

A - din - a Mon - a, Me beg Na - na wahter ; A - din - a
Mon - a, Him give me dirty wahter, A-din - a Mon-a.

Here they stand face to face in separate couples. At the beginning of one bar the boys knock their hands upon their thighs, and at the beginning of the next bar clap them against those of their partners, as in the first motion of the game of Clip-clap. As they do this the boys walk backwards, occasionally wheeling, and making, as they say, "all manner of flourish."

CIII.

"Palmer" affords an opportunity for individual display :—

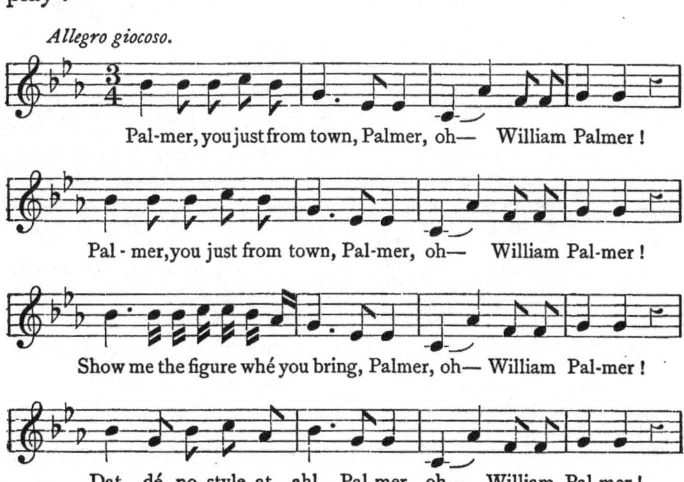
Allegro giocoso.
Pal-mer, you just from town, Palmer, oh— William Palmer !
Pal - mer, you just from town, Pal-mer, oh— William Pal-mer !
Show me the figure whé you bring, Palmer, oh— William Pal-mer !
Dat dé no style at ahl, Pal-mer, oh— William Pal-mer !

Pal - mer, you just from town, Palmer, oh— William Pal-mer !
Put on de style now more, Palmer, oh— William Pal-mer !

Palmer has just come back to his mountain home from Kingston, and is urged to show the latest step for a quadrille figure or other dance. His companions affect surprise. What! is that all? Oh, Palmer, that's not style!

CIV.

Very popular is the next one:—

Allegro.
Mo - ther Free - man, a whé me Gun - go dé?
Not a one can sow me Gun - go; Fe me Gun - go, da precious Gun-
go, Not a one can sow me Gun - go; All the
gal them a go dead 'way 'pon me, Not a one can sow me Gun -
go. All the boy a go dead 'way 'pon me,
Not a one can sow me Gun - go.

Mother Freeman, where is my Gungo (a kind of pea)? No one will sow my Gungo, or perhaps rather:—Will no one sow my Gungo? For my Gungo is precious Gungo.

As they sing and dance, the boys pretend to faint, and fall into the arms of the girls. When the words change, the girls fall into the arms of the boys, who catch them. "Dead 'way 'pon me," besides meaning to faint, has a slang interpretation equivalent to: "All the girls are death upon me."

CV.

The following is perhaps a sly allusion to some dull-witted boy:—

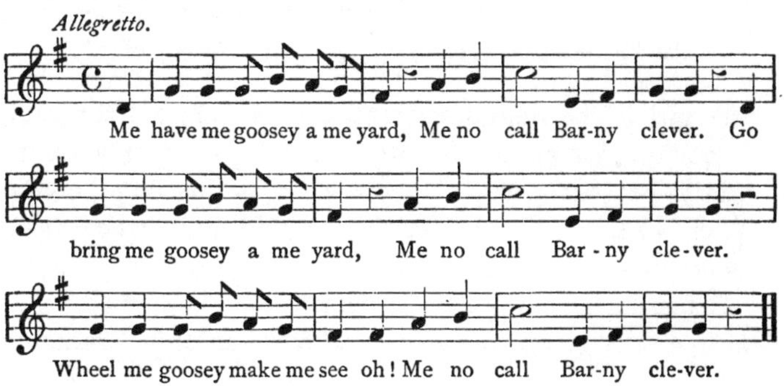
Allegretto.
Me have me goosey a me yard, Me no call Bar-ny clever. Go
bring me goosey a me yard, Me no call Bar-ny cle-ver.
Wheel me goosey make me see oh! Me no call Bar-ny cle-ver.

Thick sour milk allowed to stand and curdle is called "barnyclebber" [Irish word, F.Y.P.].

CVI.

Here we have a reference to the too common practice of stealing, which is treated more as a joke than a crime:—

Allegretto.
Drill him, Constab, drill him; Drill him, Constab, drill him; She

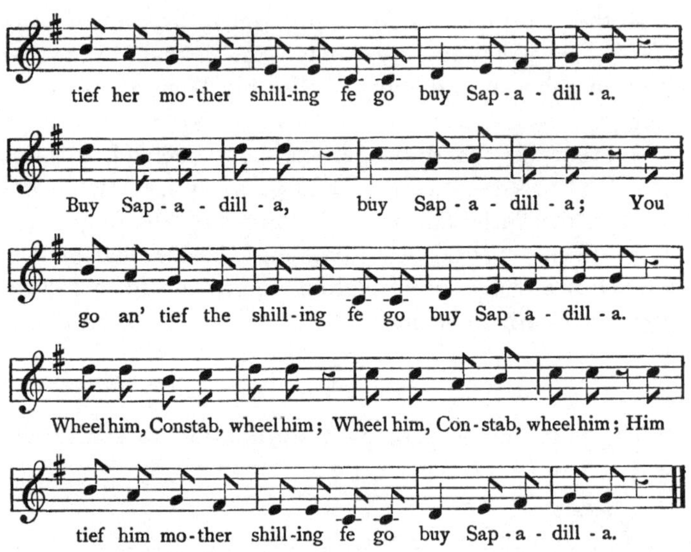
tief her mo-ther shill-ing fe go buy Sap-a-dill-a.
Buy Sap-a-dill-a, buy Sap-a-dill-a; You
go an' tief the shill-ing fe go buy Sap-a-dill-a.
Wheel him, Constab, wheel him; Wheel him, Con-stab, wheel him; Him
tief him mo-ther shill-ing fe go buy Sap-a-dill-a.

A girl is the delinquent and the "Constab" (constable, pronounce *con* as in *constant*) is inside the ring with her, lightly beating her with a twig or pocket-handkerchief. When one has been marched round and wheeled, he "sends her out" and takes another.

Sapadilla is really a fruit something like a medlar, but the name is given to all sorts of fruit, notably Granadilla.

CVII.

Another "flogging" tune, but without any dancing, is :—

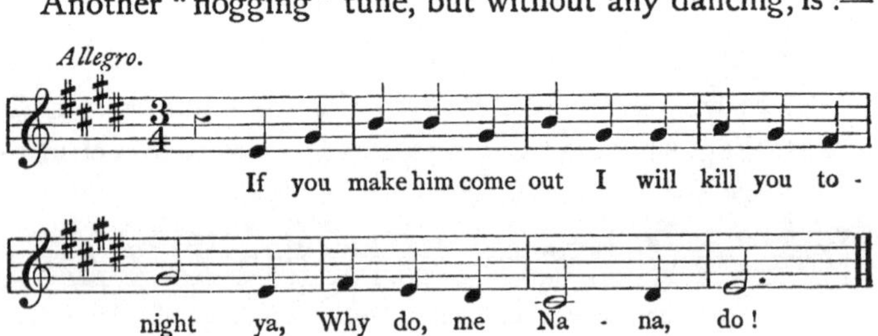
Allegro.
If you make him come out I will kill you to-
night ya, Why do, me Na-na, do!

A girl is in the ring and a boy is flogging her with a whip. The boy says to the holders of the ring:—"If you let her come out I will kill you to-night, do you hear?" The girl is going round, begging to be released, with the appeal to each one:—"Oh do, my Nana!" that is, "Do let me out."

CVIII.

The most laughable antics, "mechanic" as they call it, are indulged in in the next:—

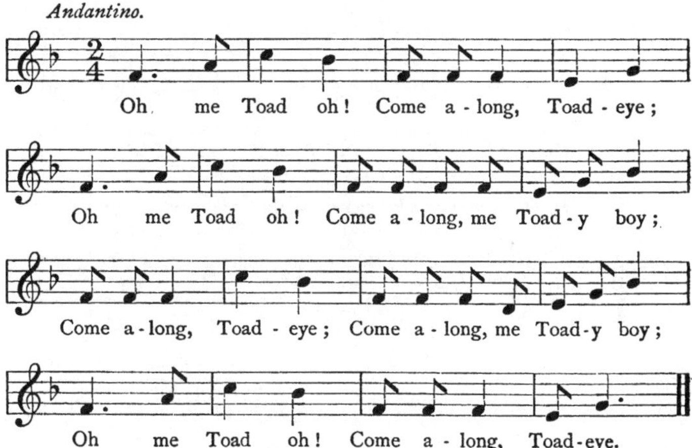
Andantino.
Oh me Toad oh! Come a - long, Toad - eye;
Oh me Toad oh! Come a - long, me Toad - y boy;
Come a - long, Toad - eye; Come a - long, me Toad - y boy;
Oh me Toad oh! Come a - long, Toad - eye.

Each girl has a "Toad" in front of her to protect her. The Toads jump about, and the one who can get past the other and capture his girl, wins. Jamaican toads, or at least the small kind, hop like the frogs of cooler countries.

CIX.

The first half of the tune which follows occurs in the story of Annancy and Screech-owl (No. XIX.):—

Allegro.
There's a black boy in a ring, tra la la la
la, There's a black boy in a ring, tra la la la
la, There's a black boy in a ring, tra la la la
la, He like su - gar an' I like plum.
Wheel an' take you pard - ner, jump sha - ma - dor !
Wheel an' take you pard - ner, jump sha - ma - dor !
Wheel an' take you pard - ner, jump sha-ma - dor ! For
he like su - gar an' I like plum.

The boy inside the ring chooses his partner, whom he leaves there after the dance. She obtains release by choosing another partner, whom she leaves behind. So there is alternately a boy and a girl in the ring,

"Shamador" is possibly a corruption of "camerado."

CX.

The next is an old tune which is going out of fashion. It is still remembered in my district, but nobody can tell me how it is danced.

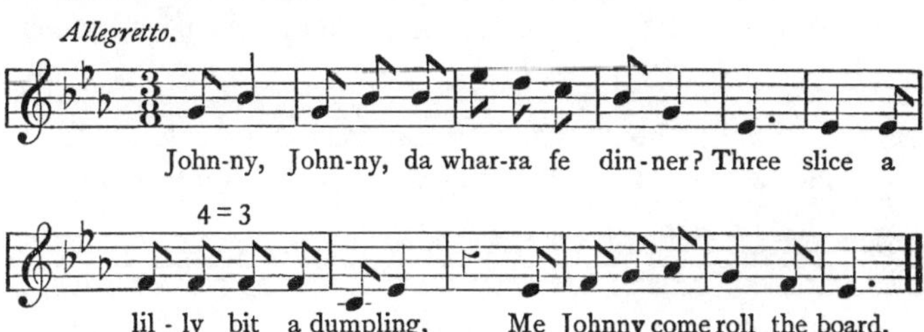
Allegretto.
John-ny, John-ny, da whar-ra fe din-ner? Three slice a
4 = 3
lil - ly bit a dumpling, Me Johnny come roll the board.

"Da wharra" literally means "is what." What is there for dinner? Three slices and a little bit of dumpling. I tried to find out whether they were slices of dumpling or slices of something else, but no one could tell me that. The dumplings are plain flour and water, innocent of suet. They are very popular, and are eaten with a morsel of salt fish or meat. Johnny is invited to come and roll them on the board.

CXI.

We all know the next tune :—

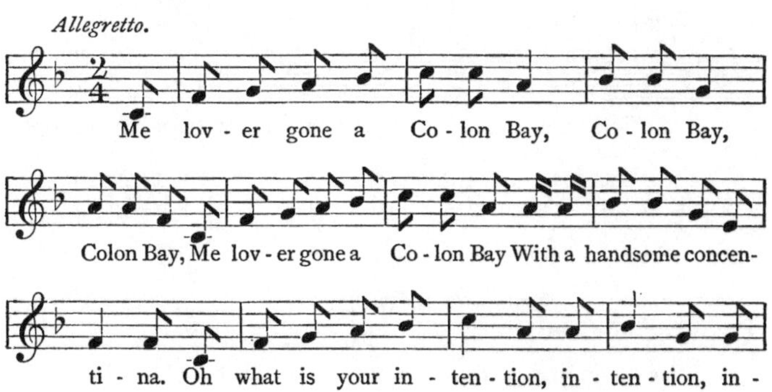
Allegretto.
Me lov - er gone a Co - lon Bay, Co - lon Bay,
Colon Bay, Me lov - er gone a Co - lon Bay With a handsome concen-
ti - na. Oh what is your in - ten - tion, in - ten - tion, in -

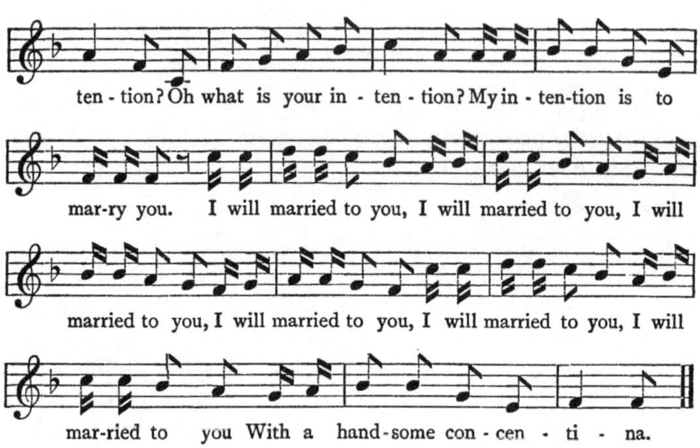
ten - tion? Oh what is your in - ten - tion? My in - ten-tion is to
mar-ry you. I will married to you, I will married to you, I will
married to you, I will married to you, I will married to you, I will
mar-ried to you With a hand-some con - cen - ti - na.

(Levi always sings:—"What is your retention, retention, retention?")

In "I will married to you" the wheeling becomes a giddy business, at least to the onlooker. The dancers never seem to feel it, nor do they appear to mind the heat. They simply stream with perspiration and put their handkerchiefs round their necks to save their white collars.

CXII.

A little breathing time is given by:—

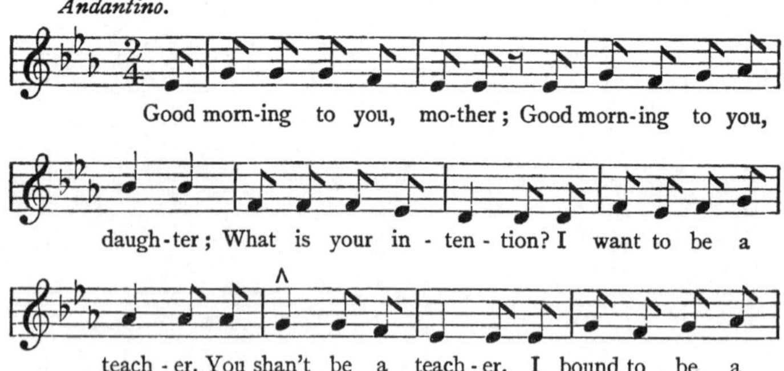
Andantino.
Good morn-ing to you, mo-ther; Good morn-ing to you,
daugh-ter; What is your in - ten - tion? I want to be a
teach - er. You shan't be a teach - er. I bound to be a

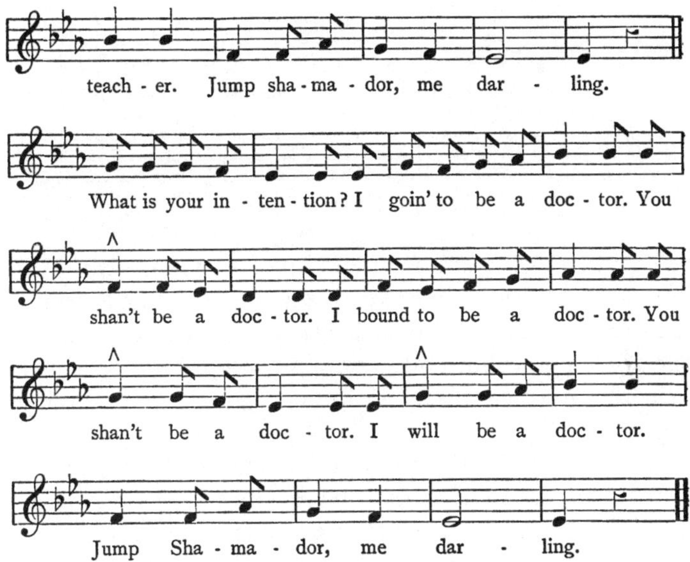
teach - er. Jump sha - ma - dor, me dar - ling.
What is your in - ten - tion? I goin' to be a doc - tor. You
shan't be a doc - tor. I bound to be a doc - tor. You
shan't be a doc - tor. I will be a doc - tor.
Jump Sha - ma - dor, me dar - ling.

There is no dancing here. The mother walks round inside the ring, the various members of which she addresses in turn. "You shan't" is emphasised by an uplifted arm swept vigorously downwards and a stamp of the foot. The answers go through the various professions until it is felt that there is a want of something more exciting, which is supplied by :—

CXIII.

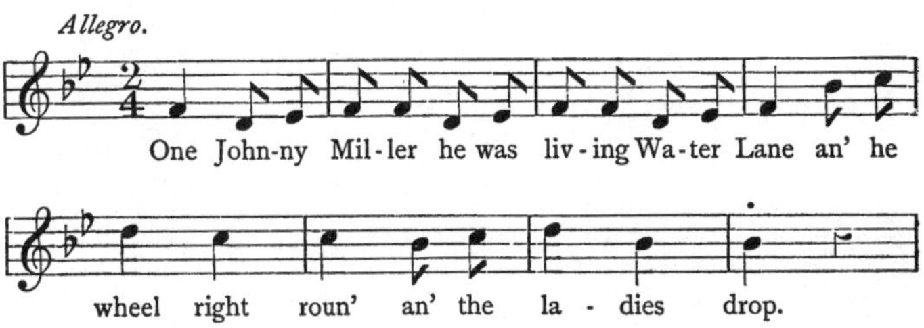
Allegro.
One John-ny Mil - ler he was liv - ing Wa - ter Lane an' he
wheel right roun' an' the la - dies drop.

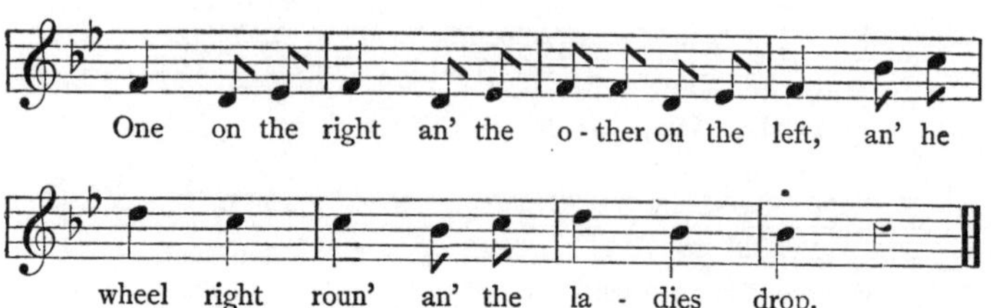
One on the right an' the o-ther on the left, an' he
wheel right roun' an' the la - dies drop.

The tune is again familiar. A boy takes two girls out of the circle, leaves one in the middle and wheels the other. Having dropped her he wheels the second one. The wheeling over, she is dropped. These two then resume their places in the circle, and the boy takes out two more.

"Water Lane." Kingston lies on ground sloping evenly to the sea. It is laid out on the American plan in parallel streets. A broad "Street" alternates with a narrower "Lane." The lanes pointing to the sea have water running down them and are called Water Lanes.

CXIV.

The next is used both as a Ring-tune and for the favourite Fifth Figure of the Quadrilles:—

Allegro.
Me go to Mo-rant Bay, Bah-lim-bo. Me
see one Coo-lie gal, Bah-lim-bo. Lard! me love the
gal, Bah-lim-bo. Me tell her wait fe me, Bah-

lim - bo. The gal no wait at all, Bah - lim - bo.
Me ride, me ride, me ride, Bah - lim - bo. Me
catch her on the way, Bah - lim - bo. Me bahss her all the
way, Bah - lim - bo. The mumma say me rude, Bah-
lim - bo. But that no rude at all, Bah - lim - bo.
For wo-man cloth so cheap, Bah - lim - bo.
Two yard fe bit, Bah - lim - bo. Man cloth so
dear, Bah - lim - bo. One pound a yard, Bah - lim - bo.

"Bahlimbo" is a nick-name for a cheap sort of cloth, *i.e.* fabric of any kind. In Africa calicoes are called *limbo.* The "two yards fe bit" kind is calico print. A "bit" is fourpence halfpenny. "Bahss" means buss, kiss.

White people pronounce Morant as it is spelt, but the Blacks always put the accent on the first syllable, and usually call it Morrum.

CXV.

As the time for dancing approaches (see note on weddings in "Gaulin" p. 76) the ring breaks up, and there is a lively marching tune or two, such as:—

Vivace.
Oh den Jack - y me knee da go ben' a
palm palm; oh me knee da go ben' a palm palm.

The couples with the right arm of one partner locked tightly into the left of the other march about bending their knees at rhythmical intervals, presenting the most ridiculous appearance. The tune has an infectious gaiety about it as its sections are sung over and over and interchanged. If you repeat them as often as they do, you will feel stealing over you that kind of intoxication which the Dancing Dervishes experience.

CXVI.

There is a great deal of laughing over "Jacky," which suggests:—

Vivace.
When me get a Mis-ter Walker gate, Me will laugh, ha, ha, ha,
ha! Me will laugh hé, hé, hé, hé! Me will laugh—ha, ha! Me will
*

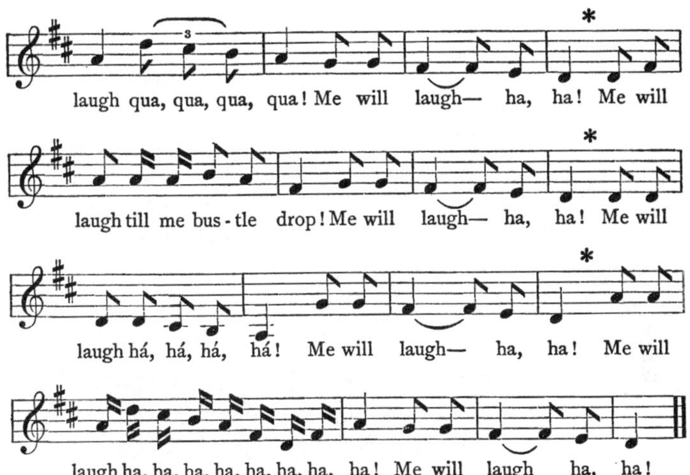
laugh qua, qua, qua, qua! Me will laugh— ha, ha! Me will
laugh till me bus - tle drop! Me will laugh— ha, ha! Me will
laugh há, há, há, há! Me will laugh— ha, ha! Me will
laugh ha, ha, ha, ha, ha, ha, ha, ha! Me will laugh ha, ha!

At the marks * a return is made to the first four bars, always substituting a new name for Walker, and the tune has many more "turnings" besides the ones noted.

A sufficient selection of Ring tunes has now been given to show their character. The number might be indefinitely increased. Every district has its own, and while some old favourites remain, new ones are constantly in process of making. These supply, or more than supply, the gaps caused by those which drop out.

PART IV. DANCING TUNES.

TURNING now to the Dancing tunes, the chief difference to be noted is that they show a more marked departure from what may be called the Jamaican type of melody. Sailors bring popular songs to the seaports, and from there they spread into the country. For a time some of the original words are kept, but before long they get changed. The change is partly due to that corruption of the text which naturally takes place as the songs pass from mouth to mouth, but mainly to the fact that the words, referring as they do to English topics, have no interest here. So we generally find that the tunes are refitted with a complete set of new words, describing some incident which has lately happened in the district, or some detail of daily life. When these reflect, as they often do, upon the characters of individuals the names have been changed and all evidence pointing to the locality destroyed. The same course has been pursued where it is thought the susceptibilities of persons or their relations might possibly be offended, even when there is nothing mentioned to their discredit.

The music consists of three "flutes" (fifes), two tambourines and a big drum. This is the professional element, which is reinforced by amateurs. One brings a cassada-grater, looking like a bread-grater; this, rubbed with the handle of a spoon, makes a very efficient crackling accompaniment. Another produces the jaw-bone of a horse, the teeth of which rattle when it is shaken. A third has detached from its leather one of his stirrup-irons, and is hanging it on a string to do duty as a triangle. The top of the music is not always supplied by fifes. Sometimes there will be two fiddles, sometimes a concertina, or, what is more approved, because it has "bigger voice," a flutina. On asking to see this strange instrument I was shown the familiar accordion.

Their chief dances are the Valse, Polka, Schottische, and Quadrilles in five figures, of which the fifth figure is the most popular, or as they would say "sweet them most." This figure goes either to $\frac{6}{8}$ or $\frac{2}{4}$ time. The $\frac{2}{4}$ figures of the Quadrilles are often used for Polka, and Polka and Schottische tunes are always interchangeable, the only difference being that the Schottische requires a slower time.

CXVII.

The ball opens with a set of Quadrilles:—

1st Figure.

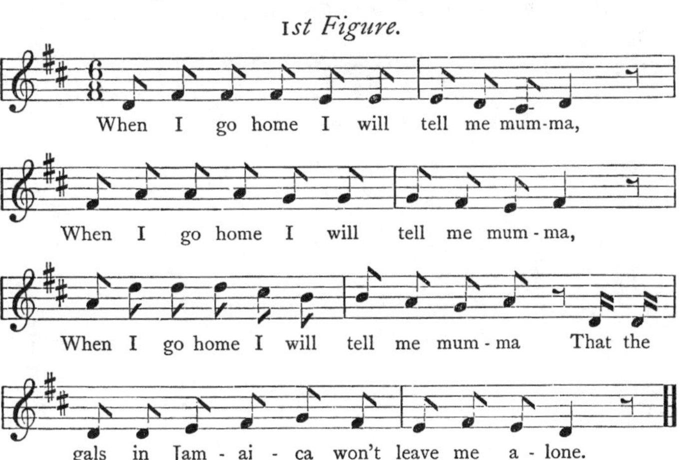
When I go home I will tell me mum-ma,
When I go home I will tell me mum - ma,
When I go home I will tell me mum - ma That the
gals in Jam - ai - ca won't leave me a - lone.

This is the production of a white musician to whom the black girls were especially attentive.

CXVIII.

2nd Figure.

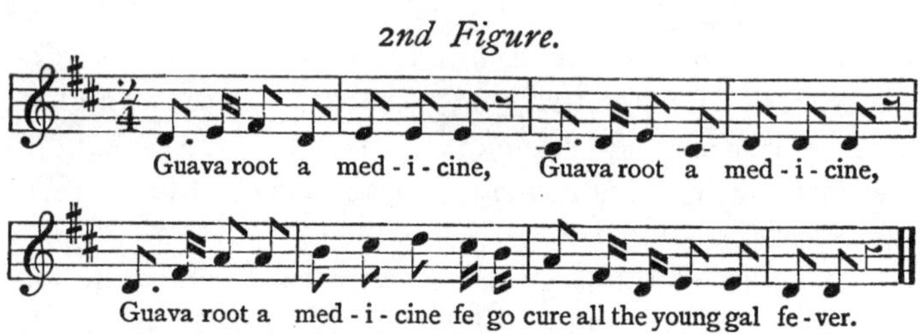
Guava root a med - i - cine, Guava root a med - i - cine,
Guava root a med - i - cine fe go cure all the young gal fe - ver.

A decoction of the root of the Guava is used in cases of fever.

"Medicine" is pronounced so as to rhyme with Edison.

CXIX.

3rd Figure.

Crahss-lookin' dog up - 'tairs, Crahss-lookin' dog up - 'tairs; I
lift up me foot an' I hit him a kick an' him roll up him tail an'
run. What you fe do with that?
What you fe do with that? I meet him up-'tairs an' I
hit him a kick an' he roll up him tail an' run.

See note to "Parson Puss and Parson Dog" (p. 93), also Author's Preface.

CXX.

4th Figure.

Goatridge have some set a gal So - so shirt them
can't wash. Give me back me soap an' blue,
Give me back me soap an' blue, Give me back me
soap an' 'tarch, So - so shirt them can't wash.

Goatridge is the name of a neighbouring hamlet. When a boy "gives out his shirts to wash" he also provides the girl with soap, blue and starch.

So-so means even. It also means only, as:—"I get so-so potato fe nyam," I only got potatoes to eat.

"Shirt" is pronounced almost "shut."

CXXI.

5th Figure.

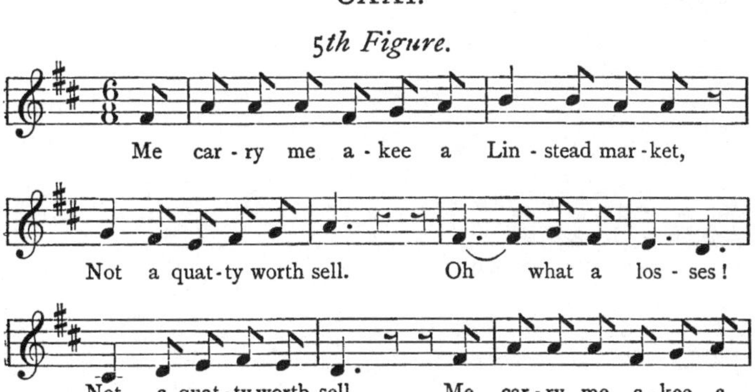
Me car - ry me a - kee a Lin - stead mar - ket,
Not a quat - ty worth sell. Oh what a los - ses!
Not a quat - ty worth sell. Me car - ry me a - kee a

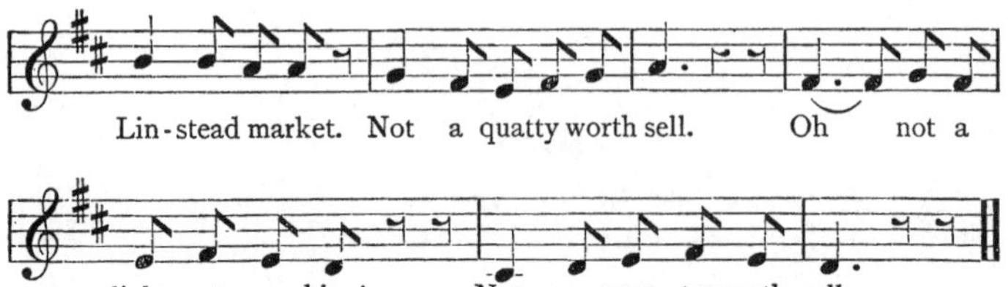
Lin - stead market. Not a quatty worth sell. Oh not a
light, not a bite! Not a quat - ty worth sell.

The Akee (*Cupania edulis*), pronounced *acky*, is a handsome tree producing something which one hardly knows whether to call a fruit or a vegetable. Besides the edible part, the beautiful scarlet capsule contains a substance which is poisonous. Deaths by misadventure through carelessness in its preparation for table occur every year.

The time of these Quadrille tunes will be pretty accurately judged. They would all come under *Allegro* except the First, which is slower than the others, and it might be headed *Allegretto* or even *Andantino*. The Third figure is not much used, and many dancers do not know the step. Its place is generally supplied by one of the other figures. The most popular of all is the Fifth, of which we have many examples to give. The step is regulated by two beats in the bar of six, so we find that they dance it also to $\frac{2}{4}$ time, as for instance :—

CXXII.

5th Figure.

Since Dor - a Lo - gan a wahk with Gal - la - woss, The
man them a beat them wife with junk-a 'tick. Why, why,

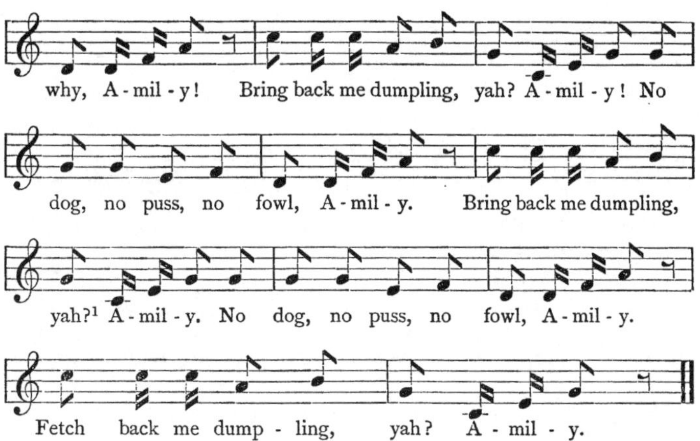
why, A - mil - y! Bring back me dumpling, yah? A - mil - y! No
dog, no puss, no fowl, A - mil - y. Bring back me dumpling,
yah?[1] A - mil - y. No dog, no puss, no fowl, A - mil - y.
Fetch back me dump - ling, yah? A - mil - y.

This has to go very fast, indeed as fast as the words of the second bar can be spoken. It will be found then to correspond to a moderate *Allegro* in six time counted in two.

Two stories are mixed up here. One of the girl who walks with the Gallawoss—a Lizard with a gold eye and an undeserved reputation for biting—which leads to an age the reverse of golden, when the men beat their wives with junka (short) sticks. And the other, of some incident connected with breakfast in the field, when Amily ate somebody's dumpling and laid the blame on the usual scapegoat, the cat.

CXXIII.

The rapid speed necessitated by some forms of $\frac{2}{4}$ time just suits the following:—

5th Figure.

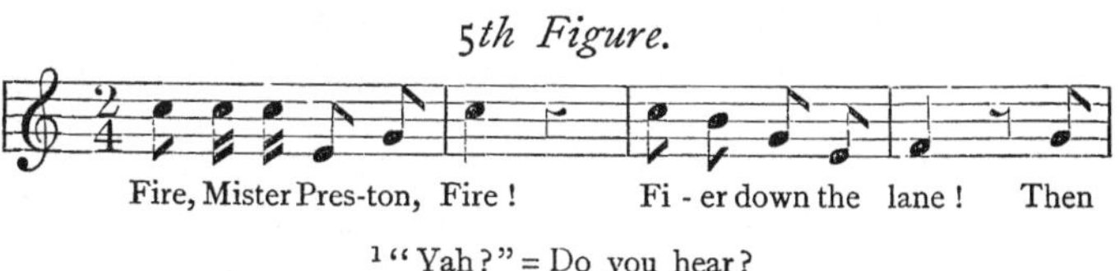
Fire, Mister Pres-ton, Fire! Fi - er down the lane! Then

[1] "Yah?" = Do you hear?

send the bri-gade fe go out the fire, The bri-gade can't out the
fire. Fire, Mis - ter Pres - ton! Fire, Mis - ter Pres - ton!
Fi - er down the lane! Fire, Mis - ter Pres - ton!
Fire, Mis - ter Pres - ton! Fi - er down the lane!

CXXIV.

Where the beat is in crotchets it sounds unduly slow :—

5th Figure.

Tief cahf - fee, Tief cahf - fee, Tief cahf -
fee, Be - nig - na Field, fe go buy silk dress, Fe go show them Gardon
boy, fe go show them Gardon boy, fe go show them Gardon
boy, Be - nig - na Field, you tief cahf - fee.

Benigna[1] Field steals some coffee to get money to buy a silk dress to show off to the Gardon boys. (Gardon is a place, not a family.)

CXXV.

5th Figure.

Fan me, sol-dier man, fan me; Fan me, sol-dier man,
fan me; Fan me, sol-dier man, fan me oh!
Gal, you char-ac-ter gone! Sake 'a ten shilling shahl,
Sake a ten shill-ing shahl, Sake a ten shill-ing
shahl oh! Make me char-ac-ter gone.

[1] Other unusual girls' names are Ambrogine, Ateline, Irene, Melmorine. These rhyme with Queen. The same Italian *i* is found in Elgiva, Seppelita, Barnita, Justina, aud the English *i* in Alvira, Marina. The next are all accented, like the last six, on the penultimate; Etilda, Iota, Clarista, Pastora, Barzella, Zedilla, Amanda, Agarta (evidently a variant of Agatha), Timinetia (like Polynesia), Cherryana, Indiana. Then there is Hettybel, and one girl has this astonishing combination—Ataria (rhymes with Samaria), Azadell (? Isabel).

CXXVI.

Schottische.

Manny Clark a you da man! Manny Clark a you da man!

So so ride you ride a Ginger Piece, All the gal them a dead fe

you. Oh you take 'not-ta boil soup, take salt fish 'tick in it,

Gal, you want fe come kill me? Oh you take 'notta a boil soup,

take salt fish 'tick in it, Gal, you want fe come kill me?

Manny Clark, a popular player of dance tunes, goes to Ginger Piece and is overwhelmed with attentions by the girls. He addresses himself as follows:—"Manny Clark, you are the man! You just ride to Ginger Piece and all the girls are dying for you." Then, turning to one of them, he adds:—"Oh, you boil the soup with your best, taking Anatto and salt fish to stick into it. Do you want to kill me with kindness?"

Anatto gives a rich yellow colour to the soup. Salt fish (stockfish) is one of the principal articles of diet of the peasantry.

CXXVII.

Schottische.

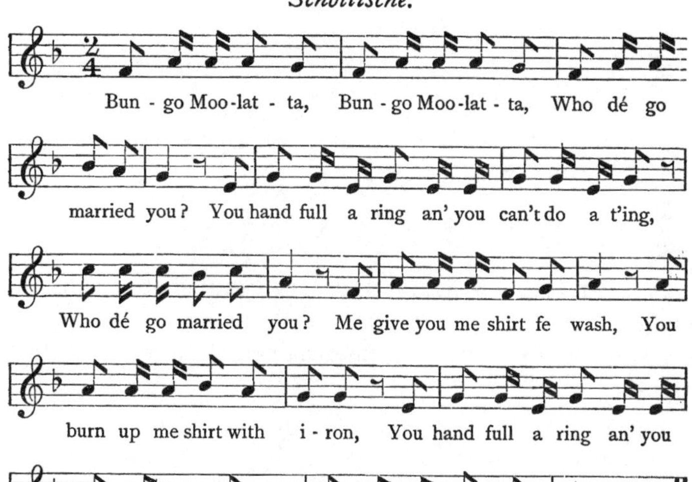
Bun - go Moo-lat - ta, Bun - go Moo-lat - ta, Who dé go
married you? You hand full a ring an' you can't do a t'ing,
Who dé go married you? Me give you me shirt fe wash, You
burn up me shirt with i - ron, You hand full a ring an' you

can't do a t'ing, Who dé go mar - ried you?

"You Bungo Mulatto, who is going to marry you? Your ring-bedecked fingers can't do anything. When I gave you my shirt to wash you burned it with an over-hot iron."

Bungo (rhymes with Mungo) means a rough un-civilized African.

A Mulatto is the child of two Brown parents, Brown being the offspring of Black and White. He has rather a yellow skin.

CXXVIII.

5th Figure.

Bahl, Ad · a you must . bahl,

Bahl, Ad - a you must bahl,
Bahl, Ad - a you must bahl, Ad - a you must
bahl till the cock say coo - coo - coo - coo - ry co.

Ada has been naughty and has been shut up for a night in the dark. The poor little thing is "bawling," crying out in terror of the nameless horrors of the night.

CXXIX.

2nd Figure.

Rise a roof in the morn-ing, Rise a roof in the
morn-ing; Tell all the nig-ger them to come, come, come,
Rise a roof in the morning. The Monkey and the Baboon them was
sit-ting on the wall, Rise a roof in the morn-ing;
I an' my wife can - not a - gree, Rise a roof in the

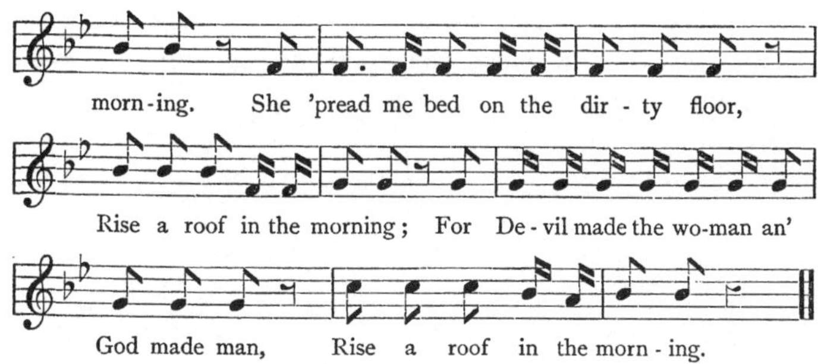
morn-ing. She 'pread me bed on the dir - ty floor,
Rise a roof in the morning; For De-vil made the wo-man an'
God made man, Rise a roof in the morn-ing.

"Rise a roof" seems to mean, as far as I can understand the explanation, "raise the roof"; as we might say, "row enough to blow the roof off."

"Baboon" always has this accent on the first syllable and a French *a*.

The Blacks do not mind calling themselves niggers, but a White man must not call them so. To say "black nehgher" is an offence not to be forgiven. The word is used again quite kindly in the following:—

CXXX.

Jig.

Oh we went to the riv - er an' we couldn' get a -
cross, We jump on the nig-ger back we think it was a
horse.[1] Then Ste - phen, Ste - phen, Ste - phen
boy, Ste - phen, Ste - phen, poor Ste - phen!

[1] A last reminder to pronounce "acrahss," "harse." The Negro rejects the sound *aw* altogether and always changes it to *ah*.

A party get to one of the bends of Four-and-twenty River, so called because the road crosses and recrosses it twenty-four times. Stephen carries them all over.

CXXXI.

Polka.

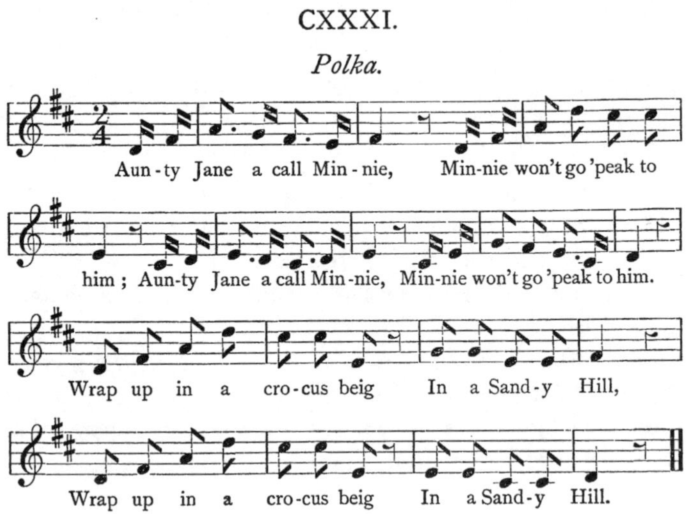
Aun-ty Jane a call Min-nie, Min-nie won't go 'peak to
him; Aun-ty Jane a call Min-nie, Min-nie won't go 'peak to him.
Wrap up in a cro-cus beig In a Sand-y Hill,
Wrap up in a cro-cus beig In a Sand-y Hill.

Aunty Jane does not want Minnie to keep company with the boys at Sandy Hill. Of course Minnie wants to go, and she does go. Aunty Jane sets off to bring her home. When she reaches Sandy Hill shc calls. Minnie hears, but will not go and speak to her. She hides in the coffee-store by wrapping herself in a crocus bag or sack. "Crocus" is a rough cheap material. Coffee ready for market is put in the finer and smaller canvas bags.

CXXXII.

Valse.

Mar - ty, Mar - ty, me wan-ty go home, Mar - ty

Mar - ty, me wan-ty go home, Mar - ty, Mar - ty, me
wan-ty go home, Me wan-ty go home back a yard.
Tell me mum - ma say me want - y come home, Me want-y come
home, Me want - y come home, Tell me mum - ma say me
want - y come home, Me want - y come home back a yard.

Martin has been flogging his wife—not an unusual condition of things—and she wants to go home to her mother. He will take her message quite loyally. The matter will be arranged and they will be good friends living apart. Before long she will go back to him of her own accord. They make up their quarrels as quickly as they fall into them.

CXXXIII.

5th Figure.

What make you shave old Hall, Rosie Fowler? What make you shave old
Hall? What make you shave old Hall, Ro - sie Fow - ler?

What make you shave old Hall? What make you shave old
Hall, Ro - sie Fow - ler? What make you shave old Hall? Mis - ter
Bar-ber have two teeth a him mout', Them sweet like a su - gar - plum.

Rosie Fowler left old Hall for Mr. Barber, and being remonstrated with, shaved him, *i.e.* gave him a good beating.

CXXXIV.

Mazurka.

Run, Mos - es, run, Mis-ter Walk - er da come;
Run, Mos - es, run, Mis-ter Walk - er da come. If you
buck your right foot, buck your left foot, Nev - er try look back; If you
buck your right foot, buck your left foot, Nev - er try look back.

To "buck" is to strike, and the word is applied to a stumbling horse, who is said to buck his foot against a stone, or simply to buck. It also means to butt with the head and is most likely a corruption of this word. Bucking, or charging stag-fashion with the head, is the favourite way for women to fight. Here is an account of such a contest:—

CXXXV.

5th Figure.

Whé you da do? Whé you da do? Whé you da do make
Sa - rah buck you? Whé you da do? Whé you da do?
Whé you da do make Sa - rah buck you? A-de - la da jump but
Sa - rah buck him, A-de - la da jump but Sa - rah buck him,
A-de - la da jump but Sa - rah buck him. Whé you da do make
Sa - rah buck you? You A-de - la ho— you ought to shame!
You A-de - la ho— you ought to shame! You A-de - la ho—
you ought to shame! Whé you da do make Sa - rah buck you?

Fights between women are by no means uncommon. This was a case of *cherchez l'homme.* The ladies both wanted to marry the same man. The "sing" was evidently composed by one of Sarah's partisans for the words are:—"What did you do to make Sarah buck you? Adela jumped, but Sarah bucked her. You, Adela, oh you ought to be ashamed!" Adela's sideway jump was not quick enough to save her from Sarah's head.

"Whé you da do?" literally, What you is do? for What you did do? meaning What did you do? So, if they were trying to talk "deep English," for "Adela da jump" they would substitute "Adela is jump" and think it was quite right.

CXXXVI.

5th Figure.

Mother William hold back Le - ah! Mother William hold back Le -
ah! Me tell you say hold back Le - ah! Hold
back Le - ah let go Jane Ann! Den a Le - ah Le - ah dead
'way, Den a Le - ah Le - ah dead 'way, Let go Jane Ann!
Let go Jane Ann! Hold back Le - ah, let go Jane Ann!

This is sung *agitato* and pulsates with excitement. We see the bustling, restless action—Mother Williams holding Leah, who is frantic to get at Jane Ann, and who faints with exhaustion as she struggles to escape from the strong arms thrown round her. "Let go Jane Ann!" cry the bystanders, which means:—Make Jane Ann go away, get her out of Leah's sight.

CXXXVII.

This seems a fitting moment to introduce:—

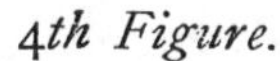
4th Figure.

Oh Gen-er-al Jack-son! Oh Gen-er-al Jack-son!

Oh Gen-er-al Jack-son! Oh you kill all the Black man them!

Oh what a wrongful judgment! Oh what a wrongful judgment!

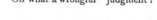

Oh what a wrongful judgment! You kill all the Black man them.

Oh what a aw-ful mourning! Oh what a aw-ful mourning!

Oh what a aw-ful mourning You bring on St. Thomas peo-ple!

This is the other side of the question, referred to in the Digging Sing, No. 88. It is the rebellion of 1865 again, from the point of view of that section of the Blacks who considered themselves aggrieved at the measures taken for its suppression.

CXXXVIII.

We get a glimpse of the doings of the soldiery in peaceable times in :—

5th Figure.

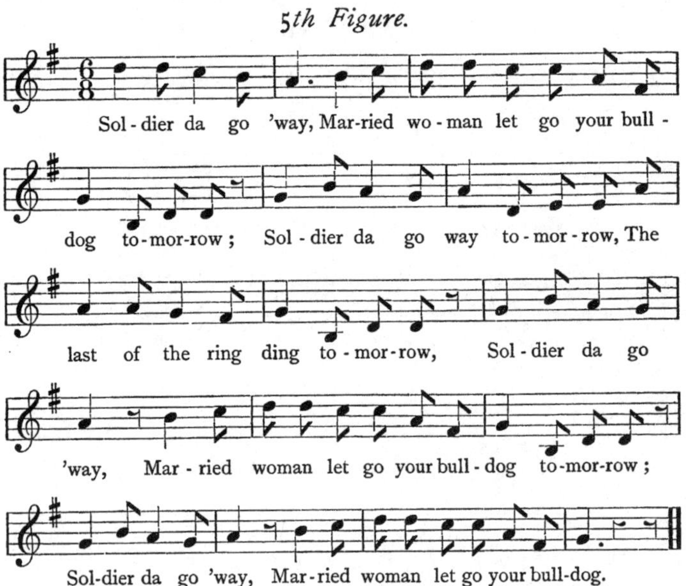
Sol - dier da go 'way, Mar-ried wo - man let go your bull -
dog to-mor-row ; Sol - dier da go way to - mor - row, The
last of the ring ding to - mor-row, Sol - dier da go
'way, Mar - ried woman let go your bull - dog to-mor-row ;
Sol-dier da go 'way, Mar-ried woman let go your bull-dog.

The soldiers are shifting their quarters. As they are apt to be rather riotous on the night before departure, the owner of the bull-dog is advised to unchain him so that he may guard her property more effectually.

CXXXIX.

There is also a tender side to the parting:—

4th Figure.

Don't cry too much, Ja - mai - ca gal, First West will soon come

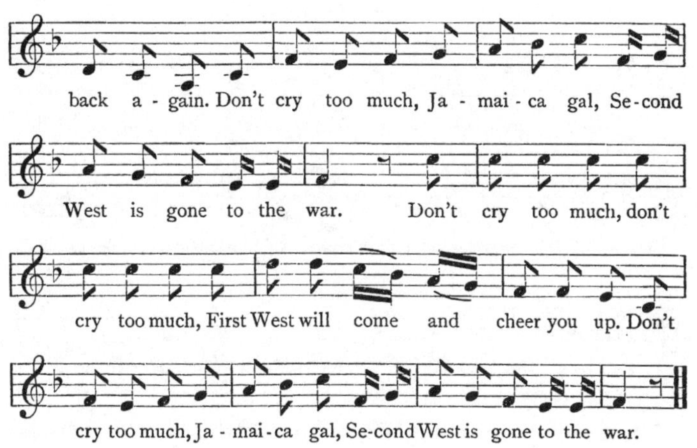
back a - gain. Don't cry too much, Ja - mai - ca gal, Se-cond
West is gone to the war. Don't cry too much, don't
cry too much, First West will come and cheer you up. Don't
cry too much, Ja - mai - ca gal, Se-cond West is gone to the war.

CXL.

A few years ago Jamaica boasted of water as efficacious as that of Mecca in the opinion of some people. It seems to have lost its repute in these sceptical days :—

4th Figure.

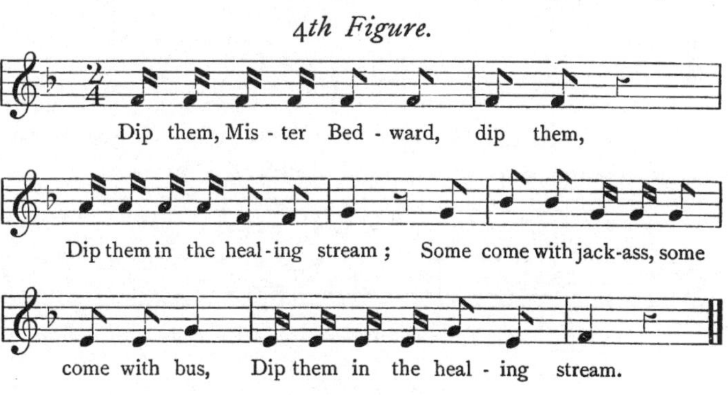
Dip them, Mis - ter Bed - ward, dip them,
Dip them in the heal-ing stream ; Some come with jack-ass, some
come with bus, Dip them in the heal - ing stream.

CXLI.

It says much for the expertness of the dancers that they can fit the same steps to tunes of such varying accent as the two last examples present. Here is another which differs again :—

4th Figure.

Ver - y well, ver - y well, Mis - ter Col - lin now, An' him

leave an' join Sab-ba - tar - ian bands, An' him lose the whole of his

mem - bers now, Oh then poor Sab - ba - tar - ian bands!

Mr. Collin was a minister who told his flock that he had made a mistake in keeping Sunday holy, and that for the future he would have service on Saturday and the people were to come to church on that day and work on Sunday. The "sing" suggests that his congregation was not persuaded by his arguments.

CXLII.

The light-hearted way in which the Negro turns serious things into fun is well illustrated by:—

4th Figure.

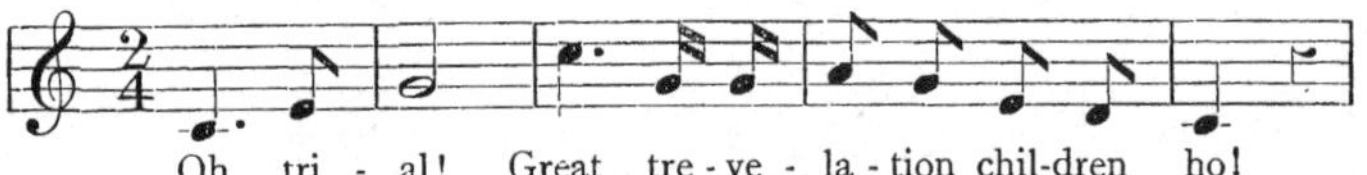
Oh tri - al! Great tre - ve - la - tion chil-dren ho!

Tri - al! We're bound to leave this world. Bap-tis', Bap-tis',

Baptis' till I die. I been grown up in the Baptis' side an' die under Baptis'

rule. Oh tri - al! Great tre - ve - la - tion children ho!
Tri - al! We're bound to leave this world. Church-light, Church-light,
Church-light till I die, I been grown up in the Church-light side an'
die un - der Church-light rule. Oh! tri - al! Great tre - ve -
la - tion children ho! Tri - al! We're bound to leave this world.

And so on through all the sects and persuasions, Wesleyan, etc., etc., among them Mettetis (Methodist).

There is no doubt about the word being *trevelation*, a mixture of Revelation, one of their favourite books in the Bible, and tribulation, for which it is intended. The wrong phrasing of two notes to "bound" is as they give it. We should allow only one.

CXLIII.

Every district has its rival churches and the various ministers have to humour their congregations, and not preach too hard things to them, so as to keep them from deserting to the enemy.

2nd Figure.

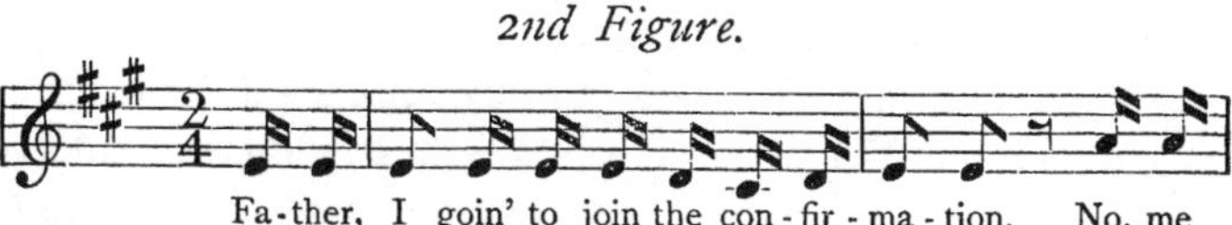
Fa-ther, I goin' to join the con - fir - ma - tion. No, me

son, you must have a lit - tle pa - tien', Why I
tell you to have a lit - tle pa - tien',
You must go an' read the Rev - e - la - tion. I
heard from my old gen - er - a - tion That they
nev - er go an' join the con - fir - ma - tion, For they
did - n' have that great oc - ca - sion To
leave an' go an' join the con - fir - ma - tion.

It will have been observed that rhyming is the last thing sought after. Here, however, we have a genius who has set his mind upon it with some success. Patience, as pronounced by the Jamaican without the final letters, is a good and new rhyme to the rest. In the old days of slavery, says the father, they did not have the occasion (*i.e.* opportunity) to leave their work to go and be confirmed.

The Black man is such an accomplished actor that he can assume any character. In these sings he throws off the stage trappings and shows his real attitude towards religion, his indifference and levity. He does not take it as a serious matter at all, and it has no effect upon his daily life. To go to church is a mark of respectability. To obtain that mark is one of his reasons for going. The other reason is to show his clothes and his boots. He will talk like a saint for the mere pleasure of rolling out words, and the ministers have to pretend to believe something of what he says. They are not, however, really deceived, and will tell you in private with a sigh that Christianity makes no progress; it is profession without practice. Of the Negro's real religion, which is bound up with Obeah, we get hardly a hint in the sings. This is what we should expect. Some things lie too deep for words and a man's religion is one of them. One general reference I have been able to find, and one particular one, and that is all. Here is the first:—

CXLIV.

5th Figure.

O-beah down dé why oh! O-beah down dé,
O-beah down dé why oh! O-beah down dé.
Gib-er-al-tar is a well fine place but O-beah down dé,
Gib-er-al-tar is a well fine place but O-beah down dé.

CXLV.

And here the second :—

5th Figure.

The o - ther day me waist-coat cut, The o - ther day me
waist-coat cut, The o - ther day me waist-coat cut, What a
pain an' grief to me. I spend me mon - ey but the
beggar don't dead, I spend me money but the beggar don't dead, I
spend me mon-ey but the beggar don't dead, What a pain an' grief to
me. All me mon - ey gone like but - ter 'gainst sun,
All me money gone like butter 'gainst sun, All me money gone like
but - ter 'gainst sun, What a pain an' grief to me !
Sake of the man me live 'pon tree, Sake of the man me live 'pon tree,
Sake of the man me live 'pon tree, What a pain an' grief to me !

Obeah (pronounced in two syllables, Ob-ya, with short Italian vowels) is the dark blot upon this fair island of Jamaica. In every district there is an Obeah-man, or Bush-doctor, as he is often called, from his supposed knowledge of herb simples. He is by no means the innocent person which this latter designation would seem to imply. He deals in magic and sorcery of all descriptions, and there is not a Black man who does not believe in his powers. They consult him on every conceivable business and he gets heavy fees. He will secure a man the favour of his master so that he shall not lose his place, or help him to revenge a wrong, real or fancied. And herein lies the danger. The puerilities of inefficacious charms and mysterious ceremonies with which he deludes his clients are not all. He keeps poison in his bag, and for sufficient reward arsenic has been obtained to put in the liqueur, or ground glass for the coffee. The Government attempts in vain to stamp out the evil.

The story of the last sing is briefly this. A has a friend who is an Obeah-man. From him he gets Obeah to injure an enemy B. The enemy does not suffer. So A says his waistcoat is torn, a figurative way of expressing the fact that he is beaten, B's Obeah turning out to be stronger than A's and able to repel it. Having indiscreetly talked about what he meant to do to B, B reports him to the police, and he has to abscond and seek shelter in the bush till the matter blows over.

CXLVI.

It is a pleasure to be able to leave the hypocrisy of Negro Christianity, and the lurid atmosphere of Obeah and to return to every-day amusements.

5th Figure.

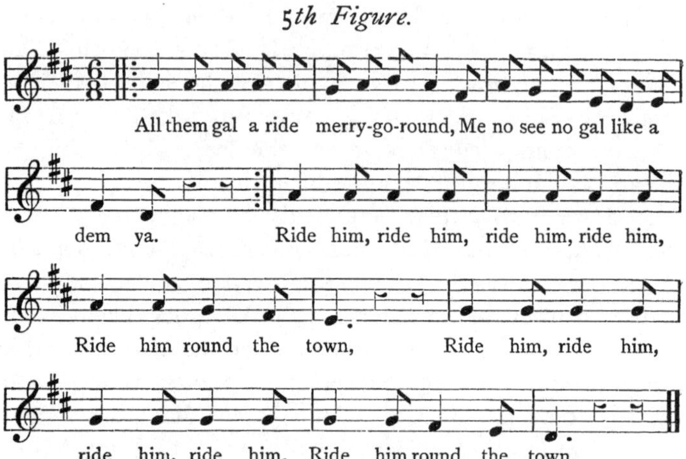
All them gal a ride merry-go-round, Me no see no gal like a
dem ya. Ride him, ride him, ride him, ride him,
Ride him round the town, Ride him, ride him,
ride him, ride him, Ride him round the town.

The merry-go-round is popular. "I never saw such girls," says an admiring bystander. Literally, "I have not seen any girls like those (here) girls." A neighbour of mine used to be made very angry when he first came to Jamaica because when he asked "Have you seen so-and-so?" the answer always was "I don't see him." This is good negro English for "I haven't seen him." It does not mean, as he thought, "I don't see him now," and the poor boy could not understand why his master got so "crahss."

CXLVII.

5th Figure.

Mer - ry - go-round a go fall down, fall down, fall down,
Mer - ry - go - round a go fall down, Sake a de worth-less

ri - der. Ri - der, ri - der, try to sit down good;
Ri - der, ri - der, try to sit down good; Ri - der, ri - der,
try to sit down good, Mer - ry - go-round a go fall down.

Grammar nowhere as usual. It was not the Merry-go-round that was going to fall down, but the worthless (*i.e.* bad) rider who was going to fall off. "Try to sit down good" is an exhortation to hold on well. This curious use of "try" is found again in :—

CXLVIII.

Mazurka.

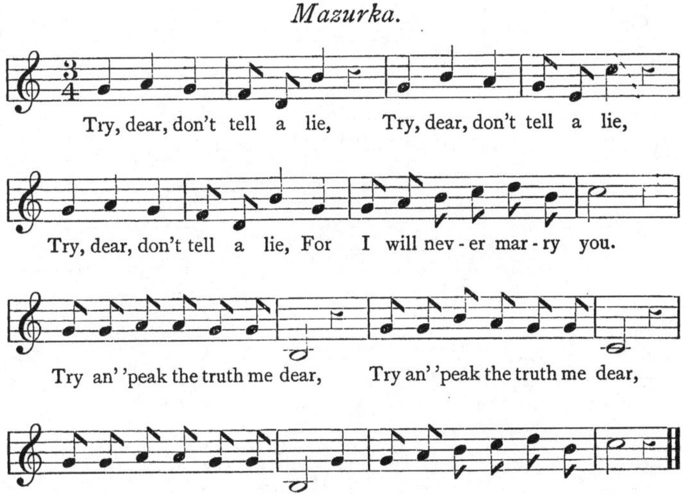
Try, dear, don't tell a lie, Try, dear, don't tell a lie,
Try, dear, don't tell a lie, For I will nev - er mar - ry you.
Try an' 'peak the truth me dear, Try an' 'peak the truth me dear,
Try an' 'peak the truth me dear, An' you shall get the ring me dear.

CXLIX.

Here are two more references to the colour question:—

1st Figure.

Look how you mout', Look how you mout',
Look how you mout' fe go kiss moo-lat - ta. Look how you mout',
Look how you mout', Look how you mout' like a pan.

CL.

Valse.

Breez - y say him no want Brown la - dy,
Breez - y say him no want Brown la - dy,
Breez - y say him no want Brown la - dy,
Af - ter - ward him go take Brown la - dy.
Why! Why! Why, Breez - y! Why! Why!

Why, Breez - y! Why! Why! Why, Breez - y!
Think you say you no want Brown la - dy.

CLI.

Here are three sings referring to Colon, the port of disembarkation for labourers on the Panama Canal:—

5th Figure.

I - saac Park gone a Co - lon, I - saac Park
gone a Co - lon, I - saac Park gone a Co - lon,
Co - lon boat a go kill them boy. Co - lon bo - low[1]
gone a Co - lon, Co-lon bo-low gone a Co - lon,
Co - lon bo - low gone a Co - lon,
Co - lon boat a go kill them boy.

It was not the boat from Kingston to Colon that killed the boys; the deaths took place on the other

[1] *Bolow*, comrade.

side. Many were due to fever, but more, if the stories current here are true, to organised assassination. The wages were very large, and when a Jamaica boy has money in his pocket he gets "boastify." This annoyed the low-class mongrels. A Coolie who was there described to me the proceedings of one night, when the 'panish (by which is meant any straight-haired people) went out in a band and murdered every woolly-haired man they met. They began at one end of the camp, a straight line of barrack huts. Some of the victims were shot through the windows, others slashed with cutlasses. Where there were no lights the assassins passed their hands over the strangers' heads, and if they felt wool, revolver or cutlass did its work. Straight-haired Coolies, that is to say, East Indians, were allowed to go unharmed.

CLII.

5th Figure.

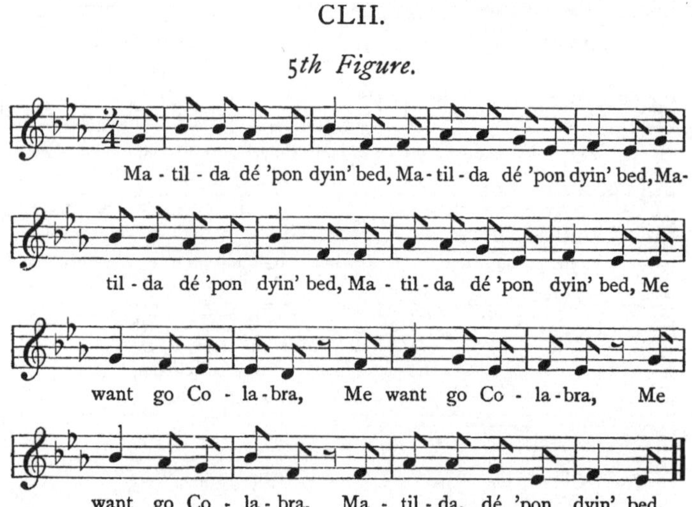
Ma - til - da dé 'pon dyin' bed, Ma - til - da dé 'pon dyin' bed, Ma-
til - da dé 'pon dyin' bed, Ma - til - da dé 'pon dyin' bed, Me
want go Co - la - bra, Me want go Co - la - bra, Me
want go Co - la - bra, Ma - til - da, dé 'pon dyin' bed.

When anybody is very ill all the members of the family, including quite distant relatives, think it incumbent upon them to go to the sick person's yard. They crowd into the house and sick-room and pour out a clatter of talk.

Colabra (Culebra) is a place near Colon. Matilda must have been an old Jamaica acquaintance who had gone over to settle there.

CLIII.

5th Figure.

Mas' Char - ley say want kiss Mat - ty,
Kiss with a will-ing mind, Me ra - ra- bum why! Colon money
done, Me ra - ra - bum why! Col-on mon-ey done.

"Me rarabum" is a nonsense phrase equivalent to "my boy." "My boy, hi! the money I made at Colon is done!"

CLIV.

Here is the lament of an out-of-work cabdriver:—

5th Figure.

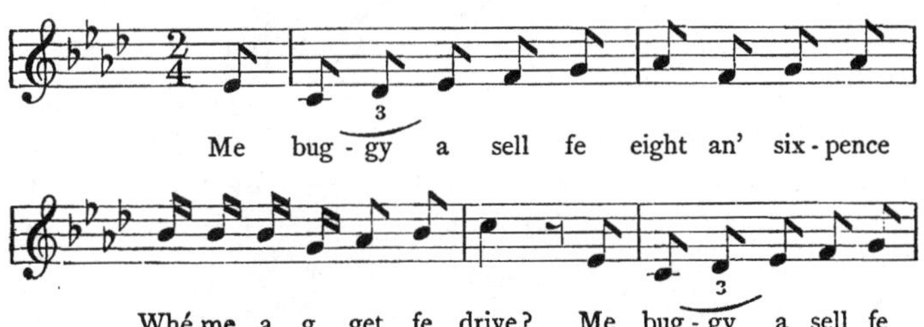
Me bug - gy a sell fe eight an' six-pence
Whé me a g get fe drive? Me bug-gy a sell fe

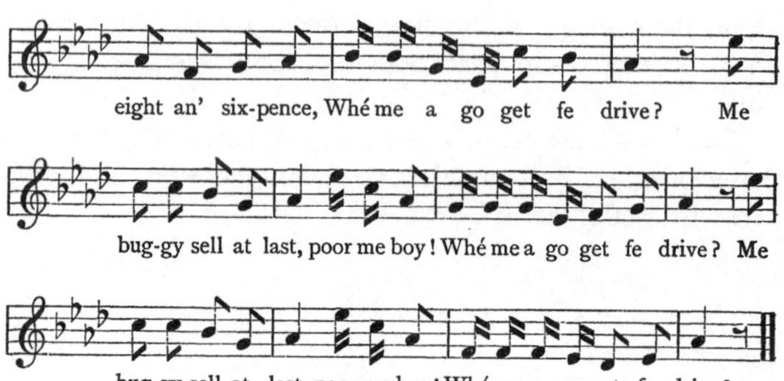
eight an' six-pence, Whé me a go get fe drive? Me
bug-gy sell at last, poor me boy! Whé me a go get fe drive? Me
bug-gy sell at last, poor me boy! Whé me a go get fe drive?

CLV.

The words of the next dance have a certain interest, but the tune is poor:—

Polka.

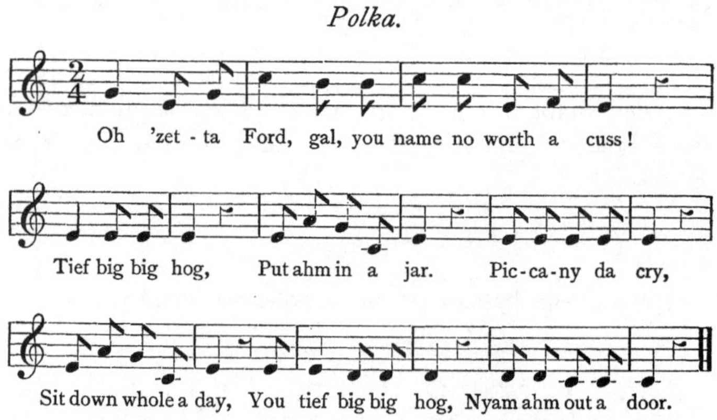
Oh 'zet - ta Ford, gal, you name no worth a cuss!
Tief big big hog, Put ahm in a jar. Pic-ca-ny da cry,
Sit down whole a day, You tief big big hog, Nyam ahm out a door.

The girl stole the pig, killed it, cut it up and put the meat into a jar. This was done out in the bush, far away from her yard, and took the whole day. Meanwhile her poor little babies were starving at home, having been left without any one to look after them.

CLVI.

There is an idyllic simplicity about the following:—

5th Figure.

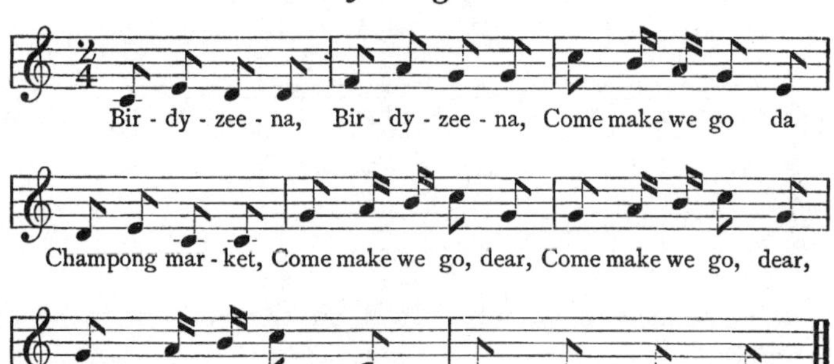
Bir - dy - zee - na, Bir - dy - zee - na, Come make we go da
Champong mar - ket, Come make we go, dear, Come make we go, dear,
Come make we go da Cham - pong mar - ket.

CLVII.

5th Figure.

Me an' Katie no 'gree, Katie wash me shirt in a sea.

If you t'ink a lie, If you t'ink a lie, Look in a Ka-tie yeye.

CLVIII.

Water seems formerly to have been scarce in Kingston, judging by the following:—

5th Figure.

Down town gal no have no wa - ter to wash them head to

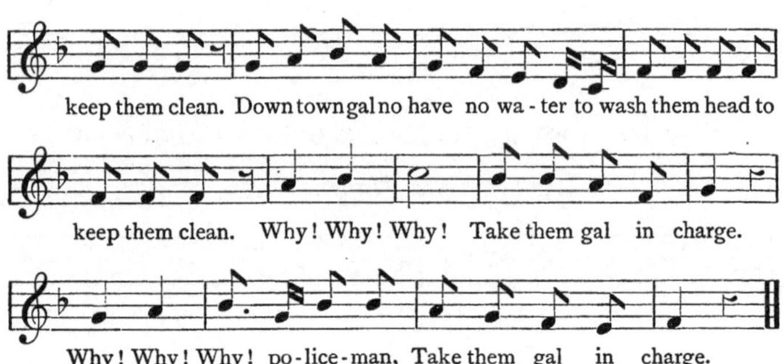
keep them clean. Down town gal no have no wa - ter to wash them head to
keep them clean. Why! Why! Why! Take them gal in charge.
Why! Why! Why! po-lice-man, Take them gal in charge.

CLIX.

The policeman is not always on the spot when he is wanted :—

4th Figure.

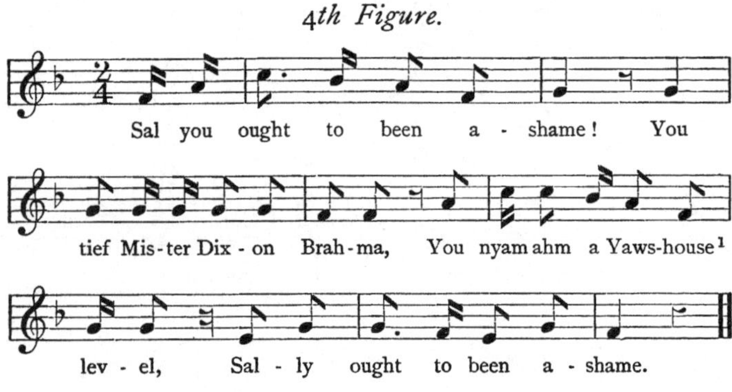
Sal you ought to been a - shame! You
tief Mis-ter Dix - on Brah-ma, You nyam ahm a Yaws-house[1]
lev - el, Sal - ly ought to been a - shame.

In this country any plot of ground that is moderately flat is called a level.

CLX.

4th Figure.

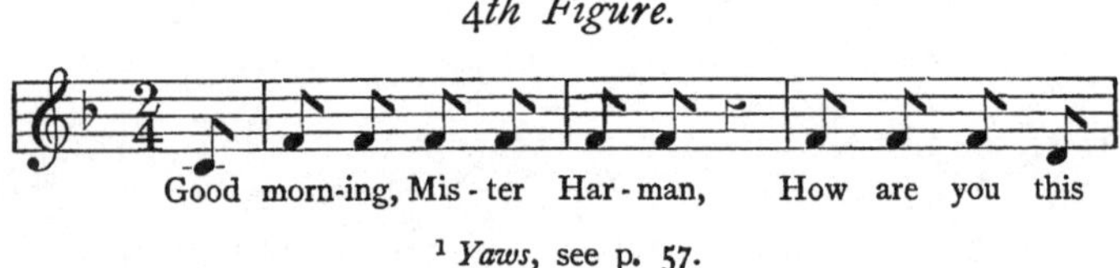
Good morn-ing, Mis - ter Har - man, How are you this

[1] *Yaws*, see p. 57.

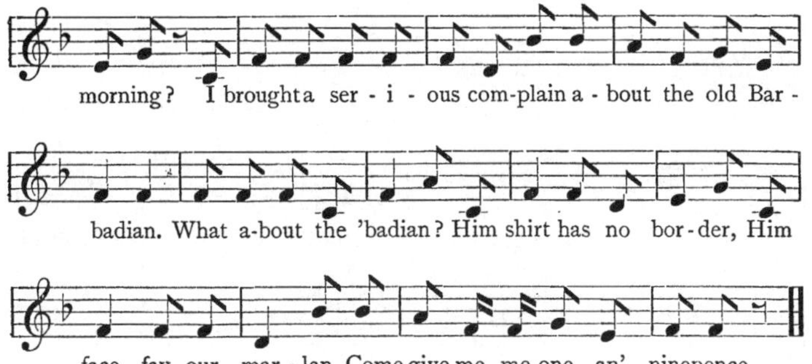
morning? I brought a ser - i - ous com-plain a - bout the old Bar -
badian. What a-bout the 'badian? Him shirt has no bor - der, Him
face fav - our mar - lan, Come give me me one an' ninepence.

The singer goes to Mr. Harman, who is employing the Barbadian (whom he accuses of wearing a ragged shirt and having a face like a marlingspike), to try and get some money which the latter owes the complainant. This is an excellent example in short of an interview between two Black men. Of the sixteen bars four are occupied with salutation, four with complaint, and four with abuse. Two are given to a question as to the cause of complaint which receives no answer, and two to a demand for money owed by another person. So we have three-quarters of the interview devoted in equal parts to compliment, complaint, and abuse; one-eighth to an attempt on the part of the person interviewed to discover what is amiss; and one-eighth to a demand for money from the wrong man.

CLXI.

The lovers' quarrel which comes next is evidently not serious:—

5th Figure.

Hul-lo me hon - ey! Hul-lo me su - gar! Hul-lo me old time

gal! Oh den, gal, if you love me, Why don't you write me?
Hul-lo me old time gal! Hul-lo me hon-ey! Hul-lo me su-gar!
Hul-lo me old time boy! Oh den, boy, I wouldn' married you,
Not for a far-din', Hul-lo me old time boy!

CLXII.

5th Figure.

When mumma dare you say you sick, Dis mum-ma gone
you get bet-ter, 'tan' 'teady till him come 'tan' 'teady,
'tan' 'tead-y till him come 'tan' 'tead-y.

When mamma tells her daughter to take her hoe and come out into the field she feigns sickness. Her brother comes in and finds her quite well. "All right," he says, "just (dis) you stand steady ('teudy, French *eu*), just you wait till she comes home and you will get a flogging."

CLXIII.

We never go far without meeting some story about petty thieving :—

5th Figure.

Oh Jil - ly oh! how you man-age a jump the win-dow?

Oh Jil - ly oh! how you man-age a jump the window? Doc-tor

Clark a one an' tan-ner, Ma-jor Black a two an' six, Mis-ter

Nel-son three an' six, How you manage a jump the win-dow?

Jilly had been "tiefing" money and made her escape by jumping out of window. "Tanner," for sixpence, is common in English slang but not here. It seems to have been derived in this case from the White soldiers at Newcastle.

CLXIV.

5th Figure.

James Brown, you mahmy call you. James Brown a shake him shoulder.

Sake a the young gal but-terdore, James Brown a shake him shoulder.

To express dissent they do not shake their heads but wriggle the whole of their bodies. It is a most expressive action.

A butterdore, more properly butter-dough, is a kind of cake.

CLXV.

The next repeats the idea of No. CXVIII., but in the mouth of a girl.

4th Figure.

When I go home I will tell me mum-ma say,
When I go home I will tell me mum-ma say,
When I go home I will tell me mum-ma say That the
boy in the coun - try love me ver - y much.

CLXVI.

The next is the only example of pure fiction that I have met with :—

5th Figure.

Feather, feather, feather, Ba - by da born with

feather. You cut off the fowl head an' boil it in a 'tew-pan,
Ba-by da born with feather. Feather, feather oh!
Ba-by da born with feather. Feather, feather oh!
Ba-by da born with feather. You cut off the fowl head an'
boil it with the feather, So the ba-by go born with feather. I
hear the news as I re'ch to Hagley Gap, Say ba-by da born with
feather. Something me nev-er hear, Something me never hear that
Ba-by can born with feather. Something me nev-er hear,
Something me nev-er hear that Ba-by can born with feather.

All the other sings are chronicles of true events, and it is an exceptional case to find one purely the offspring of imagination like this one. The compiler of the words could not get quite free of actuality; he puts in Hagley Gap, which is the name of a pass through the hills. I once asked why it was so called and was told because it was a hugly place. The cooking described savours of Obeah.

CLXVII.

2nd Figure.

When the rain an' the breeze an' the storm an' the sun I
nev-er see a man like Qua-co Sam, He live in the sun as
well as the rain, I nev-er see a man like Qua-co Sam.
Qua-co Sam was a lit-tle bit a man, I nev-er see a man like a
Qua-co Sam, For he nev-er build a house but he live as an-y man, I
nev-er see a fun-ny man as Qua-co Sam.

CLXVIII.

5th Figure.

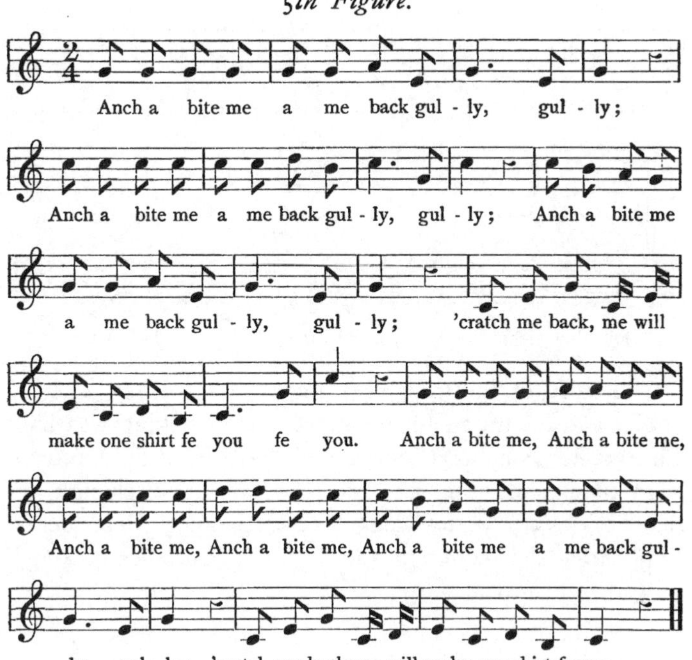
Anch a bite me a me back gul - ly, gul - ly;
Anch a bite me a me back gul - ly, gul - ly; Anch a bite me
a me back gul - ly, gul - ly; 'cratch me back, me will
make one shirt fe you fe you. Anch a bite me, Anch a bite me,
Anch a bite me, Anch a bite me, Anch a bite me a me back gul -
ly, gul - ly; 'cratch me back me will make one shirt fe you.

Small black ants often swarm on the orange-trees, and the pickers, who do not use ladders but climb the branches, get covered with them. We all know that place in the "gully" or furrow of the back which we cannot reach ourselves.

CLXIX.

4th Figure.

Me know one gal a Cross Road, Name of Lu - cy

Ban - ker, Him boil the long long cab - bage bush, Him go
long like a sai - lor nanchor. Fol - low me, fol-low me, You no
see whé the gal a fol - low me, Fol - low me, then
fol - low me, You no see whé the gal a fol - low me.

The story of the foregoing sing is this:—Lucy asked a fiddler and his friend to breakfast. The cooking was bad. The boiled bananas, which should have been light brown, were black, and the cabbage was not done enough, so that it was ropy or "long," as they aptly describe it. For these shortcomings the fiddler "put her a sing," *i.e.* put her into a sing.

CLXX.

Schottische.

Moonshine baby, don't you cry, Mumma will bring somet'ing fe you,

Some fe you, Some fe me, Fe we go boil wi' dir - ty pot.

This is a hit at another careless cook who had disregarded the time-honoured rule, "First wash your pot." A moonshine baby is a pretty baby.

CLXXI.

2nd Figure.

I have a news to tell you all a - bout the Mowitahl
men, [1] Time is harder ev - 'ry day an' harder yet to
come. They made a dance on Fri - day night an' failed to pay the
drummer, Say that they all was need of money to
buy up their August pork. Don't let them go free, drummer !
Don't let them go free, drummer ! For your fin-ger cost money to
tick - le the poor goat - 'kin. Not if the pork ev - en
purchase self Take it away for your labour, For your finger
cost money to tick - le the poor goat - 'kin.

The first of August (Ahgust as they call it) is the anniversary of Emancipation Day, and is a time of

[1] Mowitahl = Mowatt Hall.

feasting and rejoicing. As in the case of wedding festivities, they do not limit themselves to one day, and holiday-making goes on for a week or longer.

The goat-skin drum is pitied for the thumping it gets. So a man will often stroke his picker (pickaxe) and say:—"He no a come out if he t'ought him face would a jam so a dirty," he would not have come out if he had thought his face was going to be thrust so hard into the ground.

"Self" is a redundant word. It strengthens "even if."

CLXXII.

2nd Figure.

Once I was a trav'ller, trav - 'ller ov - er the
mountain, I near - ly dead for wa - ter but a
young gal show me the fountain. Why, why me pic-ny!
You shall be me wife. Show me you mammy an' you daddy, An'
you shall be me wife. I have a - nother sis - ter, she
blind she can - not see, But, if you wish to court her,

you can come with me. Why, why me picny ! you shall be me wife.

Show me you mammy an' you daddy, An' you shall be me wife.

When a Black man says he is nearly dead for water he only means that he is rather thirsty.

This sing is of an unusual form and suggests a foreign origin.

CLXXIII.

Here, on the contrary, is something typically Jamaican :—

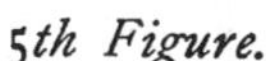
5th Figure.

Oh ! me wouldn' bawl at all, Oh ! me
wouldn' bawl at all, Oh ! me wouldn' bawl at all,

For the po-lice-man come tell a lie 'pon me.

A boy who has been arrested, conscious of his innocence, does not go through the usual pantomime of shrieks and tears. The policeman (observe the accent on the word) told a lie about me, he says.

CLXXIV.

Thoroughly Jamaican too, as to its words at least, is:—

Jig.

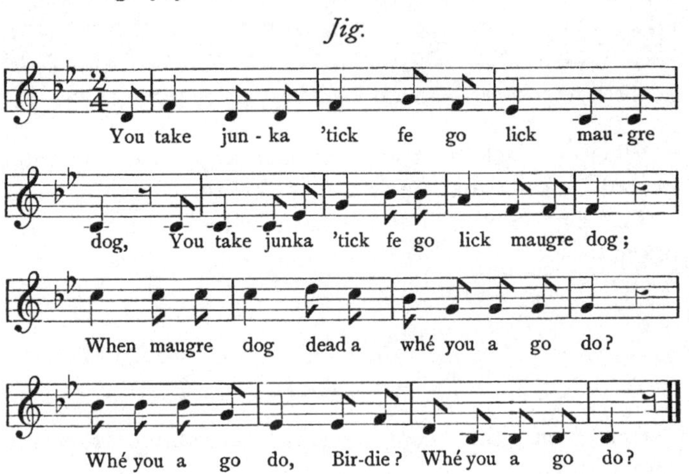
You take jun - ka 'tick fe go lick mau - gre
dog, You take junka 'tick fe go lick maugre dog;
When maugre dog dead a whé you a go do?
Whé you a go do, Bir-die? Whé you a go do?

This is a remonstrance addressed by a mother to her daughter who has taken up a short stick to beat her. "It is true," she says, that I am but a lean dog, but when the lean dog is dead what are you going to do?" (*Maugre*, French *maigre,* pronounced *mahgher.*)

CLXXV.

John Canoe dance.

Yellow fe - ver come in, Me can't walk a - gain; Him
broke me hand, him broke me foot, Me can't walk a - gain.

The "John Canoe" are masked dancers very agile in their movements. Yellow fever is now happily rare in

Jamaica. "It has come and caught me," says the patient, "and broken my arms and legs so that I really can't walk."

"Again" has a curious use here, which is perhaps better shown by the following illustration. A man was reported to be dead. Next day came the intelligence:—"He don't dead again," he is not dead after all, he is not really dead. Compare No. LXII.

CLXXVI.

Schottische.

Jim - my Ramp - y a come oh, Sal
oh! Jimmy Rampy a come oh, Sal oh! Some a
wash him foot, some a comb him hair, Some a put him to bed,
put him to bed oh, Sal oh! Jimmy Rampy a come
oh! Sal oh! Jim-my Rampy a come oh, Sal
oh! Some a wash him foot, some a comb him hair, Some a
put him to bed, put him to bed oh, Sal oh!

"Sal oh!" is perhaps a corruption of *Salut.* Tradition associates a curtsey with the word.

CLXXVII.

The next calls to mind the Ring tune (No. XC.), "Rosybel oh, why oh!"

5th Figure.

Sus - an ve - ry well, why oh! Sus - an ve - ry
well, why oh! Sus - an chop bo - low with tum - bler,
Sus - an chop bo - low with tum - bler, Sus - an go chop bo -
- low with tum - bler, Sus - an go chop bo - low with tum - bler.

A case of assault with a broken piece of glass. Here is something more serious:—

CLXXVIII.

1st Figure.

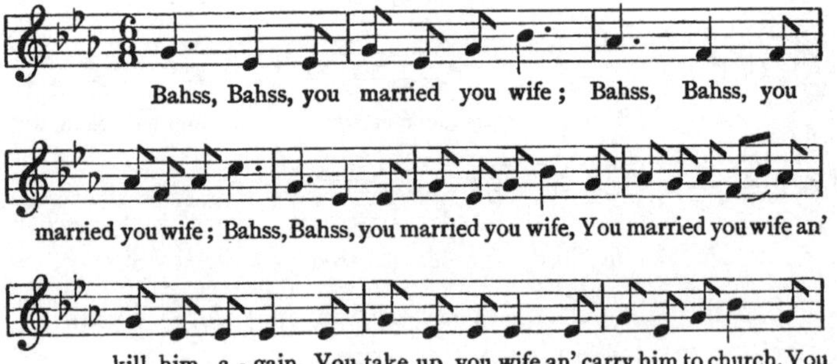
Bahss, Bahss, you married you wife; Bahss, Bahss, you
married you wife; Bahss, Bahss, you married you wife, You married you wife an'
kill him a - gain. You take up you wife an' carry him to church, You

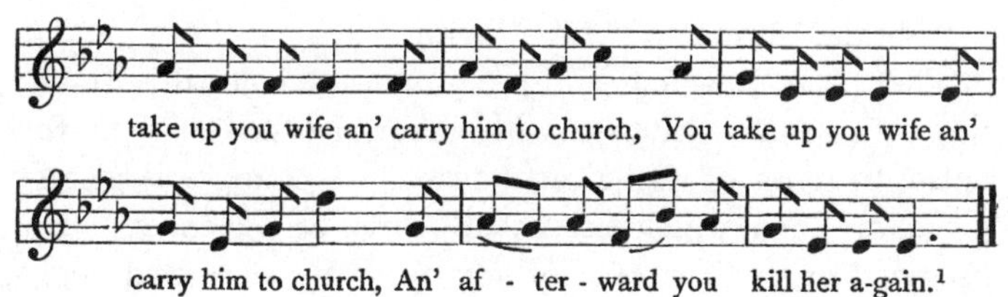
take up you wife an' carry him to church, You take up you wife an'
carry him to church, An' af - ter - ward you kill her a-gain.[1]

CLXXIX.

The next is a pretty lullaby, which they call a Nursing sing :—

Andantino.
Blackbird a eat puppa corn, oh! Blackbird a eat puppa
corn, oh! Come go da mountain, go drive them, Blackbird a eat puppa
corn, oh! Blackbird a eat pup-pa corn.

CLXXX.

Schottische.

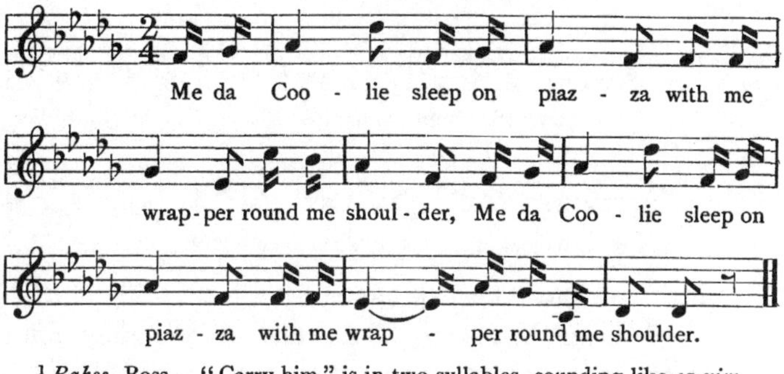
Me da Coo - lie sleep on piaz - za with me
wrap-per round me shoul - der, Me da Coo - lie sleep on
piaz - za with me wrap - per round me shoulder.

[1] *Bahss*, Boss. "Carry him" is in two syllables, sounding like *ca-yim*.

"Me da," literally, "I is," I am.

The piazza, which is not pronounced in the Italian way but nearly rhymes with razor, is the long narrow entrance-room of Jamaican houses. A wrapper is a large piece of linen which serves all sorts of purposes. It is used as an article of clothing both by day and night, and also makes a convenient bag for rice.

Many of the East Indian Coolies, originally brought over to work on plantations, have now settled in Jamaica.

CLXXXI.

Schottische.

Not-ty Shaw, you bet-ter go home; Not-ty
Shaw, you better go home; Notty, run in the garden an'
pick a bunch of flowers; Notty Shaw, you bet-ter go
home; Notty Shaw, you mother want you service; Notty
Shaw, you mother want you service; Notty, go in the garden you
see abunch of rose; Notty Shaw, you better go home.

"Notty" is short for Nathaniel.

"Rose" means any kind of flowers. When they want to indicate what we call roses they say "sweet-rose."

CLXXXII.

1st Figure.

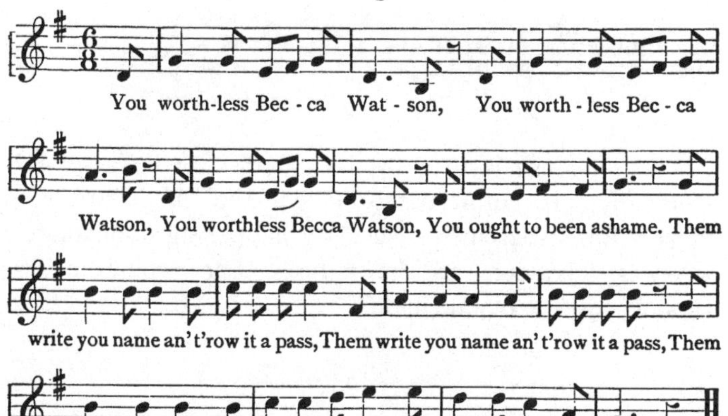
You worth-less Bec - ca Wat - son, You worth - less Bec - ca
Watson, You worthless Becca Watson, You ought to been ashame. Them
write you name an' t'row it a pass, Them write you name an' t'row it a pass, Them
write you name an' t'row it a pass, you ought to been a - shame.

A familiar tune, I think a mixture of two.

To write disparaging remarks on paper, which is then thrown in the "pass" (path, road), for anybody to pick up and read, is a common trick. The epithet "worthless" seems to imply that Becca was not altogether free from blame. They seldom say "bad." It is almost always "worthless."

CLXXXIII.

5th Figure.

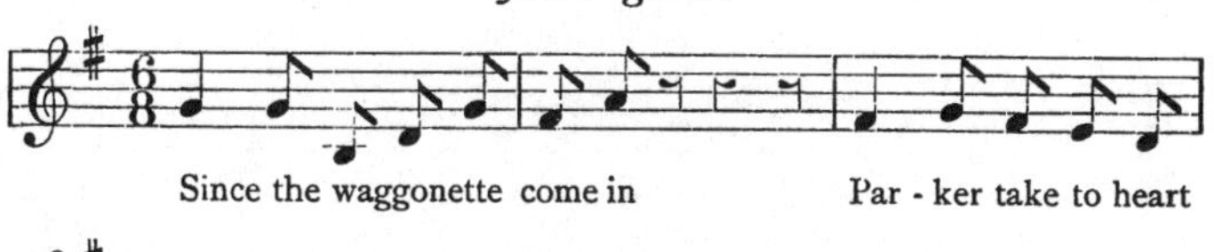
Since the waggonette come in Par - ker take to heart

dead, Since the waggonette come in Parker take to heart dead.

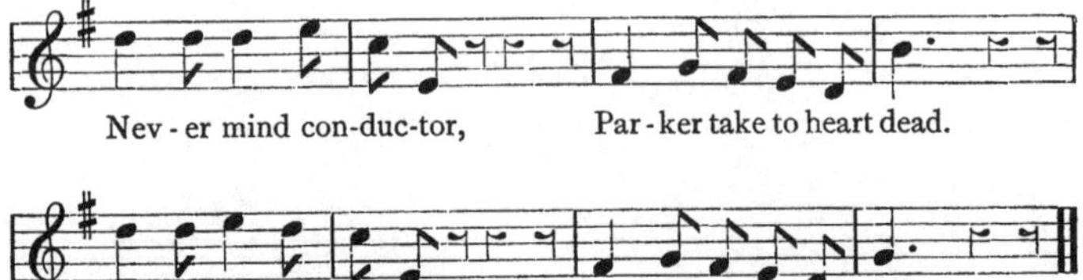
Nev - er mind con-duc-tor, Par - ker take to heart dead.
Nev-er mind con-duc-tor, Par-ker take to heart dead.

The reference is to a local enterprise, the Waggonette Company. It unfortunately failed, and the death of a person interested in its success, happening immediately after, is attributed to the failure. For "come in" we should say "were taken off."

CLXXXIV.

Schottische or 4th Figure.

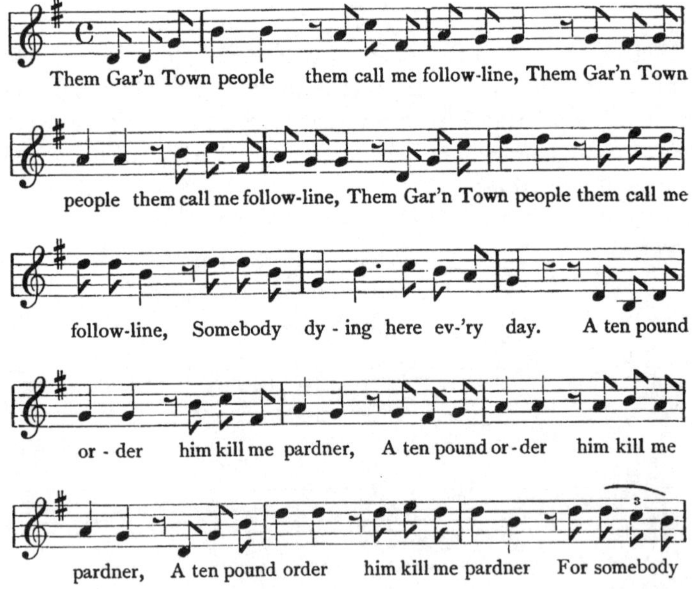
Them Gar'n Town people them call me follow-line, Them Gar'n Town
people them call me follow-line, Them Gar'n Town people them call me
follow-line, Somebody dy - ing here ev-'ry day. A ten pound
or - der him kill me pardner, A ten pound or - der him kill me
pardner, A ten pound order him kill me pardner For somebody

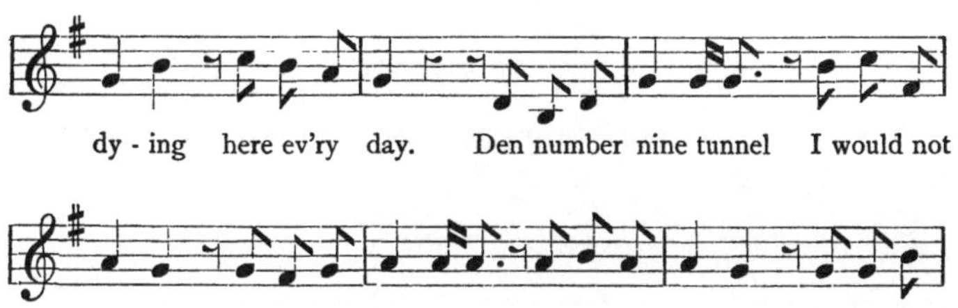
dy - ing here ev'ry day. Den number nine tunnel I would not
work dé, Den number nine tunnel I would not work dé, Den number

nine tunnel I would not work dé For somebody dying here ev'ry day.

An incident, or perhaps it were better to say an accident, in the making of the road to Newcastle. A man who undertook a piece of contract work for £10 was killed by a falling stone. The so-called tunnels are cuttings. Number nine had a very bad reputation.

Gordon Town is a hamlet nine miles from Kingston. The driving road ends there, and access to the mountain district beyond is obtained only by mule tracks.

Strangers are called "follow-line" because, as they come down from their homes in the higher hills, they walk in strings. No Black man or woman ever goes alone if he can help it. He always hitches on to somebody else, and the string increases in length as it passes along. This walking in Indian file is necessitated by the narrowness of the track, which is seldom wide enough for two to walk abreast.

The tune has the character of a march rather than of a dance, but I am assured it is used for a Schottische, which has a somewhat slower measure than a Polka, and for Fourth Figure. Their cleverness in adapting the same steps to different rhythms has been already commented on.

CLXXXV.

The last of our tragedies, a murder this time, is chronicled in:—

2nd Figure.

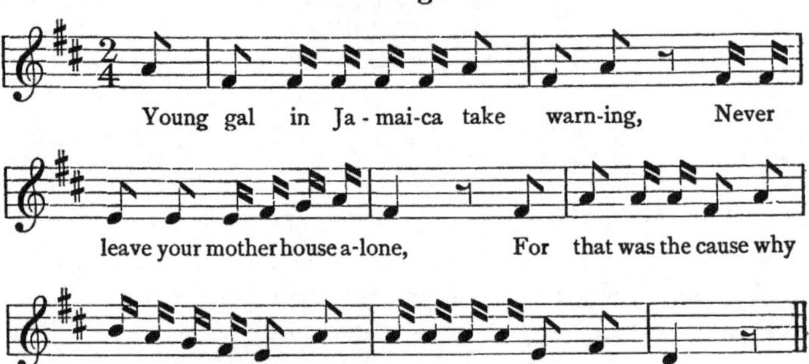
Young gal in Ja - mai-ca take warn-ing, Never
leave your mother house a-lone, For that was the cause why
Al-ice get her death while driving in the May Pen cyar.

"The May Pen cyar" is a tramway which runs to May Pen, the cemetery of Kingston.

CLXXXVI.

4th Figure.

Me no min dé a concert the night When Martha an' Pompey catch a

fight. Da Martha da Pompey, Da Martha da Pompey catch a fight.

"Me no min dé," literally, "I not been there," I was not there. Nobody hearing these words for the first time would ever suspect that they were English. People are always said to "catch fight" when they come to blows.

Few of the old classical slave names like Pompey now survive.

CLXXXVII.

1st Figure.

Complain complain complain, Complain a - bout me one, Me

daddy complain, me mahmy complain, Complain about me one.

"Me one," *i.e.* "only me." Everlasting complaints, always about me! (What child does not suffer in this way?) In Negro speech *complain* stands for complaint as well as for the verb.

CLXXXVIII.

2nd Figure.

Elderly readers will recognise a popular song of thirty years ago in the following:—

I can't walk on the bare road, cyart man, I can't walk at all;

When I re-member, When I remember, When I remember them.

Oh Captain Ba - ker, I never can walk a - gain, For
when I remember the cyart man, cyart man, When I remember them.

These words taken as a whole refer to the carts of the United Fruit Company of which Captain Baker is the manager. In defiance of rules girls may be seen perched on top of the bunches of bananas in the laden carts.

CLXXXIX.

5th Figure.

Come go da mountain, Come go da mountain, Come go da mountain go

pick co-co fin-ger, Busha Webb an' all a pick co-co fin-ger,

Busha Webb an' all a pick co-co fin-ger; Pick co-co fin-ger,

Pick co-co fin-ger, Come go da mountain go pick co-co fin-ger.

"Come let us go to the mountain and dig cocoes. Overseer Webb and everybody is digging them." A plan often adopted is to dig round the root, search for the tubers, pick them off and then push back the soil. This may be the picking referred to, only the tubers do not look like fingers. They are the shape of a peg-top.

Another suggestion is that the fingers are the young rolled-up leaves which are picked before they expand for spinach. This variety of interpretation, coupled with the fact that the word *finger*, always applied to bananas, is never used in speaking of cocoes, points to this being a very old sing.

CXC.

Valse.

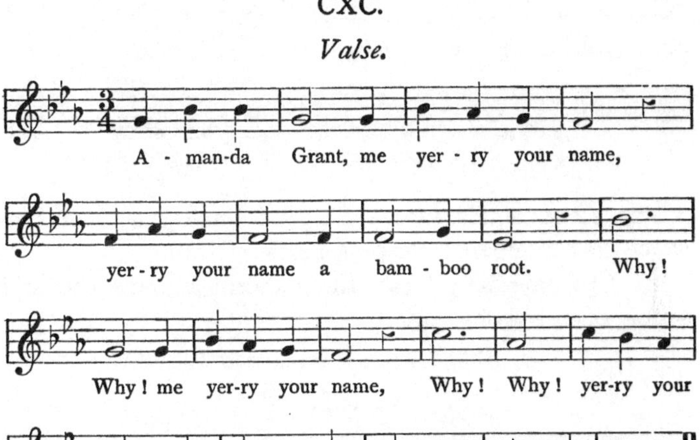
A - man-da Grant, me yer - ry your name,
yer - ry your name a bam - boo root. Why!
Why! me yer-ry your name, Why! Why! yer-ry your
name, Me yer - ry your name a bam - boo root.

Amanda stole some money and hid it at the foot of a bamboo.

CXCI.

2nd Figure.

Last night I was ly - ing on me num - ber, An' a
fool-ish man come wake me out of slum-ber, Say Why oh!
Why oh! I nev-er see a woman dancing with a wooden leg.
Bammerlichy, bammerlichy, bamby, Bammerlichy, bammerlichy,

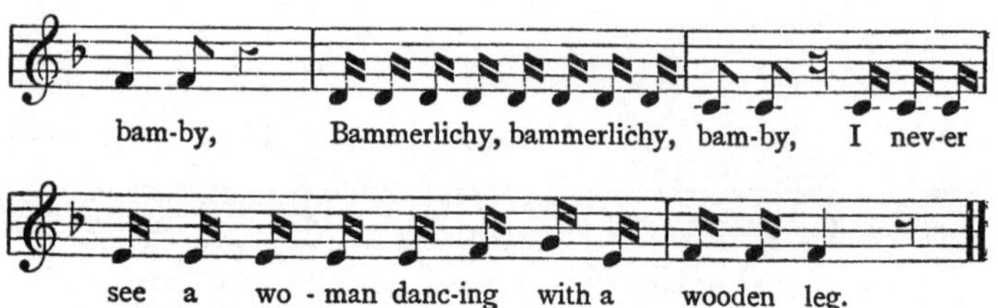
bam-by, Bammerlichy, bammerlichy, bam-by, I nev-er
see a wo - man danc-ing with a wooden leg.

The scene is laid in the People's Shelter at Kingston which has numbered sleeping-berths.

At "Bammerlichy" etc. the dancers imitate the stiff action of a wooden leg.

CXCII.

5th Figure.

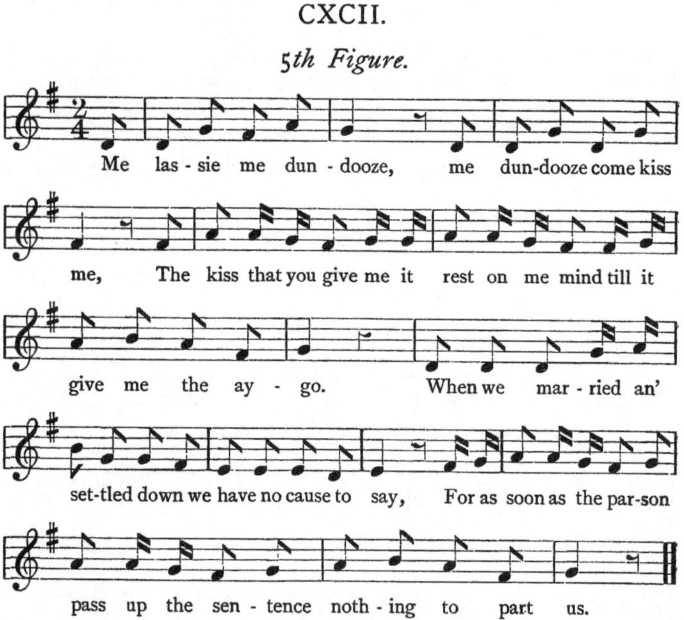
Me las - sie me dun - dooze, me dun-dooze come kiss
me, The kiss that you give me it rest on me mind till it
give me the ay - go. When we mar - ried an'
set-tled down we have no cause to say, For as soon as the par-son
pass up the sen - tence noth - ing to part us.

"Dundooze" (or dundoze, for it is rather hard to catch the vowel) is a term of endearment. Others are, honey, lover, sugar, sweety, marvel, bolow, bahzoon.

"Aygo" is ague; "say," perhaps, sunder.

CXCIII.

The next conveys an appreciative reference to a proprietor who is a large employer of labour.

Polka.

Mis - ter Dav - is bring some - t'ing fe we all,

Mis - ter Dav - is bring some - t'ing fe we all. Oh him

bring black gal, An' him bring brown gal, An' him bring yaller gal an' all.

CXCIV.

5th Figure.

A whé the use you da hang da me neck-back,

Married man me no want you. Turn back, married man,

turn back, you brute, Turn back married man, married man a dog.

CXCV.

4th Figure.

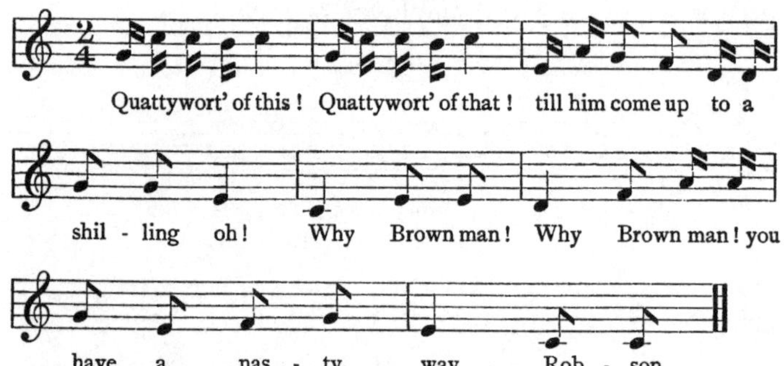
Quattywort' of this! Quattywort' of that! till him come up to a
shil - ling oh! Why Brown man! Why Brown man! you
have a nas - ty way, Rob - son.

The boy has run up a score at the shop and professes astonishment at the items and the total. Black trusts White more than Brown.

CXCVI.

We end with the pretty flowing melody:—

Schottische.

Mahngoose a come, Dory, Mahngoose a come. All them gal are
dead fe Do-ry, Mahngoose a come. Come back me dear Do-ry,
Come back me dear. All them gal are dead fe Dory, Mahngoose a come.

The mongoose was introduced into Jamaica to kill the rats. Unfortunately rats sleep in the day and the mongoose sleeps at night, so they never met. How the mongoose took instead to killing chickens has been often told. Dory is having a private interview with a girl who has another admirer. This man has announced his intention of chastising Dory. "Mongoose has come" is a preconcerted formula which means, "the other man has come, Dory, look out!" When a gang of labourers is working and one of them catches sight of his master in the distance, he will sing this song and the others understand that they must pretend to be busy.

THE END.

NOTE.—(*Accidentally omitted on page* 77 : *Cf.* Nos. 56, 67, 132, 133).

Marriage is, unhappily, often a failure. The woman, in marrying, has attained the goal of her ambition. Now that she is Mrs. Smith she "sits down" and refuses to help her husband, provision-ground food is not good enough for her, and she is always calling out for a new frock. In a few years the couple separate and the home is broken up, with disastrous consequences to the children. In the old days the custom was to defer the ceremony (as Constantine deferred his baptism) to a very late period. This plan worked very well. The couple did not marry till they knew for certain that they suited each other, and often their well-brought-up children and grandchildren danced at the wedding.

APPENDIX.

A. TRACES OF AFRICAN MELODY IN JAMAICA.

I HAVE been asked to read through this book in proof, with the object of ascertaining whether the Jamaican songs bear any traces of an African origin.

Unfortunately, it must be confessed at the outset that our knowledge of African music is scantier than that of almost any other kind of primitive music. In other regions of the globe the phonograph has been effectively utilised in acquiring accurate records of songs and dances. These records have been brought back to Europe, where they have been studied at leisure and their peculiarities of interval and rhythm have been precisely determined.

But in the case of African music (apart from a few imperfectly studied records in my own possession) we have to rely entirely on the versions which travellers have taken down for us in the field. We have to assume, in the first place, the correctness of their 'musical ear,' and in the second place, the possibility of expressing in European notation those delicate shades of pitch and time in which the characteristics of primitive music so essentially consist. And both these are unwarrantable assumptions.

However, from our study of comparative music elsewhere, we may make one statement with certainty, namely, that *an* African music does not exist. There must be almost as many styles of native music in Africa as in Europe—varieties differing not only broadly in general form and structure, but also more minutely in the intervals and rhythms which are employed.

I have been informed by travellers in West Africa that surprising differences occur in the degree of development of musical art even in closely neighbouring regions. In one district hardly any music is to be heard at all; in another the music is most uncouth; in a third it is highly agreeable to the European ear; while some parts of West Africa have advanced to the stage of part-singing.

The most erroneous notions have been expressed as to the nature of African music. I have seen it stated that African songs consist in a gradual descent from a higher to a lower pitched note. That this is far from being usually the case is shown in the following specimens, which I have gathered from various narratives of African travel.

I.
Boat Song. Congo District.
II.
Boat Song. Congo District.
III.
Song of Bawili Women.
IV.
Funeral Song. Angola.

V.

Song. Angola.

VI.

Song. M. Balunda.

VII.

Dance-Song. M. Balunda.

VIII.

Boat Song. Guinea Coast.

IX.

Song. I. of Bimbia.

Songs I. and II. from *La route du Tchad.* Jean Dybowski. Paris. 1893. pp. 198-9.

Songs III.-VII. from *Aus West-Afrika.* Hermann Soyaux. Leipzig. 1879.

Song VIII. from *Einige Notizen über Bonny.* Göttingen. 1848.

Song IX. from *A Narrative of the Expedition . . . to the River Niger.* London. 1848.

A great deal might be said about the general character of these songs, *e.g.* the simplicity and brevity of the phrases, and the fondness for triple measure.

But I pass on to consider three very interesting examples of Jamaican music which, thanks to my friend Mr. N. W. Thomas, I have found recorded in 1688 in Sir Hans Sloane's *Voyage to Jamaica.* "Upon one of the Festivals where a great many of the Negro Musicians were gathered together," he writes, "I desired Mr. Baptiste, the best musician there, to take the words they sung and set them to Musick which follows."

X.

Angola Song.

XI.

Papa Song.

XII.

Koromanti Songs.

Hobaognion
Hobaognion
Ho-ba
Ho - ba - ognion - ognion.

Loud.
Soft.
Meri Bonbo mich langa
meri wá langa.

From *A Voyage to . . . Jamaica* . . . by Hans Sloane, M.D. London. 1707. Vol. i. pp. l, li.

The words of these songs are *Hobaognion, ognion* and *Meri Bonbo mich langa meri wá langa.* Sir Hans Sloane observes that the Jamaican negroes of that time had their native instruments: (i) gourds with necks and strung with horsehair, (ii) a "hollow'd Timber covered with Parchment," having a bow for its neck, the strings tied longer or shorter.

These songs, however inaccurately recorded, are of the greatest value for the hint they give us of Jamaican music as it existed over two centuries ago. It will be observed that the songs are named 'Angola' and 'Koromanti,' according to their African *provenance.* In the present collection of modern songs, reference is made in Song CI. to Koromanti ('Cromanty'). So, too, the word 'Bungo' in Song CXXVI. no doubt refers to the large Bongo district of Africa (cf. 'Bungo talk,' p. 12, *n.*).

We can hardly expect to find considerable traces of this aboriginal African music after two centuries of missionary and of trade influence. African travellers have repeatedly told us how prone the negro is to introduce fresh tunes from other villages and to adapt them to his own purposes. Indeed, the contaminating influence which the Arabs and Portuguese have exercised upon primitive African music makes the study of the latter especially difficult.

But a community does not adopt exotic music without at the same time exercising selection. Those melodies have the greatest chance of success which, to some degree at least, follow the current canons of public taste. Revolutionary innovations are rare. The gradual changes in taste which take place are the result of such selective adoption of foreign music as we have indicated.

There is one feature in the above-quoted 'Angola' song which is also shared by the modern songs of this collection, namely, the presence of 'bobbins' or short refrains.

The simplicity in structure of the songs is still a feature of Jamaican music. I may be allowed to call attention to the repetition of single phrases in Song XVIII. and to the building up of simple phrases in Songs LXXVII. and LXXIX.

I had hoped that some light might be thrown on the antiquity of certain songs by the presence of nonsense words; but in this I was disappointed.

I quite agree with Miss Broadwood (see next page) that the majority of the songs are of European origin. The negroes have learnt them from hearing sailors' chanties or they have adopted hymn tunes.

But adoption always involves adaptation. A song is modified to suit the current canons of taste. In Song L. I observe 'Home, Sweet Home' and (in the latter half) a hymn tune which I frequently heard in the Torres Straits. Song CXXXIX. is doubtless 'The British Grenadiers.' But it, again, has not been adopted without modification.

Needless to say, a detailed study of these modifications would throw light on the characteristics of modern Jamaican music.

In Song XXXI. a typical non-European modification is the insertion of an extra (the fifth) bar, so that the phrase consists of nine bars. The five time in Song XI., the change of accent at the close of Song XXIV. and in Song XLI., are no doubt the expression of African delight in the complexities of rhythm.

In the already-quoted 'Koromanti song,' we may observe the curious temporary change of rhythm in the second air, and the characteristic measure which prevails throughout the third air with its syncopation and almost baffling changes. Such features are precisely what we should expect to meet with among a primitive people who more than two centuries ago doubtless possessed in a still higher degree that delight in complication of rhythm which according to Mr. Jekyll (p. 6) persists among their descendants of to-day. For a more detailed study of this aspect of the subject I may perhaps refer enquirers to my "Study of Rhythm in Primitive People" (*British Journal of Psychology*, vol. i. pp. 397-406).

The present taste and preferences of the Jamaican negroes may perhaps be gauged by the similarities and differences in the first bars of Songs LXIII., LXIV., and LXXVIII., by the similarity of Songs I. and VIII., XV. and XXVII., and of the bobbins in LIV. and LXVIII.

But it is not my intention to make a detailed analysis of the songs of the present volume. My object has been rather to emphasize our present ignorance of African music, and to indicate the lines along which a more intimate acquaintance with African and Jamaican songs may be expected to lead to conclusions as to their relation to one another.

C. S. Myers.

B. English Airs and Motifs in Jamaica.

By far the greater part of these Jamaican tunes and song-words seem to be reminiscences, or imitations, of European sailors' "chanties" of the modern class; or of trivial British nursery-jingles adapted, as all such jingles become adapted.

Except in the cases specified below, I have not found one Jamaican tune which is *entirely* like any one English or European tune that I happen to know. But unrecorded folk-tunes are essentially fluid, and pass through endless transformations. In all countries any one traditional ballad may be sung to dozens of distinct traditional tunes, each of these again having variants. It is therefore quite possible that versions of some of the older-sounding Jamaican airs are being sung unrecorded at this moment in the British Islands or elsewhere.

I note below such instances of modal tunes as occur in this collection. I should perhaps explain that by "Modes" are meant those ancient scales (other than our major and minor scales) which amongst European composers fell into disuse at the beginning of the 17th century, but which survive still in the ancient Church Music (popularly called "Gregorian"), and in the Folk Music of most European countries, and notably that of the British Isles.

III. **King Daniel**, p. 14.

Cf. the old ballads "May Colvin" and "Young Hunting." In the latter the parrot reveals a murder. In both ballads the lady makes the same promises to the bird (see Child's *English and Scottish Popular Ballads*).

VII. **The Three Sisters**, p. 26.

Although the story of the monster outwitted by the maiden he tries to carry off is an almost world-wide *motif*, and is found in Africa among other countries, this particular version has evidently been in contact with European (English or Scottish) sources. This is shown not only by the fact that the suitor proves to be the Devil, but by the question and answer (misplaced by the story-teller):

"What is roguer than a womankind?"
"The Devil is roguer than a womankind."

This riddle appears in three versions of the ballad of "The Three Sisters," otherwise "The Elfin Knight," or "Riddles wisely Expounded" (Child, *English and Scottish Popular Ballads*, vol. i. pp. 1-6), as:

"O what is greener than the grass?
Or what is worse than e'er woman was?"
"O poison's greener than the grass,
And the Devil's worse than e'er woman was. . . ."
"As soon as she the fiend did name,
He flew away in a blazing flame,"

says one version, but in the rest there is no disenchantment, and the youngest sister wins the visitor as her husband by her ready wit in replying, which Professor Child (*Additions and Corrections*, vol. v. p. 283), thinks a modernization of the original story. He quotes a manuscript version taken from a book of Henry VI.'s time, wherein the "Elfin Knight" is the foul fiend himself *undisguised.*

For similar survivals of Riddle Songs and Tales see "There was a Lady in the West" and "Scarborough Fair" in *English*

County Songs, and Kidson's *Traditional Tunes*, and "The Lover's Task" in *Songs of the West*, etc.

The tune is evidently an old ballad air. It is in the Aeolian Mode.

XVII. **Man Crow**, p. 54.

The tune is the same as that sung in Worcestershire by children to "A finger and thumb keep moving."

XVIII. **Saylan**, p. 59.

This is a version of "The Maid freed from the Gallows," "The Golden Ball," or "The Prickly Bush." For the latter see *English County Songs*. Child gives very exhaustive notes on the story and its variants; also a tune, noted in North Carolina, "The Prickly Bush" has a tune quite unlike Child's, and the Jamaican air is quite distinct from both.

XXI. **Tacoma and the Old Witch Girl**, p. 65.

Cf. "The Keys of Heaven" in *English County Songs*, "Blue Muslin" in *Songs of the West*, and "Madam I will gi'e you," etc., in *Journal of the Folk-Song Society*, No. 7. All these airs are distinct from each other, and from the Jamaican tune.

XXIX. **Parson Puss and Parson Dog**, p. 91.

This tune is the first half of the old French air "Ah, vous dirai-je, Maman?" used so often by English children in their games. See note in Moffat and Kidson's *Children's Songs and Games of Long Ago*, p. 42. Other adaptations of the same tune are CXVI. (p. 215), CLXXVII. (p. 264), and CLXXXIX. (p. 272).

XXXI. **Pretty Poll**, p. 96.

Cf. "King Daniel." This is again the story of "May Colvin" or "The Outlandish Knight." The tune "Come, pretty Poll" here given is rather reminiscent of one traditional air to the ballad sung still in different parts of England (where numerous tunes to the favourite story have been noted). See "The Outlandish Knight" in *Songs of Northern England* (Stokoe and Reay) for the type of tune referred to, but plentiful variants from Hertfordshire, the West of England, Yorkshire, etc., exist in MS.

XXXVI. **Leah and Tiger**, p. 108.

The tune is in the Aeolian Mode.

LXIII. **Oh, Samuel, oh,** p. 168.

This tune is in the Mixolydian Mode.

LXXXVIII. **War down a Monkland,** p. 187.

The tune is in the Dorian Mode. By far the most interesting tune in this collection. It is a fine Dorian air, I should think an old traditional tune imported by English or Irish.

There are slight modal influences in other tunes, viz.: "Bad homan oh," "Bell oh," "A Somerset me barn," "Whé me loon dé," "Me da lí," and "Since Dora Logan a wahk with Gallawoss" (Nos. 56, 57, 85, 91, 100, 122).

CXI., p. 209.

This tune is a variant of the well-known children's game-song, "Here come three Dukes a-riding."

CXIX., p. 218.

The tune is a variant of one commonly sung in the North of England and in various parts of Scotland, to a children's game, "Hullaballoo ballie," in which reference is made to lifting the right foot and the left foot.

CXXVII., p. 225.

This air is the first part of the tune of "O dem Golden Slippers," the negro revival song of some twenty years ago.

CXXX., p. 227.

This is a reminiscence of the Scotch dance-tune usually sung to the words "There's nae luck aboot the hoose."

CLXXVIII., p. 264.

This is a well-known old English dance-tune, known also in Scotland.

CLXXXII., p. 267.

The second part of this tune is merely a reminiscence of "We won't go home till morning."

CLXXXVII., p. 271.

This tune is the first part of a very commonplace modern Italian popular composition called "La Mandolinata," played on every conceivable instrument, and sung also, about the year 1876 and for some years afterwards.

L. E. BROADWOOD.

A CATALOG OF SELECTED

DOVER BOOKS

IN ALL FIELDS OF INTEREST

A CATALOG OF SELECTED DOVER BOOKS IN ALL FIELDS OF INTEREST

STICKLEY CRAFTSMAN FURNITURE CATALOGS, Gustav Stickley and L. & J. G. Stickley. Beautiful, functional furniture in two authentic catalogs from 1910. 594 illustrations, including 277 photos, show settles, rockers, armchairs, reclining chairs, bookcases, desks, tables. 183pp. 6½ x 9¼. 23838-5

AMERICAN LOCOMOTIVES IN HISTORIC PHOTOGRAPHS: 1858 to 1949, Ron Ziel (ed.). A rare collection of 126 meticulously detailed official photographs, called "builder portraits," of American locomotives that majestically chronicle the rise of steam locomotive power in America. Introduction. Detailed captions. xi+ 129pp. 9 x 12. 27393-8

AMERICA'S LIGHTHOUSES: An Illustrated History, Francis Ross Holland, Jr. Delightfully written, profusely illustrated fact-filled survey of over 200 American lighthouses since 1716. History, anecdotes, technological advances, more. 240pp. 8 x 10¾. 25576-X

TOWARDS A NEW ARCHITECTURE, Le Corbusier. Pioneering manifesto by founder of "International School." Technical and aesthetic theories, views of industry, economics, relation of form to function, "mass-production split" and much more. Profusely illustrated. 320pp. 6⅛ x 9¼. (Available in U.S. only.) 25023-7

HOW THE OTHER HALF LIVES, Jacob Riis. Famous journalistic record, exposing poverty and degradation of New York slums around 1900, by major social reformer. 100 striking and influential photographs. 233pp. 10 x 7⅞. 22012-5

FRUIT KEY AND TWIG KEY TO TREES AND SHRUBS, William M. Harlow. One of the handiest and most widely used identification aids. Fruit key covers 120 deciduous and evergreen species; twig key 160 deciduous species. Easily used. Over 300 photographs. 126pp. 5⅜ x 8½. 20511-8

COMMON BIRD SONGS, Dr. Donald J. Borror. Songs of 60 most common U.S. birds: robins, sparrows, cardinals, bluejays, finches, more–arranged in order of increasing complexity. Up to 9 variations of songs of each species.
Cassette and manual 99911-4

ORCHIDS AS HOUSE PLANTS, Rebecca Tyson Northen. Grow cattleyas and many other kinds of orchids–in a window, in a case, or under artificial light. 63 illustrations. 148pp. 5⅜ x 8½. 23261-1

MONSTER MAZES, Dave Phillips. Masterful mazes at four levels of difficulty. Avoid deadly perils and evil creatures to find magical treasures. Solutions for all 32 exciting illustrated puzzles. 48pp. 8¼ x 11. 26005-4

MOZART'S DON GIOVANNI (DOVER OPERA LIBRETTO SERIES), Wolfgang Amadeus Mozart. Introduced and translated by Ellen H. Bleiler. Standard Italian libretto, with complete English translation. Convenient and thoroughly portable–an ideal companion for reading along with a recording or the performance itself. Introduction. List of characters. Plot summary. 121pp. 5¼ x 8½. 24944-1

TECHNICAL MANUAL AND DICTIONARY OF CLASSICAL BALLET, Gail Grant. Defines, explains, comments on steps, movements, poses and concepts. 15-page pictorial section. Basic book for student, viewer. 127pp. 5⅜ x 8½. 21843-0

FRANK LLOYD WRIGHT'S DANA HOUSE, Donald Hoffmann. Pictorial essay of residential masterpiece with over 160 interior and exterior photos, plans, elevations, sketches and studies. 128pp. 9¼ x 10¾. 29120-0

THE MALE AND FEMALE FIGURE IN MOTION: 60 Classic Photographic Sequences, Eadweard Muybridge. 60 true-action photographs of men and women walking, running, climbing, bending, turning, etc., reproduced from rare 19th-century masterpiece. vi + 121pp. 9 x 12. 24745-7

1001 QUESTIONS ANSWERED ABOUT THE SEASHORE, N. J. Berrill and Jacquelyn Berrill. Queries answered about dolphins, sea snails, sponges, starfish, fishes, shore birds, many others. Covers appearance, breeding, growth, feeding, much more. 305pp. 5¼ x 8¼. 23366-9

ATTRACTING BIRDS TO YOUR YARD, William J. Weber. Easy-to follow guide offers advice on how to attract the greatest diversity of birds: birdhouses, feeders, water and waterers, much more. 96pp. 5³⁄₁₆ x 8¼. 28927-3

MEDICINAL AND OTHER USES OF NORTH AMERICAN PLANTS: A Historical Survey with Special Reference to the Eastern Indian Tribes, Charlotte Erichsen-Brown. Chronological historical citations document 500 years of usage of plants, trees, shrubs native to eastern Canada, northeastern U.S. Also complete identifying information. 343 illustrations. 544pp. 6½ x 9¼. 25951-X

STORYBOOK MAZES, Dave Phillips. 23 stories and mazes on two-page spreads: Wizard of Oz, Treasure Island, Robin Hood, etc. Solutions. 64pp. 8¼ x 11. 23628-5

AMERICAN NEGRO SONGS: 230 Folk Songs and Spirituals, Religious and Secular, John W. Work. This authoritative study traces the African influences of songs sung and played by black Americans at work, in church, and as entertainment. The author discusses the lyric significance of such songs as "Swing Low, Sweet Chariot," "John Henry," and others and offers the words and music for 230 songs. Bibliography. Index of Song Titles. 272pp. 6½ x 9¼. 40271-1

MOVIE-STAR PORTRAITS OF THE FORTIES, John Kobal (ed.). 163 glamor, studio photos of 106 stars of the 1940s: Rita Hayworth, Ava Gardner, Marlon Brando, Clark Gable, many more. 176pp. 8⅜ x 11¼. 23546-7

BENCHLEY LOST AND FOUND, Robert Benchley. Finest humor from early 30s, about pet peeves, child psychologists, post office and others. Mostly unavailable elsewhere. 73 illustrations by Peter Arno and others. 183pp. 5⅜ x 8½. 22410-4

YEKL and THE IMPORTED BRIDEGROOM AND OTHER STORIES OF YIDDISH NEW YORK, Abraham Cahan. Film Hester Street based on *Yekl* (1896). Novel, other stories among first about Jewish immigrants on N.Y.'s East Side. 240pp. 5⅜ x 8½. 22427-9

SELECTED POEMS, Walt Whitman. Generous sampling from *Leaves of Grass*. Twenty-four poems include "I Hear America Singing," "Song of the Open Road," "I Sing the Body Electric," "When Lilacs Last in the Dooryard Bloom'd," "O Captain! My Captain!"–all reprinted from an authoritative edition. Lists of titles and first lines. 128pp. 5³⁄₁₆ x 8¼. 26878-0

MY BONDAGE AND MY FREEDOM, Frederick Douglass. Born a slave, Douglass became outspoken force in antislavery movement. The best of Douglass' autobiographies. Graphic description of slave life. 464pp. 5⅜ x 8½. 22457-0

FOLLOWING THE EQUATOR: A Journey Around the World, Mark Twain. Fascinating humorous account of 1897 voyage to Hawaii, Australia, India, New Zealand, etc. Ironic, bemused reports on peoples, customs, climate, flora and fauna, politics, much more. 197 illustrations. 720pp. 5⅜ x 8½. 26113-1

THE PEOPLE CALLED SHAKERS, Edward D. Andrews. Definitive study of Shakers: origins, beliefs, practices, dances, social organization, furniture and crafts, etc. 33 illustrations. 351pp. 5⅜ x 8½. 21081-2

THE MYTHS OF GREECE AND ROME, H. A. Guerber. A classic of mythology, generously illustrated, long prized for its simple, graphic, accurate retelling of the principal myths of Greece and Rome, and for its commentary on their origins and significance. With 64 illustrations by Michelangelo, Raphael, Titian, Rubens, Canova, Bernini and others. 480pp. 5⅜ x 8½. 27584-1

PSYCHOLOGY OF MUSIC, Carl E. Seashore. Classic work discusses music as a medium from psychological viewpoint. Clear treatment of physical acoustics, auditory apparatus, sound perception, development of musical skills, nature of musical feeling, host of other topics. 88 figures. 408pp. 5⅜ x 8½. 21851-1

THE PHILOSOPHY OF HISTORY, Georg W. Hegel. Great classic of Western thought develops concept that history is not chance but rational process, the evolution of freedom. 457pp. 5⅜ x 8½. 20112-0

THE BOOK OF TEA, Kakuzo Okakura. Minor classic of the Orient: entertaining, charming explanation, interpretation of traditional Japanese culture in terms of tea ceremony. 94pp. 5⅜ x 8½. 20070-1

LIFE IN ANCIENT EGYPT, Adolf Erman. Fullest, most thorough, detailed older account with much not in more recent books, domestic life, religion, magic, medicine, commerce, much more. Many illustrations reproduce tomb paintings, carvings, hieroglyphs, etc. 597pp. 5⅜ x 8½. 22632-8

SUNDIALS, Their Theory and Construction, Albert Waugh. Far and away the best, most thorough coverage of ideas, mathematics concerned, types, construction, adjusting anywhere. Simple, nontechnical treatment allows even children to build several of these dials. Over 100 illustrations. 230pp. 5⅜ x 8½. 22947-5

THEORETICAL HYDRODYNAMICS, L. M. Milne-Thomson. Classic exposition of the mathematical theory of fluid motion, applicable to both hydrodynamics and aerodynamics. Over 600 exercises. 768pp. 6⅛ x 9¼. 68970-0

SONGS OF EXPERIENCE: Facsimile Reproduction with 26 Plates in Full Color, William Blake. 26 full-color plates from a rare 1826 edition. Includes "The Tyger," "London," "Holy Thursday," and other poems. Printed text of poems. 48pp. 5¼ x 7. 24636-1

OLD-TIME VIGNETTES IN FULL COLOR, Carol Belanger Grafton (ed.). Over 390 charming, often sentimental illustrations, selected from archives of Victorian graphics–pretty women posing, children playing, food, flowers, kittens and puppies, smiling cherubs, birds and butterflies, much more. All copyright-free. 48pp. 9¼ x 12¼. 27269-9

PIANO TUNING, J. Cree Fischer. Clearest, best book for beginner, amateur. Simple repairs, raising dropped notes, tuning by easy method of flattened fifths. No previous skills needed. 4 illustrations. 201pp. 5⅜ x 8½. 23267-0

HINTS TO SINGERS, Lillian Nordica. Selecting the right teacher, developing confidence, overcoming stage fright, and many other important skills receive thoughtful discussion in this indispensible guide, written by a world-famous diva of four decades' experience. 96pp. 5⅜ x 8½. 40094-8

THE COMPLETE NONSENSE OF EDWARD LEAR, Edward Lear. All nonsense limericks, zany alphabets, Owl and Pussycat, songs, nonsense botany, etc., illustrated by Lear. Total of 320pp. 5⅜ x 8½. (Available in U.S. only.) 20167-8

VICTORIAN PARLOUR POETRY: An Annotated Anthology, Michael R. Turner. 117 gems by Longfellow, Tennyson, Browning, many lesser-known poets. "The Village Blacksmith," "Curfew Must Not Ring Tonight," "Only a Baby Small," dozens more, often difficult to find elsewhere. Index of poets, titles, first lines. xxiii + 325pp. 5⅝ x 8¼. 27044-0

DUBLINERS, James Joyce. Fifteen stories offer vivid, tightly focused observations of the lives of Dublin's poorer classes. At least one, "The Dead," is considered a masterpiece. Reprinted complete and unabridged from standard edition. 160pp. 5$\frac{3}{16}$ x 8¼. 26870-5

GREAT WEIRD TALES: 14 Stories by Lovecraft, Blackwood, Machen and Others, S. T. Joshi (ed.). 14 spellbinding tales, including "The Sin Eater," by Fiona McLeod, "The Eye Above the Mantel," by Frank Belknap Long, as well as renowned works by R. H. Barlow, Lord Dunsany, Arthur Machen, W. C. Morrow and eight other masters of the genre. 256pp. 5⅜ x 8½. (Available in U.S. only.) 40436-6

THE BOOK OF THE SACRED MAGIC OF ABRAMELIN THE MAGE, translated by S. MacGregor Mathers. Medieval manuscript of ceremonial magic. Basic document in Aleister Crowley, Golden Dawn groups. 268pp. 5⅜ x 8½. 23211-5

NEW RUSSIAN-ENGLISH AND ENGLISH-RUSSIAN DICTIONARY, M. A. O'Brien. This is a remarkably handy Russian dictionary, containing a surprising amount of information, including over 70,000 entries. 366pp. 4½ x 6⅛. 20208-9

HISTORIC HOMES OF THE AMERICAN PRESIDENTS, Second, Revised Edition, Irvin Haas. A traveler's guide to American Presidential homes, most open to the public, depicting and describing homes occupied by every American President from George Washington to George Bush. With visiting hours, admission charges, travel routes. 175 photographs. Index. 160pp. 8¼ x 11. 26751-2

NEW YORK IN THE FORTIES, Andreas Feininger. 162 brilliant photographs by the well-known photographer, formerly with *Life* magazine. Commuters, shoppers, Times Square at night, much else from city at its peak. Captions by John von Hartz. 181pp. 9¼ x 10¾. 23585-8

INDIAN SIGN LANGUAGE, William Tomkins. Over 525 signs developed by Sioux and other tribes. Written instructions and diagrams. Also 290 pictographs. 111pp. 6⅛ x 9¼. 22029-X

CATALOG OF DOVER BOOKS

THE STORY OF THE TITANIC AS TOLD BY ITS SURVIVORS, Jack Winocour (ed.). What it was really like. Panic, despair, shocking inefficiency, and a little heroism. More thrilling than any fictional account. 26 illustrations. 320pp. 5⅜ x 8½. 20610-6

FAIRY AND FOLK TALES OF THE IRISH PEASANTRY, William Butler Yeats (ed.). Treasury of 64 tales from the twilight world of Celtic myth and legend: "The Soul Cages," "The Kildare Pooka," "King O'Toole and his Goose," many more. Introduction and Notes by W. B. Yeats. 352pp. 5⅜ x 8½. 26941-8

BUDDHIST MAHAYANA TEXTS, E. B. Cowell and others (eds.). Superb, accurate translations of basic documents in Mahayana Buddhism, highly important in history of religions. The Buddha-karita of Asvaghosha, Larger Sukhavativyuha, more. 448pp. 5⅜ x 8½. 25552-2

ONE TWO THREE . . . INFINITY: Facts and Speculations of Science, George Gamow. Great physicist's fascinating, readable overview of contemporary science: number theory, relativity, fourth dimension, entropy, genes, atomic structure, much more. 128 illustrations. Index. 352pp. 5⅜ x 8½. 25664-2

EXPERIMENTATION AND MEASUREMENT, W. J. Youden. Introductory manual explains laws of measurement in simple terms and offers tips for achieving accuracy and minimizing errors. Mathematics of measurement, use of instruments, experimenting with machines. 1994 edition. Foreword. Preface. Introduction. Epilogue. Selected Readings. Glossary. Index. Tables and figures. 128pp. 5⅜ x 8½. 40451-X

DALÍ ON MODERN ART: The Cuckolds of Antiquated Modern Art, Salvador Dalí. Influential painter skewers modern art and its practitioners. Outrageous evaluations of Picasso, Cézanne, Turner, more. 15 renderings of paintings discussed. 44 calligraphic decorations by Dalí. 96pp. 5⅜ x 8½. (Available in U.S. only.) 29220-7

ANTIQUE PLAYING CARDS: A Pictorial History, Henry René D'Allemagne. Over 900 elaborate, decorative images from rare playing cards (14th–20th centuries): Bacchus, death, dancing dogs, hunting scenes, royal coats of arms, players cheating, much more. 96pp. 9¼ x 12¼. 29265-7

MAKING FURNITURE MASTERPIECES: 30 Projects with Measured Drawings, Franklin H. Gottshall. Step-by-step instructions, illustrations for constructing handsome, useful pieces, among them a Sheraton desk, Chippendale chair, Spanish desk, Queen Anne table and a William and Mary dressing mirror. 224pp. 8⅛ x 11¼. 29338-6

THE FOSSIL BOOK: A Record of Prehistoric Life, Patricia V. Rich et al. Profusely illustrated definitive guide covers everything from single-celled organisms and dinosaurs to birds and mammals and the interplay between climate and man. Over 1,500 illustrations. 760pp. 7½ x 10⅛. 29371-8